Under Cover for Wells Fargo

THE WESTERN FRONTIER LIBRARY

UNDER COVER

for

WELLS FARGO

The

Unvarnished

Recollections

of FRED DODGE

Edited by CAROLYN LAKE

Foreword by Neil Morgan

Introduction by Casey Tefertiller

Illustrated with Photographs

UNIVERSITY OF OKLAHOMA PRESS
NORMAN

Library of Congress Cataloging-in-Publication Data

Dodge, Fred, 1854–1938.
    Under cover for Wells Fargo : the unvarnished recollections of
  Fred Dodge / edited by Carolyn Lake ; foreword by Neil Morgan ;
  introduction by Casey Tefertiller.
        p.   cm.
      "Illustrated with photographs."
      Originally published: Boston : Houghton Mifflin, 1969.
      ISBN 0-8061-3099-7 (cloth : alk. paper)
      1. Wells, Fargo & Company.   I. Lake, Carolyn.   II. Title.
  HE5903.W5D6   1998
  363.28'9'092—dc21
  [B]   98-24222
                                                                        CIP

Under Cover for Wells Fargo is Volume 63 in The Western Frontier Library.

The paper in this book meets the guidelines for permanence and durability of the Committee on Production Guidelines for Book Longevity of the Council on Library Resources, Inc. ∞

Published in 1998 by the University of Oklahoma Press, Norman, Publishing Division of the University. Reprinted by special arrangement with Houghton Mifflin Company. Manufactured in the U.S.A. First printing of the University of Oklahoma Press edition, 1998.

1 2 3 4 5 6 7 8 9 10

*To those whose lives
are the unique history
of the American West*

*To those writers
who have sought to keep
the record accurate*

ACKNOWLEDGMENTS

It is with appreciation that I acknowledge the assistance given me in bringing Fred Dodge to his readers. My sincere thanks:

To Mr. and Mrs. Fred J. Dodge, Jr., for their sanction of the project and for providing me with the original of the only photograph I could locate of Fred Dodge.

To Wells Fargo Bank and the staff of their history room who generously gave of their photographs for illustrations, captions of which credit Wells Fargo.

To the collector who wishes to remain anonymous for permission to photograph the Stilwell gun.

To numerous people including E. Robert Anderson and Kenneth D. Zumwalt, both of the Copley Newspapers, who helped me search far-flung files for the Dodge name which, unfortunately, eluded us all.

To Neil Morgan, prominent and perceptive newspaperman on the San Diego *Evening Tribune*, author of the widely syndicated column, "Assignment West" and numerous magazine articles, whose book titles include *Westward Tilt: The American West Today*, and a forthcoming analysis, *The California Syndrome*, for his kind foreword to introduce Fred Dodge.

To Houghton Mifflin, in the early stages Austin Olney and later Mrs. Ruth K. Hapgood whose advice and encouragement along the way gave unusual pleasure to the winding road of details which leads ultimately to press and publication.

C. L.

FOREWORD

THE NAME of Fred Dodge seems curiously familiar, and yet even historians of the American West may be hard pressed to identify him. He is not the Dodge of Dodge City. There is no evidence that he ever visited Dodge City in Kansas, and in any case Dodge City was a landmark of the westward push before Fred Dodge was born. But the name leads the mind down an appropriate path; Fred Dodge, heretofore almost unnoticed in history, helped more than most men to push the Southwest across the threshold of time away from the tyranny of the badman in mining camps where law and order found scant vogue.

Now the story of Fred Dodge emerges from a padlocked old wooden Wells Fargo box found on the bottom of a closet in San Diego by the daughter of the late Stuart N. Lake, the distinguished biographer of Wyatt Earp. It was Lake who brought Earp into perspective in 1931 with publication of *Wyatt Earp, Frontier Marshal*. That volume extricated the violent events of Tombstone mining days from a soggy mush of recalled braggadocio and journalistic romanticism. Fred Dodge found his way briefly into its pages in his role as undercover detective for Wells Fargo; but Lake was saving Dodge for another volume he hoped to write. This was to have been a history of Wells Fargo itself, one to which the figure of Dodge would have added much.

But Lake was meticulous. Documentation for much of the history of Wells Fargo had been lost in the fire that fol-

lowed the San Francisco earthquake in 1906. Lake recoiled
from a task that would rely heavily on nostalgia to fill major
gaps. As a child, Carolyn Lake remembers, she suggested to
her father that to do the best he could with what was available should be better than nothing. "The answer was an un-
equivocal no," she recalls, and she went back chastened to her
homework.

So the story of Fred Dodge lay in the Wells Fargo chest in
the closet of Lake's littered studio, a sanctum in which Lake
found communion with the Southwest of half a century earlier,
and where his wife and daughter seldom ventured. Lake kept
his own counsel as he pondered the world of Fred Dodge. No
one close to Lake knew what the Wells Fargo box held. When
Dodge died in 1938 at the age of 84, one of the last peace
officers of the frontier, Lake knew he was sole custodian of an
important historical link in the American West. Shortly before the Second World War, Dodge's widow turned over to
Lake the last of his diaries and notes. But wartime service and
bad health intervened. Lake died in 1964 without bringing
Dodge onstage. His daughter, as scholarly as Lake and possessed by a rare familial loyalty to her father's work, began
to inventory his hoard of Americana. Thus Dodge has finally
come out from under cover in the total sense.

He emerges as a character of monumental sturdiness with
the detective's disciplined passion for anonymity. It is part
paradox, and his story unfolds compellingly in his own low-
key journals, buttressed by Miss Lake's terse and unobtrusive
notes. Dodge always succeeded in evading the limelight. His
nature and his job required that he be just off the stage of
tumult but never out of action; he was the prompter in the
wings, the conductor in the pit, the scrim man high in the
flies.

At Tombstone in 1881 he steps off a stagecoach, sent from San Francisco as undercover agent to protect Wells Fargo banking and commerce against a deadly concentration of frontier outlaws, and he is met by Wyatt Earp — but only because Wyatt is expecting his brother Morgan, and Dodge closely resembles him. Dodge takes up a career posing as gambler, but we see him teaming with the Earp brothers to bring order to Tombstone — as constable, deputy sheriff and political lobbyist. We find him watchful in a Tombstone courtroom, his double-barreled shotgun across his knees, assigned to protect the person of the judge and jury during a murder trial. "Everything around the courts at that time was simply rotten," he tells us, and then mentions casually how his jury was ambushed by a defense-hired gunman on their way from breakfast. Shot at in another ambush but unwounded, he remarks only that "serious mistakes were happening in that country all the time."

Again he is riding hard in posses, shooting to kill with deadly aim and employing the intuition that every great detective must have. Dodge is a man of honor, but killings are relative. He is peevish at men who sometimes "did not question the fairness of a killing." He has finesse. Now he gets the draw on an outlaw by making small talk until the badman relaxes enough to use both hands in rolling a cigarette from paper and tobacco that Dodge has tossed him.

Always Dodge is looking up to Wyatt Earp as the bravest and most fearless man he has known and admiring Earp for his calmness and persistence in the cause of justice. We see Dodge through his journals as he makes nightly visits to the rear of the Tombstone express office to appraise events of the day. We find unexpected depths of tenderness in Dodge as a family man when his first child is born amid the uproar of

Tombstone — and again, much later, when he writes to congratulate Lake on the birth of the daughter who has edited this volume.

Train robberies and holdups became less frequent as mining grew less rewarding. Tombstone began to seem dull to Dodge. He left in 1888 and tried to resign from Wells Fargo and go into business for himself. He lost his life savings almost immediately in the fire of a Fresno livery stable and was promptly back with Wells Fargo to stay.

The scene of action shifted to Oklahoma, Texas and Kansas, and the villains of the piece became the Dalton brothers. Dodge went through the rest of his career sleeping on counters in train stations or lying out in marshy bottoms on night stakeouts, plagued with mountain fever, but bringing bank robbers and embezzlers and killers to justice. He never forgot the frenzy of Tombstone. Late in life he read that the county seat had been moved from Tombstone. "Am sorry," he wrote, "for it was all she had left."

Dodge prided himself on being "known among reporters from New York to San Francisco as the man who could not be interviewed." But late in his life when Stuart Lake brought him back in touch with his old idol Wyatt Earp, Dodge decided he had found a spokesman in whom he could trust his knowledge of the frontier Southwest. Even then Dodge did not give information to Lake until Earp advised him to do so. Lake earned Dodge's confidence and even persuaded him, for the first time, to lend for exhibit the sawed-off Wells Fargo gun and the six-gun that had been the more persuasive tools of his trade.

Because a daughter has inherited her father's sense of history, Dodge's own narrative can take its place among other classic journals of the American West. It is not too much to compare Dodge's contribution with those of Francis Parkman and Josiah Gregg and even, in his own workaday way, with that of Lewis and Clark. The earlier journals tell how the West was opened. Dodge shows how a handful of disciplined and fearless men helped guide the transition of the Southwest from anarchy toward republic. His journals should become a basic source for the historian.

More, they will provide the layman reader with moments of agonizing suspense. In an era when the fictional image of the detective is glossy and superficial, and when he moves through a world of plastic girls and computerized gadgetry, it is refreshing to find it told the way it was, when death from a gunman was the payment for an error in judgment, and a boardinghouse meal and a bath were the reward for being right.

NEIL MORGAN

La Jolla, California
October 15, 1968

INTRODUCTION

FRED DODGE LIVED LONG ENOUGH to see the West go from real-life adventure to a few minutes of cinema entertainment. He didn't much like the movies, and he made his opinions clear in a letter he wrote to his old friend John Clum: "We old timers know that the battles fought for law and order in Tombstone were no moving picture affairs. Good men, who were our friends, met wounds and death there. It is an offense to us and to them to reproduce these things as an entertaining spectacle, and incident, for it is not possible to show what necessity lay back of them and made them inevitable." (Fred Dodge Collection, September 24, 1930. Huntington Library, San Marino, Calif.)

In *Under Cover for Wells Fargo*, Fred Dodge does much to show what made those battles for law-and-order a necessity, and he tells his story in a way that could never be glorified in the motion pictures. This is no bloodthirsty tale of guns-a-blazing; rather, it is an insightful look at law enforcement during one of the most difficult periods in history to carry a badge. Dodge spent most of his life working for Wells Fargo—both undercover and without cover—solving mysteries, chasing criminals and resolving problems. This is not the West of the celluloid gunslinger; it is the real, authentic story of a true frontier detective, one who used his mind more often than his pistol to bring criminals to justice.

Perhaps more important than the stories themselves is the passion for law and justice revealed in Dodge's writings. He constantly voices his distaste for mob vengeance. He helped prevent lynchings in Tombstone and chastised the citizenry who committed one elsewhere. Yet he was an ardent supporter of Wyatt Earp, a man who fashioned his own kind of justice when the courts could not control lawlessness.

Fred Dodge also provides important insights into many of the personalities who cross the pages. Dodge did not approve of Wells Fargo special officer John Thacker, whom he believed took kickbacks, nor of Tombstone district attorney Lyttleton Price, who held too close an allegiance to sheriff John Behan. Dodge tells what occurred behind the scenes with them and with many others, what the newspapers could not report.

My appreciation of Fred Dodge's recollections grew as I researched *Wyatt Earp: The Life Behind the Legend*. Other sources, often unseen for decades, continually confirmed Dodge's recollections. The newspapers and various documents considered him a gambler who rode with posses and became involved in local politics. It would not be for a half century that he would tell Earp and Clum his true role in Tombstone: that of a special agent for Wells Fargo, stationed in Tombstone to report back directly to Wells Fargo president John J. Valentine.

In the years since this book first appeared in 1969, some students of the West have doubted Dodge's actual role as an undercover agent in Tombstone. No actual proof exists beyond his word that he did hold such a position, nor is it likely that there would be. In such a position, Dodge would have to report not only on outlaw activities but also on the effectiveness of law officers and Wells Fargo employees. It would serve no purpose to let others in on the secret of Dodge's position, because that could undermine his effectiveness and cause him to lose his secret status. After Dodge came out from undercover work, there is no question of his authenticity. While the evidence of Dodge's undercover role in Tombstone is slim, Dodge is honest and accurate in the rest of his memoir, and his

verifiable facts in Tombstone check out. I am convinced that
Fred Dodge's role in Tombstone was exactly as said: a secret
agent for Wells Fargo.

I do not always agree, however, with Dodge's conclusions.
Much of Dodge's Tombstone information came from outlaw
Johnny Barnes, who was wounded by Wyatt Earp in the Iron
Springs gunfight. Barnes eventually died from the wounds, but
not before telling Dodge a number of details about the cowboy
operations. One of these stories was that Doc Holliday had
helped plan a stage robbery on March 15, 1881, in which a gun
battle led to the murder of driver Eli "Bud" Philpott. My
suspicion is that the cowboys mounted a propaganda campaign
to discredit the Earps by tying them and their friend Holliday to
criminal activities. While Barnes actually may have believed
that Holliday was involved, it seems unlikely that he was part of
the planning or execution of the murder and robbery attempt.
Holliday was disliked even among his associates, and most of
them were willing to believe the worst of him.

Barnes himself is a most interesting case. He told Dodge of
his involvement in several major crimes in the Tombstone area,
yet his name had not surfaced in other records until 1996, when
Mario Einaudi, a historian at the Arizona Historical Society,
unearthed some long-lost documents on Barnes's activities.
They revealed that Barnes had been paid for posse service by
Cochise County Sheriff John Behan, who deputized such
characters as Barnes, John Ringo, and Fin Clanton to aid in the
pursuit of Wyatt Earp, Doc Holliday, and others who staged
what was known as the Arizona Vendetta. These documents
indicate that Barnes was actually a deputy while riding with
outlaw leader Curley Bill Brocious and being wounded by Earp
in the battle of Iron Springs. The story of Tombstone is a very
difficult puzzle, and the significance of Fred Dodge's contri-
butions becomes more apparent with new discoveries.

Carolyn Lake has done a great service for students of the West by providing Dodge's memoir in his own words, rather than rewriting it into a stylized biography as has been done with so many other western characters. Too often these first-person memoirs have turned out to be more fiction than fact. In researching my book on Wyatt Earp, part of the job was to determine which memoirs actually stood up to historical scrutiny. While many supposedly first-person accounts turn out to be badly flawed or mostly fictionalized, this book stands out as one of the most accurate, important works ever published concerning the Earps and Tombstone.

As fascinating as the memoir itself is the collection of letters in the final chapter. Dodge responds to the questions of Stuart Lake, Carolyn's father and the author of *Wyatt Earp: Frontier Marshal*, on many of the difficult issues surrounding the events in Tombstone. Most important, Dodge often provides more information and tells how he reached his conclusions.

This is the type of book where the more knowledgeable the reader is on a subject, the more they will appreciate Fred Dodge's recollections. From a dusty Wells Fargo box on the floor of a closet in Stuart Lake's home has emerged a treasure that helps us understand the forces that created law and order in the American West. This is an adventure story written in the vernacular of the West, the "unvarnished recollections" of a man who lived the adventure. It is an essential tool in learning the workings of the real West, not the cinematic West that Dodge so deplored.

CASEY TEFERTILLER

San Francisco, California
February, 1998

CONTENTS

ILLUSTRATIONS

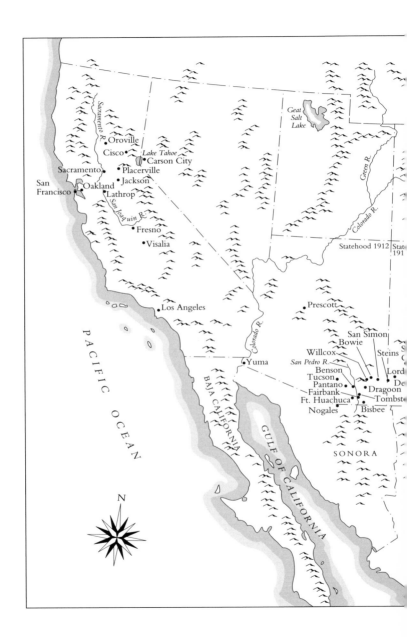

Oroville
Cisco
Lake Tahoe
Carson City
Placerville
Sacramento
Jackson
Sacramento R.
San
Francisco
Oakland
Lathrop
San Joaquin R.
Fresno
Visalia
Los Angeles

Great Salt Lake

Green R.

Colorado R.

Statehood 1912 | State 191

Prescott

San Simon
Bowie
Willcox
Steins
San Pedro R.
Benson
Tucson
Lord
Pantano
De
Fairbank
Dragoon
Ft. Huachuca
Tombst
Nogales
Bisbee

Colorado R.
Yuma

PACIFIC OCEAN

BAJA CALIFORNIA

GULF OF CALIFORNIA

SONORA

N

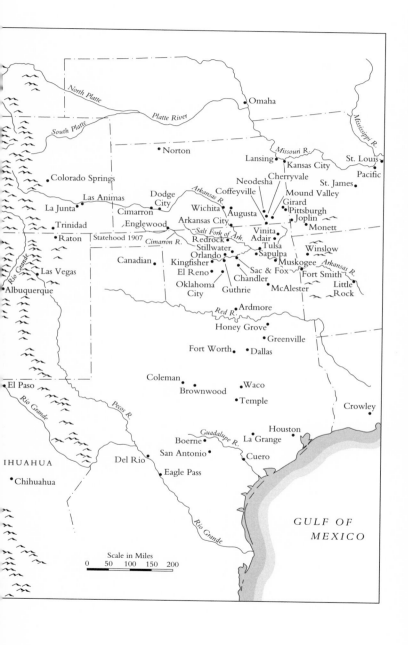

North Platte

Platte River

South Platte

•Omaha

Missouri R.

•Norton

Lansing•   •Kansas City

Mississippi R.

St. Louis•
Pacific

•Colorado Springs

Neodesha   •Cherryvale
Coffeyville•   Mound Valley

•St. James

Las Animas

Dodge
City

Arkansas R.

Wichita•   •Augusta
•Girard
•Pittsburgh

La Junta•

Cimarron•

Arkansas City•

Joplin•

•Monett

•Trinidad

Englewood•

Salt Fork of Ark.

Vinita•
Adair•

•Raton   Statehood 1907   Cimarron R.   Redrock•   Tulsa•
Stillwater•   Winslow
Orlando•   •Sapulpa

Las Vegas•

Canadian•

Kingfisher•
El Reno•   •Sac & Fox
Chandler•

Muskogee•

Arkansas R.

Fort Smith

•Albuquerque

Oklahoma
City

Guthrie   •McAlester

Little
Rock

Red R.   •Ardmore

Honey Grove•

•Greenville

•El Paso

Fort Worth•   •Dallas

Rio Grande

Pecos R.

Coleman•
Brownwood

•Waco

•Temple

•Crowley

Houston•

Guadalupe R.   •La Grange
Boerne•

IHUAHUA

Del Rio•

San Antonio•   •Cuero

•Chihuahua

Eagle Pass•

Rio Grande

GULF OF
MEXICO

Scale in Miles
0   50   100   150   200

INTRODUCTION

BY ITS VERY NATURE, the creative mind of a writer will produce ideas throughout his lifetime — many more ideas than the man has hours or physical energy to pursue to fulfillment; time imposes its limits not on the spirit, but on the hand which takes up the pencil. So it was with Stuart N. Lake who saw in Fred Dodge the possibilities for a biography which would fascinate the casual reader and at the same time record for posterity the story of a man, Fred Dodge, and a company, Wells Fargo, whose places in the history of the Southwest were of great import.

The ideal is not always realized however, and now Fred Dodge must be his own biographer through notes and journals and letters he left, hopefully for Stuart Lake to develop.

For some time after my father's death in 1964, I was sorting out his studio of more than forty years, and when I came to an old wooden Wells Fargo box on the floor of a closet, I wondered what I was going to find. It was one of the last things I investigated because the box had a heavy padlock on it and no key around the studio would fit. I put off prying loose a board. Eventually, when I did and saw the contents, I recalled the Dodge letters in the files and upon rereading one from Mrs. Dodge (see her letter of April 1, 1941) laughed to find her saying *she* had pried a board off that box too, as there was no key to fit. She just nailed the board back on and shipped the box that way. Stuart Lake had opened it once again and later put it back as it was. So I had to break in too.

What I found was a small but valuable piece of American history in Fred Dodge's journals, written in an inimitable style by a man of great character, subtle wit, compassion, and loyalty. That he was a born detective is only part of his story.

Fred Dodge has told of his mid-nineteenth century childhood in the Sierra Nevada Mountains of California and his adult life under and out from under cover for fifty years as a detective for Wells Fargo, which gave him his wide acquaintance on both sides of the law. The words are his and the era — an era while not distant historically, yet scarcely within the comprehension of anyone alive today. Fred Dodge was there himself when Wyatt and Virgil Earp were meeting the stage in Tombstone looking for their brother, Morgan. Fred Dodge in the quiet capable way of a master detective solved the mysteries behind numerous holdups of both stagecoach and train — and law and outlaw knew he would get his man.

Fortunately, he was prompted in his later years to record details he recalled of his exciting life of loyal service to Wells Fargo and adventure on the American frontier. These reminiscences are offered to the reader as they occurred to Fred Dodge. They are purposely not rewritten in terms of the late twentieth century, though I have made a few cuts and a few changes for the sake of clarity; I have also done some punctuating and paragraphing. Otherwise this stands as Fred Dodge wrote it. My occasional explanations are italicized and enclosed in square brackets.

A final chapter presents some letters between Fred Dodge and Stuart N. Lake, showing how a friendship sprang up between two men who wanted to see the truth told.

CAROLYN LAKE

San Diego, California
September 1968

Part I

Under Cover in Tombstone, 1879-1888

CHILDHOOD AMONG MINERS AND INDIANS

OF THE SIERRA NEVADA

Born August 29th, 1854, at Spring Valley, Butte County, California, (Oroville is the County Seat.) I was the first White Child to be Born in the northern part of Butte County. The Indians in that Section were a mixture of Digger, Modoc, and Piutes and Ranged along the border between California, Oregon, and Nevada. These Indians were the off shute of the mixture of Digger Indians — Only tribe that, in all my Experience, the men worked, done washing etc. (Many years later there were many Tribes in the United States that become more or less Educated and the men were made useful in different persuits.) This Tribe were very friendly to the White People, Especially to my Father and Mother. My Father gave them much help, and he was looked up to by them and they were very loyal to him. When I was Born they had never seen a White Child and they come for many miles to see me and bring me presents. There were a selected few who had made their Camp near us and assumed what they thought was the Sole Charge of me. Untill I was a Lad of 12 years of Age, we remained in the same Teritory of these Indians, and there was always some of them that were looking after me. My father usually had a number of the men working for him. While I was growing up these Indians taught me many things among which was the use of the Bow and Arrow and Also the Sling Shot of which they were experts of high efficiency. For the first few years of my life, I only had Indian children to play with.

When about one year old, my Folks moved to Yankee Hill in the same County. This was a rich Placer Mining District that had just been discovered. I was, at the start, the only white child there. And between the Indians and the Miners I was very much in demand and ruled supreme. My Father was interested in Several Mines. He and my Mother administered to all that were sick or hurt and at an Early Age I become thougherly used to all kinds of wounds from Mining Accidents and from Gun shots.

I recall a few incidents at that Early Age, Three of which are still fresh in my mind. The first was when I got my first Pair of Red top Boots. There were not any where I lived and a Partner of my Father's took me on his Back and Carried me Indian fashion to a place 5 miles away called Spanish town and got me my Red top Boots. When he got me home I was quite a Sensation, especially among the Indians. I also become the possessor of a large Straw Hat. Indian fashion, I laid down anywhere when I got sleepy and went to Sleep and one day I went to sleep in the Shade of the Store. My Hat was laying on the ground and some Hogs got hold of it and tore it up. Then the Miners said that I had got Drunk and down and the Hogs eat up my Hat — I was mad for a long while.

Another incident was when a friend of my Father's was Shot. His name was Ned Fuller. It was in the Evening, and about my Bed time for I was undressed and had on my Night gown. They brought him into our House and laid him on the floor while they were making Examination of the Wound. He was a favorite friend of Mine and I wanted to go in and see him. They tried to dissuade me from doing so but I was insistant and He told them to let Fred come in that he wanted to see me. I went into the Room where he was laying and had hold

4

of his hand while I stood looking at the wound which was a large ragged hole in the abdomen. I finally put my Big Toe into it and said to him, "Ned, that is a Damn big hole." By the attention and good care taken of him by my Father and Mother he got entirely well and some years later gave me my best lessons in Wresteling.

We moved from Yankee Hill to a place my Father had bought just above Bangor, a Small town in the same County, Butte. The next few years of my life was put in on that Ranch — with Cattle, Going to School some, Packtrains, fast freight handling fruit into the Mining Camps, and it was at that that I learned to Drive — 2, 4, and later on, 6. A few years was put in driving and then Father sold the Ranch and I went with him and Mother to Sacramento, Cal. My Brother was then living there — he had married. I went to School a little more. Then I went to work tending Store for a Cigar Wholesale and retail Store and there I took some writing lessons.

Father sold his business in Sacramento and we took the Cisco Hotel at Cisco. It was a Railroad Eating house 14 miles from the summit of the Sierra Nevada Mountains on the Central Pacific Railroad. I was Manager there a Couple of years and then we Sold out and come back to Sacramento. My father and Mother bought out the Crescent City Hotel there and were in the Hotel Business, but I was lonesome for the Mountains and the Excitement of the Mining Camps. I was a restless fellow and I had learned to play cards and of Course I wandered around some. My father had bought out my Brother in the Hotel business and he had a Man whom he trusted implicitly and this fellow run off with all the money Father had. I heard of it and went right to Sacramento. I got back part of the money and then Started to straighten out things at the Hotel. I worked there untill I was taken with the Typhoid fever. When I got so I could, I went to the mountains again and I soon regained my health. Father sold the Hotel and they got a nice little Home on G Street, Sacramento where they lived and both Died there.

2

WELLS FARGO, TOMBSTONE,

AND WYATT EARP

[When the stagecoach carrying Fred Dodge as a passenger
arrived in Tombstone, Arizona, Wyatt Earp and his brother,
Jim, had been in town not quite a month. Until September 8
of the year 1879, Wyatt had been Marshal of Dodge City,
where with characteristic efficiency, he had succeeded in bringing order to the cowtown until his job as marshal there left
him more time for faro dealing than he would choose. As he
turned in his badge, he told Mayor Dog Kelley he was through
with the marshal business.

Virgil Earp was already in Arizona and half owner of a mine
near Prescott. He had written letters saying he was certain that
Arizona mining was going to boom, so the Earp brothers gave
up an idea they had had of cattle ranching in the Texas Pan-
handle and set out on the trail for Arizona. Wyatt, at that
time, had no idea of another job with the law, but contemplated establishing a stage line to connect Tombstone with the
railroad. If a mining town was going to boom, he figured, the
transportation business would follow suit. Virgil would look
after the family mining interests, Jim, the stage station and
animals, Morgan would come from Montana and he and
Wyatt would divide the job of riding shotgun on the stages.
All profits would be shared equally.

But before the family enterprise materialized, Wyatt found
first that there were already two stage lines out of Tombstone,

and then found himself, at the urging of Pima County (Arizona) Sheriff Charles Shibell, Deputy Sheriff of that county which at that time included Tombstone. Morgan came anyway, as Fred Dodge notes later.]

In the winter of 1879–1880 I went to Tombstone, Arizona, as undercover man for Wells Fargo & Co. President John J. Valentine. And there I met with many new faces — *good* and *bad*. It was a wild and turbelent town, but not nearly as bad as it has been pictured to be by *many* writers. There I become aquainted with the Earp Brothers — Wyatt, Virgil, Morgan, Jim, and Warren — Warren come later than the others. Morgan and I become close friends — we favored each other in looks.

It would probably be well now to give the reasons for my Close Connection with the Earps. I arrived in Tombstone Dec. 7th, 1879 — I come in on the Stage and Lou Cooley was the driver. I had allready made friends with him by putting on a Silk Cracker on the End of his Whip and then he Knew that I had Driven Stage — that friendship lasted all through the years that Lou Cooley lived.

When the Stage pulled up, there were many there. I was sitting on the front Dickey right behind the Driver. I always felt "hunches" and I could feel that there was some one looking intently at me. I carefully looked arround and I saw two men who were carefully sizeing me up — It was plain to be seen that they were Brothers and that they were outstanding *Men*. There was no one to meet me, and as far as I knew, no one there Knew me. I got down from the Stage like the rest of the Passengers and was standing there, when these 2 men started towards me — I could plainly see that there was nothing wrong in their movements. One of them stepped up to me and put out his hand and said, "My Name is Wyatt Earp," and I said, "My name is Fred Dodge."

8

We shook hands and he then introduced to me his brother, Virgil Earp — and said, "I suppose that you noticed that we were both looking at you very carefully," and I told him that I had noticed them. So they told me that they were expecting another Brother on any Stage and that He and I looked enough alike to be twins. And as we three moved off a little, we heard several say, "There is another one of the Earp Boys." Our friendship Commenced right then.

The next day, I think, this other Brother Come — Morgan Earp — and before he got off of the Stage, I could see there was a strong resemblance to Each other. We become very close friends. Morg would sometimes be called Fred and likewise I would be called Morg — this of course was not from our closer friends and associates.

I had written to Mr. Valentine in Answer to a request from him for me to select someone to look after Wells Fargo and Co.'s interest — Run Shot Gun Messenger and Guard heavy shipments of Bullion and Money. I recommended Wyatt Earp, giving what I knew at that time of his past record, and advising Mr. Valentine that with this appointment, the Company would receive the Cooperation of all the Brothers. Jim Hume Shortly come there and Made the Arraingements with Wyatt Earp — Wyatt did not know anything at that time about any connection that I had had in this appointment. That my judgment was good in this Selection was proven in many ways by future Events. This also made it more serious regarding myself, as an Undercover Man. *I must be undercover* and I can assure you that it required all my resources to remain So.

This appointment of Wyatt Earp by W. F. & Co. took place in January of 1880.

On November 6th, 1880, City Marshal Fred White was Killed by an Outlaw named William "Curley Bill" Brocius. This killing took place right at the rear End close by the

9

Chimney of a Cabin occupyed by Morgan Earp and My self
and Wyatt E. at times. Bird Cage Theater afterwards built on
this lot. Wyatt Earp was the first to reach the scene. Morgan
Earp and My self reached there together allmost at once. Virgil Earp and others got there immediately. The Rustlers were
Shooting from an Arroya close by and the Bullets were hitting
the Chimney. We all Squatted down on our feet to Escape as
much as possible the dainger. Curley Bill had shot Fred
White at Close quarters and set fire to his clothing. Wyatt
said, "Put the fire out in Fred's clothes." My name was Fred
also and they thought it was me. The Guns clicked fast and
they would have Shot Curley Bill, had I not spoken and said,
"It is Fred White, not me." Wyatt Earp had got Curley Bill
at once when he killed White and was holding him there waiting for the fusilade to Cease some. When it did, We took
Curley Bill to the Lockup which was very close by. This
Lockup was about 10′ by 12′ and made of 2x4^s — one on top
of the other and Each one spiked down to the other — it was
quite Strong and Secure for the ordinary purpose.

Morgan Earp and My Self was left to Guard this Lockup.
We had a consultation with Wyatt and Virg and we Estab-
lished a Deadline, inside of which no one was allowed to
come. Then After agreeing on a signal, Wyatt and Virg Earp,
accompanyed by several more, Started to Round up the town
for the Rustlers. When they would get one or more they
would bring them to this Lockup, Stopping at the Deadline
and giving the Signal. They kept this up untill we could not
put in any more. It was a wild and rather desperate night, for
at any time, the Rustlers that had got away was liable to get
help and make an attempt to liberate those that we had under
arrest. But we passed through the night without another killing. And in the morning everything was quiet and orderly, as
all things were that Wyatt Earp had anything to do with.

A short while after this, there was a hard character called Johnny-Behind-the-Duce Killed a man in Charleston about the middle of 1880, 10 miles from Tombstone. The man that he Killed was named Henry Schneider, an Engineer at the Mills Smelter — he was an employee of the Grand Central Mill at Charleston. Soon a mob gathered to hang Johnny-Behind-the-Duce. The Constable who had him under arrest started for Tombstone to turn him over to the Officers there.

Virgil Earp, then City Marshal of Tombstone was out on the Charleston Road near what was Known as the "last Chance" where Earp had a claim upon which he was having the assessment work done. He saw this mob coming and saw the 2 men ahead and he rode down to the Road. The Constable knew him and he turned Johnny over to Earp. The 2 Horses that had come from Charleston were all played out. Virgil Earp was mounted upon a big Strong Horse that was a Race Horse. Johnny was a small man and Virgil took Johnny up behind him and started for Tombstone which was 2½ miles away.

Virgil was soon leaving the mob behind. He brought Johnny to Vogan's Saloon where his brother, Jim Earp, was tending bar and in 2 or 3 minutes Wyatt, Morgan, and several others were there also, myself among the number. Wyatt was a Deputy U.S. Marshal and he at once took charge. He sent to the Corral and had a Team hitched up to take Johnny to Tucson, then the County Seat, 75 miles from Tombstone. (The closest point on the Railroad was Benson 30 miles from Tombstone.)

The Grand Central Mine was at Tombstone and the Mill had telephoned the Mine and the Miners were coming in to join the mob and in a very few minutes there was several hundred men ready to take Johnny away from the Officers and Hang him.

When Wyatt Earp was ready to go, he put Johnny into a

11

hollow square headed by Wyatt and arround Johnny was Virgil and Morgan Earp, Jack Salmon, Shot Gun Collins, Turkey Creek Jack Johnson, Doc Holliday, Sherman McMasters, My Self, and one or two more that I do not now recall. No one was to do any talking except Wyatt. All marched out of the Saloon and Wyatt said to those in front of him, "Stand back there and make a passage. I am going to take this man to jail in Tucson." He did very little talking, only to give a very few orders to some one of the Guards to keep back this or that fellow who were being pushed up from the rear, or to say to some one of the Guards to look out for so and so, or look out for that fellow on your right or left as the Case might be. Wyatt made his principal talk to Dick Gird.

There was a few Bragadocia ones who were in the mob that would have something to say but it was noticeable that they were always in the Back Ranks. There was little said considering the Class and number of the Mob — But they allso knew the men who were arround Johnny and if there was a break made, it would surely result in the death or injury of many in the mob. Without any serious obstruction Wyatt and party reached the Corral and He and 5 or 6 more started in the rig to which was hitched a good fast team and then the balance of the Guards went about their business —

I did not go with the party to Benson. My reason for not going was that in front of Vogan's Saloon I was hurt. There was a Shoe Shine Stand there. It had Iron foot rests and some of the mob must have pushed this Stand over for it fell against me and one of the foot rests cut a Deep gash in my right leg just above the ankle. I was bleeding freely. My Boot was soon nearly full of Blood and I had to attend to it at once. But Wyatt took Johnny to Tucson and put him in Jail.

There were many Stage Robberys during the Early days of Tombstone. It was not Profitable, and later on there were several Train holdups. I had gone to Tombstone as an Undercover man for Wells Fargo & Co. and it was a hard role to assume. I had to have some reason for being there — Something to do that could work in with my main job and give me a free hand to go and come as I pleased — So I took up Gambling. Wm. Breakenridge in his Book, "Helldorado," in telling of a Stage Robbery of the Bisbee Stage, Sept. 1881, refers to me as a Gambler.

I was a member of the Posse that went out from Tombstone when the Bisbee Stage was held up by 2 men near Hereford. The Posse consisted of Wyatt and Morgan Earp, Marshall Williams (Wells Fargo & Co.'s Agent at Tombstone) and My Self.

Shortly after we arrived at the scene of the Robbery, Dave Neagle and Wm. Breakenridge, Deputy Sheriffs, who was sent out by Sheriff Behan shortly after we had left, arrived on the scene. We had no trouble in locating the Trail that was left by the Robbers — it showed that there was two men on Horses. The Trail started towards Tombstone — but we soon lost it by reason of a bunch of Cattle crossing it. Breakenridge and Neagle then left us.

I had had considerable Experience in trailing, having been raised among the Indians. Breakenridge and Neagle when they left us headed towards the Road that went to Bisbee. I had a talk with the men of our Posse and told them that I felt sure we could cut the trail. Wyatt Earp also had Experience in trailing, So we rode off to quite a distance so as to put us outside of where the Cattle had obscured the trail. Wyatt went one way and I the other to make a Circle. Before we met, I had found the trail and it soon turned toward Bisbee through the Mule Mountains and then the trailing was hard. Wyatt and I were both off of our Horses and trailing on foot when we were nearing the summit. I found a Bootheel — it

13

was a long heel and one like all Cowboys and men who were much in the saddle used. It showed that it was freshly detached from the Boot.

Much depended on the trail for Evidence. Dark coming on we made a dry Camp and laid out that night. As soon as we could see, we were on the trail again, and it was a sure thing that they were going to Bisbee, where it went into the Main Saddle Trail that was between Bisbee and Tombstone. We went right into Bisbee and Wyatt Earp went to the Shoemaker's and I went down to the Corral to look arround to see if I could find any New Heel on a pair of Boots. I did — a new heel on one of Frank Stilwell's Boots.

I come back up town and met Wyatt and the Balance of our Posse. Wyatt said that the Shoemaker had told them what I had seen of Frank's boots. Pete Spence was with Stilwell when they were at the Shoemaker's — they were Partners and Always together. Breakenridge and Neagle come to us then, and we told them all the Evidence that we had. We then got a John Doe warrant — Wyatt Earp and I arrested Frank Stilwell, and Morgan Earp and Dave Neagle arrested Pete Spence.

There was a little Excitement and Several Horses were quickly saddled and the talk was among the Class of Rustlers and their kind that they would take Stilwell and Spence away from us before we got through the Mule Mountains. Morgan Earp, Dave Neagle, and Myself Guarded the Prisoners while Wyatt and Williams and Breakenridge got our Horses. Wyatt had allready got Stilwell's and Spence's Horses. Dave Neagle was a good Officer and we were friends of long standing. (I had known Dave Neagle in Nevada before either of us had thought of Tombstone.) He and I had a little talk just before we left Bisbee. Wyatt was present at this talk and we agreed on a little proceedure in case we were attacked.

14

I had known Spence ever since I had been in Tombstone. And I also knew Frank Stilwell but not so well as Spence. Morgan Earp rode with Stilwell and I rode with Spence. Wyatt Earp and Dave Neagle rode ahead, Breakenridge and Williams rode last. Although Breakenridge was back and forth nearly all the time. We finally got through the most daingerous part of the mountains.

When a halt was had to adjust a Saddle and while we were together — Wyatt, Morgan, Williams, and My Self — Stilwell and Spence both Swore they would get every one of us four — How near they come to it Shows later on.

After we got to Tombstone, they were given a hearing and admitted to Bond — Marshall Williams had got out a U.S. Warrant after we reached Tombstone, as there was no U.S. Commissioner in Bisbee — and Stilwell and Spence made Bond also before the Commissioners. They never come to trial in either case. Both of these men were killed later on —

[Known stage robber though he was, Frank Stilwell was appointed a deputy by Sheriff Behan who has been accused of keeping outlaws on his staff, and Stilwell's beat was the territory around Charleston, a notorious outlaw hangout.

In March 1882, after a career of lawlessness, Stilwell was Morgan Earp's cold blooded murderer and a federal warrant was issued for him. Wyatt ran him down in Tucson and shot him as he resisted arrest in the railroad yards there.

Pete Spence was no candidate for a glowing character reference either. Like Stilwell, he was in on the Tombstone-Bisbee stage holdup and involved in the murder of Morgan. Eventually, Spence surrendered himself to Sheriff Behan on an old charge of stage robbery. What he wanted, he said, was protection in the jail. His request was granted but the place was no luxury hotel and his endurance lasted two nights. Finding

security overpriced, he stole a horse and headed for Tucson. A
territorial court sentenced him to lengthy "protection" in the
Yuma Penitentiary.]

Marshall Williams, the Agent of Wells Fargo & Co. was a
crook and was robbing the company. It was a hard matter to
get next to him — but by getting an interest in a Faro game
where Williams had his money played, I finally got next and
reported the matter to San Francisco, and Jim Hume and
John Thacker were both sent out there. Williams was never
Known to put a Bet down on the Faro Layout but had one
man do his playing for him. This man did not know that the
money was taken from the Company — he was a close friend
of mine, but I did not dare to let him know that I was after
Williams. It took a long time to get the evidence on him, and
Thacker come back several times from San Francisco to work
on the case. I had to send all my reports to San Fran, and
then they would be told to Hume or Thacker. Williams was
finally got, but he made partial restitution and there was not
evidence enough to convict him unless I come out from Under
Cover, and that would not do, as I would then be useless as an
Undercover Man.

Thacker never did know about me, for if he had, he surely
would have told it as he could not Keep anything — but I
have always been Satisfied that Jim Hume Strongly suspicioned it. But the good old Sport, even in after years when I
was out from Under Cover and an officer of the Company and
closely associated with Hume, never did he intimate what he
suspicioned.

Jim Hume was an honest man in all his work and loyal to
the Company and one of the best Express Detectives that I
ever knew. He specialized on Seals and was the best man the
United States had as an expert of Seals. He made many trips

into Arizona on Wells Fargo business — On one of his trips, after he left the Railroad at Benson and took the Stage for Tombstone, he had the back Seat. It was very hot, and Jim, who was getting along in years and pretty tired from his long trip, fell asleep, to awake at the Command "Throw up your hands" and he found 2 Guns leveled on him, one on each side. They then disarmed him — taking a fine pair of Pistols and a Short Doublebarrelled Shot Gun from him.

The Robbers made him get out and line up with some more Passengers but the Old Man had his head and Eyes working all the time. He was a man who made many very "Dry" remarks — and he kept up quite a String of Banter with the Robbers and they were quite pleased with him. He worked to such good advantage that when the Stage finally got to Tombstone (which was the first time any one there had heard of the hold up) Hume got out and looked arround and spotted me in the doorway and asked me where Wyatt Earp was.

I sent for Wyatt at once, and Jim Hume called me into the back Room where Wyatt soon joined us, and Hume gave such an accurate description of the Robbers — which were 4 in number — such as Height, build, and Voice and other details, that I could name the men that were in the Robbery for I knew them all. And they always held out at Charleston 10 miles from Tombstone — at J. B. Ayers' Saloon, the Headquarters of all Outlaws and Rustlers.

[*In reality, J. B. Ayers, for all his keeping of bar and outlaw, was another of Wells Fargo's shrewdly located undercover men.*]

We told Hume about this and cautioned him not to go there, for we were affraid they would kill him, and he said, "All right, I won't."

Wyatt and Morgan Earp, Charlie Smith, and My Self were soon on our way, for it was a long hard ride to get into the Section of the Country where these men made temporary homes — on the west side of the Huachuca Mountains — and it was late in the P.M. when we were leaving Tombstone.

We reached the vicinity about 2 A.M. next morning after interviewing a friend who lived on that side. We then made a Secluded dry camp and rested untill nearly day light. Then we proceeded to Round up these socalled homes of the Robbers and got the families out of bed — but the Robbers had not returned there after the Robbery. They had got only a small amount at the Robbery, and we failed to get the evidence there that we hoped to. We then determined to go to Charleston — which was back towards Tombstone.

We reached Charleston about 2 P.M. and rode speedily straight to J. B. Ayers' Saloon. As we dismounted, we saw Hume in the Saloon Standing leaning with his back against the Bar, and as we entered, I saw 2 of the men who were in the Robbery, one on Each side of Hume. Hume gave us no Salutation, only to say, "We were just about to have a Drink when you speeding Gentlemen rode up. Will you join us?" Which we did.

This was not the Safest place in the world for us to be in, and we took our places at the Bar that were the most advantageous to us in Case anything Started. I took a Schooner of Beer and when Ayers was waiting on me, he was joking me about drinking slop etc. — and in the meantime managed to indicate to me with his Eyes the two men that were in the Robbery.

Shortly we went outside as there was nothing to Conceal, for all Knew who we were and what Hume was. So we had a little private talk, but I did not tell any of them about the tip that Ayers gave me, for I would not, under any circumstances

18

whatever, tell Any one of Any connection between Ayers and My Self.

Hume had armed himself again and that morning had got a team and driven down to Charleston alone, and was at Ayers' Saloon when the 2 Robbers rode up. He was satisfied about them being 2 of the men — but it was not of Sufficient Evidence to warrant an arrest, for all 4 of the Robbers were masked. Hume advised, and rightly so, that no Arrest should be Attempted. We all returned to the Saloon and another round of Drinks were had in which Everybody was invited that was in the Saloon and we Shortly left for Tombstone.

Hume invited anyone of the party to ride with him and Charley Smith availed himself of the invitation. I led Charley's Horse for a short distance and then put him behind the Buggy. Charley had went with Hume more as a safeguard, and we did not want the Horse arround the Buggy if anything did start. (I afterwards quite a while succeeded in getting Hume's Pistols back for him but we never did get the Shot Gun although I knew who had it.) I did not want to ride with Hume for I was affraid of him — as it was only the day before that he gave me my first suspicion that he felt I was in the Employ of the Express Co. — when he called me into the Back room of the Express office to tell me about this Stage Robbery.

[*According to Wyatt Earp, Jim Hume's prized pistols and holsters were on Curly Bill at the Iron Springs encounter when Brocius and his crowd of eight other outlaws ambushed Wyatt's posse and came out somewhat subdued. Warrants had been issued for the outlaws and Wyatt was scouring the chaparral for them. His posse came upon them unexpectedly at Iron Springs and the bandits opened fire. Wyatt answered with both barrels, and Curly Bill died from gunshot on the* scene while his friends including Pony Deal and Johnny Barnes ran. Fred Dodge comments on the occasion in his letter to Stuart Lake dated October 8, 1928.]

The first City Officers were Elected in Tombstone Jan. 5th, 1881. John P. Clum, the founder of the Paper named the *Tombstone Epitaph* was elected the first Mayor of Tombstone and Ben Sippy, City Marshal. Sippy soon absconded and Mayor Clum and City Counsel appointed Virgil Earp Marshal.

Cochise County become a County in January 1881. John H. Behan was appointed Sheriff of Cochise County by the Govenor — Govenor Fremont — and Behan appointed Harry Woods as Under Sheriff and William Breakenridge a Deputy Sheriff.

3

FIGHTS AND FARO GAMES

[The hierarchy of the express business, taken from top to bottom, began with the Superintendents, the General Superintendent being the head of the outfit. He had an Assistant General Superintendent who was in charge of a grand division and under the Assistant was the Division Superintendent who supervised a relatively large territory, often comprising one or two states. He traveled the routes in his territory personally, supervised personnel, and settled most losses and claims.

A general accounting department with obvious responsibilities was, of course, part of the organization.

A Route Agent had immediate charge of and responsibility for all agencies on his route, which might mean, in a few cases, as many as four or five hundred offices; his headquarters was at some central point in his territory. At least once a month and more often when possible, the Route Agent examined each office in his charge and checked the paper work and accounts of all agents and messengers. All company property was in the charge of the Route Agent and it was he who worked out details of claims for submission to the Division Superintendent.

The Transfer Agent at a junction was a hard-working man with long erratic hours based on train schedules. Trains arrived; transfers of freight had to be made quickly; trains departed, perhaps simultaneously, perhaps at hours scattered liberally among the twenty-four. The Transfer Agent accepted his job and performed it with the well-known loyalty and pride characteristic of good expressmen. Bad weather and personal inconvenience weren't considered. A Transfer Agent's schedule was the same as that of the trains. When they were due, he was due; if they were late, he waited.

The local Agent received all freight whether outgoing for forwarding or incoming for delivery. He made receipts for both and keep scrupulous accounts. He was charged with making prompt delivery of arriving freight and collecting what money might be due. He was expected to be courteous to customers both on and off his job, with a thought to building up business.

The Messenger had charge of the freight while it was in transit. In the days of the stagecoach, the Messenger "rode Shotgun" seated on the box beside the Driver. The green wooden treasure box was beneath his feet; his ear and eye had to be sharp. In the West particularly, trouble could arise at any moment. Many is the Messenger who has given his life defending his charge against marauders.

On trains, the Messenger rode the express car, acting as the entire express business in that car — porter, receiving and way-bill clerk, money clerk, freight deliveryman, transfer agent, route agent, cashier and auditor for the contents of his car, not to mention defending the company's safe from train robbers who always outnumbered him. He was necessarily a good man. Actually, there wasn't room in the express business for any other kind.

The Driver, in the city, was responsible for his load and made, in 1881, $40 to $75 per month depending on his ability and experience, also whether or not he drove a money wagon. In stagecoach days of the West, the job was a hazardous one, indeed, with impossible roads, Indians, bandits, the snows of the Rockies, and the blazing heat of the desert. How many men today would seek the job? Still, for those drawn by the frontier, the position of Stage Driver with a six-horse hitch might seem unrivaled, unless by that of Shotgun Messenger, for adventure in the West.

These are the jobs as outlined by A. L. Stimson in his book, History of the Express Business, published in 1881.]

March 15th, 1881, The Tombstone-Benson Stage was held up about ten o'clock at night. Bud Philpot, the Driver, was Killed and one man on top of the Stage, whose name I have forgotten, was also Killed. Bob Paul, the Shot Gun Messenger, who was a brave and fearless man, was, at the time of the holdup, driving the Team. Bud Philpot had been taken sick after leaving Tombstone. He had cramps in his Bowels and they become so severe that he had to get Bob Paul to Drive for him — this was told to me by several passengers on the Stage — and when the Fusilade opened, Bud Philpot was Killed and was slipping down and would have fallen at the heels of the Wheel Horses, but Bob Paul reached out with his left hand in which were three lines and Caught Bud and pulled him back into the front boot. The team, frightened by the Shooting and the fact that there was no Controll of them by reason of Bob Paul's hand being used to pull Bud Philpot back, was in a Sure Enough runaway — But Bob Paul being an Old Driver Steadied them out and kept the Road till he had the team under Controll, which was close to the Stage Station at Drews.

There were Six men in the hold up and they scattered at once and the Identity of the Robbers was not known for some time. It was evident that the Shot that Killed Bud Philpot was intended for Bob Paul, for the Robbers Knew that he was the Shot Gun Messenger and that he would surely fight. The arrest of Doc Holliday was premature and was instigated by some one in the Sheriff's Office who worked on Kate Elder, the mistress of Doc Holliday — there were suspicions but it

23

was not Evidence. I got the Sure enough Evidence, but at a much later day.

The Names of the Men that were in that hold up Were Billy Leonard, Luther King, Jim Crane, Doc Holliday, Harry Head, and Johnny Barnes. Later on Johnny Barnes was Shot and very badly Wounded in the fight at Iron Springs in which Curley Bill was Killed by Wyatt Earp. Barnes got better of his wounds but never Well and finally Died from them — And Before his Death he told me personally all About the Holdup, who planned it, and all details (Billy Leonard and Doc Holliday were the men who planned it) and it was he that also gave me the Names of the others in the Robbery — All of these were Killed or died Natural Deaths.

Wyatt Earp Appointed a Posse to go after these Robbers and Murderers. Wyatt led the Posse which Consisted of Virgil and Morgan Earp, and Bob Paul — I did not go in this Posse, for my work was thick and fast at that time trying to get Evidence arround Tombstone and Charleston and from the Cow Boys and Rustlers that come in to these places. None of these Robbers and Murderers were ever apprehended only one — Luther King — and Sheriff Behan fixed it so he could escape.

John P. Clum, in his Paper, the *Tombstone Epitaph*, was a fearless writer and he spoke right out in "Meetin" with reference to this attempted Robbery and murder. The *Nugget* (Behan and Rustlers, owners) took up the other side of this affair which was to lead to desperate 1½ hour trouble in the Near future. This Paper, the *Nugget* was responsible for nearly all the trouble that Ensued.

Dayly the situation become more intense. Morgan Earp and I were still living in the Cabbin on the lot that the Bird Cage Theater was later built. Wyatt was with us most of the time, but he was desirous that we give up living there for the reason

that we were too much exposed to assassination. And I feel
sure that that was the main reason that Wyatt Stayed with us
so much — and I was marked by Spence and Stilwell, with the
others, for Death. (See above.)

After the Bud Philpot Murder and attempted Stage holdup,
March 1881, it was hard to get anyone to drive the Stage and
for a very Short time while Wyatt Earp was on the trail of
these Robbers and Murderers, I drove when no one else was
available. And When the Earp Bros. got back — for there
were 3, Wyatt, Virgil, and Morgan — Morgan and I held the
Stage down for a few days untill things righted. Soon after
this Jimmie Harrington was made Driver. Harrington was a
fine Driver and was also a fearless Man.

Between the Crooked Sheriff, the Rustlers, and the *Tombstone Nugget,* things were getting bad. Attempt to Assassinate
John P. Clum, Mayor of Tombstone & Prop. *Epitaph,* while
on the Stage. (See John P. Clum's "It all happened in Tombstone," Page 58 of the *Arizona Historical Review,* Vol. 3, No.
2, October 1929.) Many other Combinations made life in
Tombstone somewhat risky to those who had been marked for
Death. It was to all intents a regular Vendetta — and usually
we were in pairs. Morgan Earp and I were together most of
the time. Everything seemed to trend towards an open Collision between the two factions in the near future — Things
Kept rocking along and getting more strained all the time. I
had a room at Mrs. Young's Rooming house where I could go
into from the outside.

I had sent for my old Partner, Dan McCann, Early in 1881
— I wanted him to look after my interest whenever I was
away. Dan was a good, and square Gambler and as soon as he
got acquainted, he become very popular for he was a Man that
you just had to like — Small of Stature, Irish, and witty —
and a Game little fellow — He was rooming with me —

I had been Sick for Some time with a slow fever that was called mountain fever — was up some of the time but weak and down some of the time.

In the Evening of Oct. 25th, 1881, I was up, and down town. I Knew that the town was full of Rustlers — Ike Clanton and Tom McLowery were among those present, having come in that afternoon. I got word from Ayers in Charleston that Frank McLowery, Billy Clanton, & Billy Claiborne were there, and they were going to go to Tombstone to be with Ike Clanton and Tom McLowery — I got up and went out so as to See Wyatt or Morg and tell them about who were coming.

Sometime before midnight, Morgan Earp and I were in the Alhambra — and opposite the Bar in the front part was the Can Can Lunch and Eating Counter Kept by a man named Welsh, Who I Knew in Bodie where he had a place of the same Kind and same name. While Morg and I were sitting in the rear part, Ike Clanton come in and set at the Lunch Counter. It could be seen that he had been Drinking Sufficiently to loosen up his tongue and make him talkitive. Soon after, Doc Holliday come in and Seeing Ike, he went over to him and Said, "I hear you are going to Kill me, now is your time to go to work." Ike Clanton said that he did not have any Gun. Doc called him a liar. Doc's vocabulary of profanity and obscene language was monumental and he worked it proficiently in talking to Ike. Morg was going to take me to my room, I was sitting in a Chair and Morg was sitting on the Edge of a Table when these men Come in. Morg remarked, "This won't do," and stepped over to Doc Holliday and took him by the Arm and led him away to the door where he met Wyatt and Virgil Earp and they took Doc Away.

Morg assisted me to my room and he said that he would go and see what had become of the Boys and Doc — And tell Wyatt about the message that I had received from J. B. Ayers in Charleston. Morg said that this did not look good — but some of the Cow Boys had left town.

Next day, Dan McCann come running into my room about 2 P.M. and told me that the Earps and the Cow Boys had come together on Fremont Street and the fight was going on now. I had been somewhat worse all night and had not been well enough to get up that day at all — but before Dan had hardly finished telling me about it, I was dressed and Started down town. Dan went with me and when I got to the scene of the fight, I found Morgan and Virgil Earp both wounded. Wyatt was as Cool and Collected as usual, and was quietly giving directions for the removal of Morg and Virg to their home. I helped them all that I could and when they were fixed as Comfortable as possible, Wyatt and I started up town. When about opposite of the Sheriff's Office, Johnny Behan Come across the Street and Said to Wyatt, "I will have to Arrest you."

Wyatt looked at him for 2 or 3 Seconds and then Wyatt told him — more forceably than I had Ever heard Wyatt talk before — that any decent officer could arrest him. But that Johnny Behan or any of his Kind must not try it. (For full account of this fight, see Stuart N. Lake in his *Wyatt Earp, Frontier Marshal*, Chapter XXII, Page 292–95) — Every interest of Every body was now turned towards the trial.

I was a busy man during all this time and had good oppertunity to get much information but unfortunately, I was Sick much of the time — I had what the Doctors called "Intermittent Fever."

It was Known to Many that the Rustlers and Sheriff's Deputys would assassinate any of the Men who were opposed to them, if there was an oppertunity and they could make their get away.

There was a Gambler called Scotty that come there from

the Black Hills with Bill Freeze, another Gambler. Scotty was no good — he was a Spy and a fixer and he had been trying to get an interest for him and Freeze in a Faro Game that myself and Dan McCann owned. He called me one night as I was coming out of the Crystal Palace Saloon and wanted to talk to me. Most Everybody walked in the Middle of the Street, so we walked slowly west on Allen Street — I noted that there were not many in the Street.

I knew that the Grand Hotel was the hangout for the Rustlers, Murderers, and Robbers and I noted that Scotty cast his Eye up at the upper windows of the Hotel — I was Suspicious at once. I had a Short Colt 45 Double Action in my Coat Pocket and my hand in that Pocket. I just jammed the Muzzle of that Gun into Scotty's Side and quietly told him to turn arround and go back up the Street and if he made one false move that I would pull the Trigger — he turned and we went back to where we was out of range from the Windows of the Hotel. Then I told Scotty that he ought to be Killed. And told him that he had only tried to get me where I would be assassinated. He, of course, denied it — but he could not remove the doubt in my mind. And afterwards I learned through Johnny Barnes that I was right, that it was arrainged with Scotty to get me down there opposite the Hotel and with some excuse he was to Step aside and then I was to get it — I had been very fortunate in not getting Killed. Scotty soon left Tombstone.

Morgan and Virgil Earp were both wounded and Confined to their Beds. Morgan was the most Seriously Wounded of the two — He had been Shot in the Shoulder and it ranged across the Back and just missed the Backbone and Come out on the other Shoulder. A very Close Call. Virgil was Shot in the Leg and got along much faster than Morg. Wyatt continued about his business — Coming and going as usual and by his Appearance no one would think that he had been through an ordeal like the one just passed but any one Knowing Wyatt well could see that there was nothing at all that Escaped his Eyes. As Soon as Morg and Virg was able, they all moved to the Cosmopolitan Hotel for better protection — Times were very serious for all that were on the Side of Law and Order.

Opposite the Cosmopolitan Hotel on Allen Street, was a Saloon called "Levy's Saloon" Kept by a Jew, Ike Levy, and it was a place where there was Information to be got as there was much going on there in the way of Crooked work. I was getting some of it through Gus Williams, the Night Bartender — who was a pretty good friend of mine — but all he could get was what was dropped at the Bar. Ike wanted me to open a Faro Game there and finally I did open a Branch Game — Ike Levy was an inveterate Faro player — and things rocked along for several days. Wyatt did not want me to take the chances there and wanted me to quit the place as there were too many chances for me to be assassinated, but I took some chances and told Wyatt that I would quit there in a few days.

One Night the Proprietor, Ike Levy, Started to play Faro and he was quite lucky — he would win 25, 30, or 35 And then go up to the fast Houses and buy wine. After Several trips, the Wine was getting to make him feel Lucky and he started in to play Faro Bank in Ernest but luck changed after a while and he Commenced to loose and he lost 5 or $600.00 in Cash and then wanted to put up colateral — Bar, Fixtures, Billiard Table, and Stock, then the Lease. I would take these different things at an agreed price and give him Faro checks for the amount — I won the whole Saloon in that way. The last thing that he put up was the Billiard Table. I Knew that the Table Belonged to Hatch and Campbell, I knew that Ike was a Crook and I did not know but what some of the other things were of questionable ownership and I wanted some hold on Ike that I could count on, so I took the Bill of Sale of the Billiard Table which would give me a club to use in making a Settlement if there was one to be made, for I certainly did not want a Saloon.

Ike made quite a Spurt on these last Faro Checks which I issued to him but finally luck turned again and he got broke. He got up and stood still, seemingly in thought. I did not think for one moment that there would be any trouble with him. He said — "I am ruined. What shall I do? I know what to do — I will Kill you and then myself." He had a Gun in his Pocket and let loose at me. A man who worked there named Tim Lynch caught him instantly and then I found out that I had had a close Call. The Bullet Cut my Shirt Collar and went into the wall back of me.

In Tim Lynch's hands, Ike had become very docile and Commenced to Cry. I did not know what this shot would bring. So I was ready for Action — I did not intend to allow any one to come into the Saloon, only those that were there, and I was casting my Eye arround them not knowing what would come next, and in an increditably short time Turkey Creek Jack (Johnson) jumped through the door. Then I requested all in there to leave and asked Jack to not allow any one in there and we Closed the door.

I discharged everybody including the Bar Keeper who was a friend of mine, Gus Williams by name, and took full possession — I hired Gus Williams then as Bar Keeper and we opened up. I had Breakfast for Gus Williams, Tim Lynch, and Turkey Creek and myself sent in from the Can Can Resturant — I was not going outside at all but was going to hold possession personally. Bob Hatch come in and told me a lot more information and I went out and looked arround and got all that the Jews were doing — they had gone in town Except Dave and Ike Cohn who were of the other kind.

After a while, Solomon, the man who had a Bank and a large Mercantile Store on the Corner, and who was really the head of the Jews in Tombstone, Come along and said he wanted to see me and he asked me outside. But I was not giving any chance for possession to leave me and I invited him into the Back room and when we were alone he had a hard luck talk to me about Ike. He said that Ike was his nephew and he had cost him a lot of money. He Said that he understood the hole that Ike was in, giving Bills of Sale to property that did not belong to him, and asked me what I would take and turn back the property and the Papers. I told him I would take $2500. Then he blew up and offered me $750. I told him No — then he told me that he would take it back even if he had to take it with Shot Guns. Then he said, "You had better take what I offered you," and I said, "No, Solomon. You have made your talk and if you want to take this place with Shot Guns you can try it, but I am going to tell you now that if you Start it, there is going to be the largest Jew Funeral that has ever been in this country."

He left and I told Turkey Creek Jack and Charlie Smith and some others that were there, what Solomon had Said and what I had told him. We then took strategic places — but I remained in the door and would not alow any one who was not a sure friend to Enter the place. Nothing happened. I knew they were getting out a Writ of Replevin, and about 2 P.M., Harry Woods, Behan's Under Sheriff and editor of the *Nugget*, come and he started to Come in. I stopped him and told him that he must not attempt to Come into that place — He and I had a few words and from my point of view they were quite Emphatic. He left and we supposed that he had gone to get a Posse — but he did not come back.

So after a while, Solomon come back and wanted to talk to me again. He wanted me to Come out, but I was taking no chances on losing possession and told him he could come in —

but I had to give him my word that there would be no harm come to him. He come in and we talked privately. He said that Harry Woods had told him that there were too many chances to take and if I was ejected by Law that I would and could send Ike to the Pen. So Solomon went up on his offer And I finally Settled for $1750. He wanted to give me a check. (on which he would have payment Stopped as soon as he got possession) As it was then past Banking hours, I would not take Any thing only Cash which finally he went and got. I gave him possession, Closed the Faro Game and moved Table, layout, and checks away. Solomon closed the House and It was not used as a Saloon any more.

I had not had a chance to ask Turkey Creek Jack how he got there so quick. So I asked after it was all over, and he told me that he was in Bed in a front room at the Hotel and he could not sleep and when he heard the Shot he come out on the front porch and saw the commotion across the Street and was affraid that I was Killed, So he just slid down a Post and run across the Street. I want to take occasion here to say That Turkey Creek Jack (Johnson) was an awful good friend of mine and I Believe that he would not have shown any quarter to Ike Levy.

[*Turkey Creek Jack, a deputy marshal under Wyatt Earp in Tombstone, and well known around the West, was as fast on the draw as he was on his feet. He thought nothing in particular of a duel which he, himself, elected to fight with two opponents — not one at a time either. It was in Deadwood, and he chose a road by the cemetery as the location since he figured there'd be two bodies, and there were, conveniently located for the gravediggers Turkey Creek hired. Wyatt Earp, who was there in the wood hauling business, was among the spectators and it is his account of the incident which has sur-*

vived. He couldn't recall Turkey Creek setting up drinks for anybody afterward; people drifted away after the excitement and Wyatt went on unloading a cord of wood.

Later, after the dust began to settle on Tombstone, Turkey Creek turned up in Utah.

Like Turkey Creek Jack, Sherman McMasters, whose fluent Spanish must have been useful around that country, was one of Wyatt Earp's deputy marshals in Tombstone. The three men were in the posse ambushed at Iron Springs by Curly Bill who paid with his life for firing on an Earp posse. Again like his friend, Turkey Creek, Sherm McMasters left Arizona for Utah.]

4

SMOKE FROM THE TOWN,

THE POLLS, AND THE O.K. CORRAL

In June 1881, Tombstone had a big fire and the town was nearly burned down. Ben Sippy, the Marshal, had decamped and Virgil Earp was appointed to fill his Place. The next Morning after the fire, Lot jumpers were much in Evidence and were Squatted on many good business lots. The titles to all Tombstone lots were in dispute and were waiting the result in the Courts. The men who had lost all that they had in the businesses that they were carrying on, had over night lost possession of the lot — the Lot jumpers were now in possession. It looked to all of us that the man who was in possession when the fire wiped him out Should be put in possession and when the Courts adjusted the Controvverses over the title, the occupant would then have to abide by the Court decision. Virgil Earp and Wyatt Earp talked with Several of the leading business men and the head ones of the Safety Committee. And the Above was the Consensus of opinion —

So Virgil Earp Selected the Posse of which I was one. We Started on Allen Street — Many of these Lot Jumpers were supposed to be Gun Men and some of them were sure enough Gun Men — we proceeded up one side of Allen Street and Come down on the other side. On all lots that there was a Lot jumper on, we took him off and put back the man who had been on the lot before the fire. Fremont Street had not had the Damage that Allen Street had, and by the time we were through with Allen Street, the Lot jumpers on Fremont Street were quitting the lots on that Street. It was a fair and just proceeding.

On the upper End of Allen and on 6th Street to 7th, there were Many Women of the Sporting Class that had their Houses and the best of these lots had a jumper on the lot. They put up little round Tents and the jumper was going to sleep in his Tent. That Night, there was a selected number of men on Horseback and when the night was far enough Advanced and all was as quiet as it was at anytime, these Horsemen rode arround and just dropped a Lasso Rope over a Tentpole and then on a Gallop, they jerked the tent free from its holding and left the Lot jumper lying there. There was also another Smaller Committee that started the Cry, "Lot jumper, you *Git*," and they did. The Names of these men who done the riding and roping, and the Committee who started the Cry of "Git" were not at that time given out and will *not* be given out now.

Tombstone was at once rebuilding and it was a lively place — in more ways than one. All indications pointed to the fact that Soon there would have to be a Showdown and a Call down — for the Deputy Sheriff, Outlaws, Cattle thiefs, Stage Robbers, and Murderers. This finally Come to a Head on October 26, 1881, and the Fight at the OK Corral.

[*The notorious Battle of the O.K. Corral was, in brief, a 30 second showdown between the law as represented by the Earp brothers plus Doc Holliday (the graduate dentist turned frontiersman, gambler, killer, what have you) and the outlaw element, this time, brothers McLowery, brothers Clanton, and Billy Claiborne.*

On arriving in town, Ike Clanton had made it known that his gang had come after the Earps. Sheriff Johnny Behan had said the rustlers were disarmed, but after Virgil Earp, who was Tombstone City Marshal, told them they were under arrest, the outlaws opened fire.

Tangling with the Earps generally meant coming out second best; both the McLowerys were killed as was Billy Clanton. Ike Clanton, credited with perpetrating the fight, wound up begging, "Wyatt, don't kill me, don't kill me." Wyatt let him run, along with Billy Claiborne who also turned coward. Though Morgan and Virgil were both hurt and Doc Holliday scratched, their wounds were not serious.

Sheriff Behan trailed with his outlaws to the point of joining Ike Clanton in swearing out warrants charging the Earps and Doc Holliday with murder. But the Grand Jury indicted no one and the case was thrown out of court as the judge ruled the actions justifiable homicide necessary in the enforcement of the law. Had murder been the Earps' intent, Ike Clanton and Billy Claiborne would have been forced to finish what they started, with or without their courage.]

The men who were marked for death were all Keeping a Sharp look out to guard against assassination. The next move made by the Renegades was on the night of Dec. 14, 1881, when they attempted to murder John P. Clum — our Mayor and proprietor of the *Epitaph*.

[Editorially, the Epitaph had stood with the Earps after the O.K. Corral battle, and on this night of December 14, 1881, an attempt was made on the life of editor John P. Clum while he was traveling from Tombstone by stage. In the holdup, the horses were frightened by the shots and a fortunate runaway followed. The team had run a mile before the driver could bring them to a halt. Mr. Clum, feeling that the attack was made on him and not wishing to endanger the other passengers, left the stage and set out on foot. According to the account in the Epitaph, he walked about seven miles and after a rest at the Grand Central Mill, a horse was provided for him there.

Mr. Clum is quoted in the news story in his paper dated December 16, 1881: "I have lived in New Mexico and Arizona for the last ten years, and circumstances have always thrown me amongst the very worst classes of Americans and Indians. I have never murdered or robbed anyone, or intentionally caused anyone a serious injury, and things have come to pretty pass when a good citizen cannot travel three miles from home without danger of assassination; and now that people realize that such is the fact, I believe they will speedily provide a remedy which will insure protection to good citizens, and swift and retributive justice to outlaws."]

The next to get it was Virgil Earp, our City Marshal, the night of Dec. 28, '81.

[About midnight, December 28, 1881, Virgil Earp, on duty as marshal, was shot as he came out of the Oriental bar and crossed Fifth Street. His left side and arm were seriously wounded, and that night as he worked over Virg, Dr. George Goodfellow could give Wyatt no assurance of his brother's recovery. But Virgil did live, badly crippled for life.

Across from the Oriental, in a building under construction where the shots were fired, Wyatt, later that same night, found a sombrero with Ike Clanton's name in it. Frank Stilwell had run by with a shotgun, according to a witness who had seen, in addition, Clanton, Hank Swilling, John Ringo, and a fifth man, all armed and running. Sheriff Behan, as might be expected, did nothing to apprehend them in town and sent no posse out into the cactus. Stilwell was one of his

37

own deputies; some sheriffs would have found the situation embarrassing.

Fred Dodge makes further comment in his letter to Stuart Lake dated September 30, 1929.]

Virgil Earp was very seriously wounded and it took a long time for him to recover and then he was a cripple for life — He had no joint at the Elbow of his left arm.

I afterwards got the name of the man who fired the Shot that Got Virgil's Arm — Johnny Barnes was the man and he was dying slowly at the time that he told me. He was wounded by Wyatt Earp at the fight at Iron Springs. (Stuart Lake gives on Page 310 of his book *Wyatt Earp,* the names of four men who were in this attempt at assassination — the fifth man who was not Known was Johnny Barnes.)

Morgan Earp was playing billiards the night of March 17, 1882, with Bob Hatch, owner of the billiard hall on Allen Street. Hatch was making a shot and Morg was standing with his back to a glass-paned door which opened on to an alley when guns roared and glass shattered. Morgan fell to the floor. The bullet had broken his back and he lived but a few hours. Wyatt, acting on the intuition he said he always heeded, had accompanied his younger brother but the shots intended for him went into the wall above his head. Both men had been marked for assassination earlier by the outlaws, as Fred Dodge notes, and had received another warning that afternoon. But, being Earps, they were intimidated by no one, had attended a theatrical performance early in the evening, and Morgan had arranged a game of billiards. So it transpired that Morg paid with his life for Wyatt's having deliberately spared ring leader Ike Clanton's life at the O.K. Corral five months before.

History was repeating itself to the point of stammering. Frank Stilwell, Pete Spence, and the half-breed Indians, Hank Swilling and Florentino Cruz (Indian Charlie), with Curly Bill, Ike Clanton, and John Ringo were all involved either in the planning or in the actual murder itself. Wyatt Earp, with warrants for the lot, caught up with Indian Charlie and got the story from him. With Sherman McMasters as interpreter, Charlie admitted no Earp had ever harmed him, and that he had been led by the gang to believe he would make money if he helped kill the Earps; Curley Bill had started him with twenty-five dollars. Disgusted, Wyatt gave him a count of three in Spanish to draw his guns after which Wyatt's Buntline Special dealt finally with the second of Morg's murderers. The first called to account had been Frank Stilwell. Curley Bill was the third and the Earp posse found him at Iron Springs, wearing Jim Hume's favorite pistols, as mentioned earlier.]

Dave Neagle, whom I had Known for several years prior to the discovery of Tombstone, was a Square Man and he could not in any way tolerate the work of Johnny Behan and there was a sure and final break between the two. Virgil Earp was on the Citizens' ticket for Marshal against the Behan Clique ticket, and when Virg was Shot it precluded any further Service as a peace officer — for some time at least — and Dave Neagle was named on the Ticket in place of Virgil Earp. And at the Election Jan. 3, 1882, Dave Neagle was Elected City Marshal — first set back in an Election for the Sheriff's Clique.

Now we were to have another Election in November — for County officers and it was necessary that good men be elected regardless of Political faith. So After much Consultation with the Leading men of the town and County as to who we were to put up for the Different Officers, we wanted most of All a good honest Sheriff, Dist. Attorney, Treasurer, and Board of Supervisors — So I went into Politics.

I had had some experience before in Politics and did not like it. I went to San Francisco and consulted Mr. Valentine, Pres. W.F. & Co., and returned to Tombstone. J. B. Ayers and I had a very thorough talk over the Situation and we Concluded that we could handle it. So we openly joined forces to that End and went to Work. R. L. Ward was up for the Republican nomination for Sheriff. Ben Goodrich — Brother of Briggs Goodrich — was a Democrat and was going before the Dem. Convention for the Nomination for the Office of Treasurer and Mark A. Smith, a Democrat, was up for the Nomination for Dist. Attorney — these were the 3 principal Offices that was wanted, and these 3 men were the ones agreed upon — Ayers and I were both Republicans but the *men* were what was wanted.

So Ayers and I both went into the Repub. Convention and done hard work — the Convention nominated Ward for Sheriff. Then we wanted the weakest men we could get to run against the 2 Democrats, Goodrich, and Smith, and the Convention nominated Littleton Price for Dist. Attorney, who was the present incumbent appointed by the Govenor. Price was a man of no standing whatever — A moral Coward who was affraid to prosecute any bad man — and for Treasurer, the Convention nominated John O. Dunbar, another present incumbent. The other offices were filled, and was used by Ayers and my self as trading timber — only the Supervisors We nominated — J. M. Vickers and two more that I do not recall, but Vickers was our man.

J. B. Ayers and F. J. Dodge were appointed on the Central Committee — I represented the Tombstone Dist. and J. B. Ayers, the Charleston precinct. (There was one man from each precinct in the county.) And this Central Committee held a meeting that same night.

40

There was many of these members who lived a long way from Tombstone and it was evident that there would be many Proxys given, So we canvassed the Committee to see who could and would be in Regular Attendance. Ayers and I both Agreed to be present at all meetings, Also several others. Then there was a motion made to allow no one only a member of the Committee to hold a Proxy and it Carried. I had quite an aquaintance over the County, so the giving of Proxys resulted in Ayers and Myself having sufficient Proxys to Controll the Committee. As the whole Committee was present, all the organization, assessing the Candidates, etc. was attended to.

Then in a few days come the Democratic Convention and from underground wires, Ayers and I about controlled that Convention. They nominated a weak man from Benson to run against Ward for Sheriff then we made safe the nomination of Mark Smith for Dist. Atty. and Ben Goodrich and they were nominated — Both of these two Democrats were close friends of mine, Mark Smith Especially so.

The Conventions being over the Race was on — they were off and on a long track. Now to bring our men under the wire. Winners. Dave Neagle Come out Independent for Sheriff and he was surely going to give Ward a run for his money — Dave had been a miner and could count on a heavy vote from the Miners. Bisbee was a Copper Camp and it was Solidly for Dave Neagle. Now here shows the friendship of Dave Neagle and myself. All during that Campain, we rode together and went to all the Cow Camps, Villages, and Mines, He working for Dave and me working for Ward. It was a Red hot Campain — In the Cow Camps I had him bested, with the Miners he had me bested, and the towns I got a little the best of him. Only in Bisbee and that was a very hard nut to crack — but I went after it. I opened a Saloon there and made it the Political Headquarters. Pat Holland, an old friend of mine who I had known in Nevada and California who was present in the Billiard Hall when Morgan Earp was assassinated, had the Nomination on the Democratic ticket for Coroner and for a further ad for the Headquarters, I had a large Sign Painted on a Canvass Streamer and Hung it across the Street in front of the Saloon, "Pat Holland for Coronor." Ayers was doing likewise in Charleston. West Howell, the Foreman of the Bisbee Mine, "The Copper Queen," was a friend of mine and a Dave Neagle man — but finally he told me that he would Keep his hands off and say nothing to the men.

I had a Competent Man to run the Saloon and I was not there much, only when there was Speaking there which would be a big meeting. I was in the Saddle most of the time — I visited Every wood Cutter and Prospector and outlying Ranch in Cochise County. I had to be at all the meetings of the Central Committee and we had some Rolicky meetings, I can assure you — one of which I will make mention.

As before Stated, Littleton Price was the Republican Candidate for Dist. Atty. and everybody was giving him the Merry go round. The Candidates were invited to this particular meeting as it was near Election time — and of course Price was there. We had advanced information that Price was going to make a Spread Eagle talk and the Committee was ready for him. He had been a tool of the Sheriff's Office during their supremicy — I certainly did not owe him any good will to say the least. And wanted to be rid of him.

All the Candidates at that meeting were quite Complimentirary to the Committee and we had saved Price for the last. He got up and said that he, for himself, was not at all Satisfyed with his treatment. He said that it was a well known fact that 2 of the Committee were openly working the whole County against him. He went into detail very thougherly — And for once he lined right along quite truthfully. When he

42

had finished, it was up to me to Answer him and I did. I told the Committee (they were nearly all there at this meeting as it was the last before Election) and the Candidates That Littleton Price had come nearer telling the Truth than I had ever known him to since, unfortunately, I had first known him — That it was a well known fact that two of the members of this Committee were opposed to him and working as hard as they could to Elect his opponent, Mark A. Smith — That Littleton Price had never Prosecuted any one who had money or was a really bad man for he was a Coward and a Grafter — That he was in Every way a very incompetent man — That he owned no property in the County — was a Carpetbager and was only after the office for what there was in it and what could be "Got out of it." I went into his record and showed him up, by his work and afilliation with the Sheriff's Clique, etc. I then told all present that with Mark Smith as Dist. Atty. we would have a man who was an Able Lawyer, one who could not be bribed, and a man that was absolutely not affraid to Prosecute anyone — and that he would be Elected three to one over this man Price.

Then J. B. Ayers followed me and Said, "I am the other man mentioned by Price who is supporting Mark Smith. I know Littleton Price and know what he has been and I want to support in any way All and Everything that Fred Dodge has said." The first Central Committee that Cochise County ever had then unanimously gave us a vote of thanks for our very efficient work. (At the Election, Price was beaten by More than three to one — And he left Tombstone and Cochise County was finished with him.)

The Election — I had started in with only one vote in Bisbee that could be counted on. It was the consensus of opinion that I could do more at Bisbee on Election day than any one else. Tombstone was running smooth, and Charleston was being handled very satisfactory by J. B. Ayers — and in November 1882, Cochise County had her first Election. I was at Bisbee and I brought in the returns and we had for Ward for Sheriff a *little* less than 100 votes — Dave Neagle and the Democratic Candidate Split up the balance of the votes. The Gen. result was Ward for Sheriff, Mark A. Smith for Dist. Atty., and Ben Goodrich for Treasurer — And the Balance of the ticket satisfactory. (But as future events showed we made one mistake and that was the Sheriff — Ward.)

I soon after disposed of the Saloon in Bisbee and Again made Tombstone my home. I had made many friends in Bisbee, for they all liked the way Dave Neagle and I had Conducted our selfs in this campain — remaining friends all the way through.

Dave Neagle soon after left Tombstone and he later on become Body Guard for U.S. Judge Fields — and Killed Dave Terry, a very prominent Attorney in California. Terry had threatened Judge Fields and was about to make an assault upon him in the Dining Room of a Southern Pacific Eating house at Lathrop, San Joaquin County, California, when Dave Neagle shot Terry and killed him. Dave Neagle Died at his home in Oakland in 1926.

The newly Elected County Officers of Cochise County, Arizona took their offices on Jan. 1st, 1883. Sheriff Ward made Judge Wallace his Under Sheriff and Bob Hatch his head Deputy Sheriff. Sy Bryant, Charley Smith, and myself held Special Deputy Sheriff Commissions and could be Called upon at any time and as a matter of fact we did do considerable work. I was very busy working on matters for Wells Fargo and this outside Dep. Sheriff business gave me a good cover for my W.F. work and things rocked along quite Smoothely for some time.

5

TRAILING IN THE CHAPARRAL

On the night of December 8th 1883, I was away from Tombstone on work of my own and rode into Tombstone about 2 O'Clock A.M. Dec. 9th — I stopped on the Corner of 5th and Allen Sts. and got off my Horse to talk to Frank Ryan, an Officer of Tombstone. I heard Horses Coming, seemingly to be riden fast — I called Frank's Attention to it, and we soon could see some men at the head of Allen Street, about two Blocks away, coming right down the Street. I moved my Horse arround the corner and was close to him when they rode up. One of them Asked Frank where Fred Dodge was — I knew him by his Voice and answered, "I am right here," and stepped right over to him and then they told us that Bisbee had been held up and Johnny Tappinier, D. T. Smith, Joe Nolley, Indian Joe were killed, and Mrs. Bob Roberts and her unborn child had been shot, and some others wounded — these two messengers had been sent to me to get the Doctor and the Priest and bring help. Bob Roberts and his wife were close friends of mine and were Catholics but I also knew the others.

The Horses of these men were all in and Could go no further — I sent Ryan after Sy Bryant and I went right to Bob Hatch's house and woke him up and gave him the News. I told him to get George Goodfellow, the Doctor, and I would get the Priest and meet him at the Livery Corral where he would have to get a Team. I woke Charley Smith and he got right out to get the Posse that was the ones whom we called

upon when needed — Charley Smith and I always rode together when urgent. I got the Priest and met Hatch and Dr.
Goodfellow at the Corral — Hatch and I had an understanding and they left via the Wagon Road — the Road through
the Mule Mountains had not been built yet — and I was to
take the Posse through the Mule Mountains as I Knew Every
trail and pass in them.

I kept 3 Saddle Horses — one for town work and Two for
outside work — I changed my Saddle onto a fresh horse and
was ready by the time the balance were and there was no time
lost. Hatch was going to drive hard and would reach there
ahead of us and he was going to get what information that he
could just as soon as he got there and be ready for us when we
got there, but we were riding hard also and were there soon
after sunrise.

When we did arrive, Bob Hatch come to me and took me
aside and told me that there was a young fellow down at the
Corral who could imitate the Voice of the Man who was giving the orders to the People to get back into the Houses and
remained outside during the holdup — and that he, Hatch,
Knew that Voice and wanted to see if I also would recognize it
for he said that I knew the Man. We went down to the Corral and the young fellow gave us the demonstration. I knew
the Voice and Language at once. Hatch and I went asside and
I told him that it was Jack Dowd and he agreed — but right
then I knew what had made Hatch So Careful.

This man Jack Dowd had been a mule Skinner and had
Driven a 20 Mule Team for Jimmy Carr and had always been
a square man and had never been mixed up with anything un-
lawful — but it was surely Jack Dowd. I told Hatch that we
must think a little, for with this man as our starter, we surely
could figure out the balance of the Men.

Dowd was a large man, and my mind went back a few days,

and I told Hatch that last Saturday night I had stayed all night at Mike Gray's who lived at the East End of Rucker Canyon, that I come on into Tombstone that Sunday, and when I come out of Rucker Canyon, off to my right at an old abandoned Ranch which had the cabin standing, I had seen 5 men who were shoeing some horses. This cabin was off of the road about an 8th of a mile — the road run nearly Straight, and I was then coming into the Sulphur Spring Valley and the Canyon wash made an Elbow and the Cabin was at the End of the Elbow. 2 or 3 of the men stepped arround the Cabin and one of them, a large man, seemed to be familliar to me but I could not recognise him as my view of him was short. I passed on, but this man come into my mind several times and I told Hatch that I now believed it was Dowd, and that was the outfit that had done the Bisbee work and He thought so too — After developments Show this to be right.

About a couple of weeks before the holdup, there was a man and his supposed wife come into Bisbee and opened up a Saloon and Dance Hall — his name was Heath, and he seemed to have some money. He had a fine horse and Saddle to attract anyone's Eye and he done quite a bit of riding, presumably for Exercise.

Bill Daniels, the man who bought my Saloon, was made a Dep. Sheriff for Bisbee and he was out with 3 or 4 men when we got there and He Come Just as Hatch and I finished our Conference. Bill Daniels was an awfully good man and he told us that they had followed the Trail out of Bisbee Canyon and that they then headed North but right there the trail was lost on account of a big bunch of Cattle and the Robbers seemed to split up amongst the Cattle.

I had, at that time, a Trailer that was part Yacci [*Yaqui*] Indian and part Mexican. He was known to many in that vicinity as an Expert trailer and I told Daniels that I had

47

Manuel with me and perhaps he could work the trail out —
Daniels knew him and was pleased. Hatch allready knew that
I had Manuel. The balance of the Posse were allready finishing their Breakfast and feeding the Horses as we got a hasty
meal, and was ready to go. We rode right along on the trail
and Manuel a little Distance ahead so he could pick out any
irregularities that there might be with the Shoes or tracks of
the Horses of the Robbers.

This man Heath had been discussed by Hatch and I and
when Daniels come we talked to him about it and Heath had
been in his mind also — Heath was one of the men to Volen-
teer to go with the Posse and was along. When we got to the
Cattle mix up, I told Manuel to make a close in circle to see if
he could pick up the trail and to watch Heath. Sy Bryant with
4 men, one of which was Heath, took one Section. Bill Daniels another, and 4 more men another Section of the Circle
being cut by Manuel. Charley Smith and I went to the
Center — I was counted a good trailer myself. I had previ-
ously told Sy Bryant about Heath and Heath was being
watched.

Soon Manuel got a chance to pass me and he told me Heath
was trying to throw the trail. Soon Bill Daniels and I were
together and I told him about Heath. Soon Sy Bryant come
to us and told us that Heath was trying to throw the trail and
offering many suggestions as to where the men could go, etc.
We told Bryant to keep a close watch on Heath and get him
right and when he did, arrest him and send him to Tombstone. — Bryant was a sure getter and there was no need to
bother about him.

A little while after, while we were some distance away, Daniels and I saw Bryant's bunch closely gathered and we looked
through our Glasses and Saw Bryant taking Heath's Guns
away from him. Right away, 2 men left with Heath and in a

48

little while, Bryant was with us and he told us that there was one horse track that he had seen, and Heath was down off his horse and deliberately tried to obliterate the track with his foot — So Bryant throwed down on him and arrested him and had sent him to Tombstone.

We had got the trail of 3 men who were headed North East, And at the opposite side of the Circle, we got the trail of 2 men who were headed South — The latter two were surely headed for Sonora, only a few miles away. We marked this trail and held a Consultation and the result was Sy Bryant and his outfit were to take the trail of the three going North, and Bill Daniels, Charley Smith, and Manuel, and I were to take the Trail of the two heading towards Sonora.

The Next night, Charley Smith was taken sick — he had been shot in Texas some years before, the Ball passing through him on the Right Side just below the Nipple, and he had taken cold on this trip. Manuel told us of a friend of his near where we were camped on the trail of the two men, and that they would care for Smith. We got him there, and they were fairly well to do and would take good care of Charley, as he was Manuel's friend — So we parted from him there. He could talk Mexican and was sure to get along all right.

We took up the trail again at Daylight, and at noon we come to the parting of the ways — the Trail Split. One Man was heading straight for the Minas Prietas Mine and the other was headed towards the Sierra Madre Mountains. After a talk, it was agreed that Daniels go toward the Minas Prietas Mine and Manuel and I take the wandering trail — we agreed to get back to this point as soon as we could and if the sign agreed upon was not there, we would take the trail of the other and give him help.

Manuel and I followed our trail and the Second day we lost it in a Creek and it Stayed lost. Manuel had some friends among the Mexican Indians and finally after losing nearly a week's time, we found a Mexican who gave us the first news as to the identity of the man we were following — (for we had had no news as to the others) And when this Mexican described the man who had come there and wanted food, etc., I knew that it was Jack Dowd. He had got the Mexican to go and get him a Supply of Grub and also he had bought from the Mexican a good horse and left his worn out one.

I got a very bad cold and was quite sick for 3 days, but during that time Manuel was browsing arround among the Mexicans who were part Yacci Indians — and finally got another lead.

There was a sort of a mine about 15 miles from where we were — it was owned by Mexicans. There was about 25 or 30 Peons working there and living there, and the fellow that Manuel got hold of told him that he had seen a Gringo come in there a couple of times and get some things and leave soon after — the description that he gave was the same as the Mexican where the horse had been left.

We went over there and camped in a secure place and that Night, Manuel went in to this little town and he found an old friend from whom he got a lot of good information — Dowd was out at some Mexican place and come in and got supplies, and the Mexican where he was, was helping him for Dowd was Paying him. We found a hiding place at Manuel's friend's and after 3 days Dowd come in, and we had him. He did not offer to make any resistance. He knew me, and I have always thought that he was glad to see me — Dowd had, as before stated, Always been Straight and this was his first attempt at a Crime.

The little Jail that they had there was a very miserable Excuse and only used to Confine a Drunken Mexican in. It was made of Adobe and was in a poor State of Repair and Alive with vermin — The Jeffe Politico did not amount to much. But it was necessarry to have the head official of the District give his consent to the removal of anyone who had committed a Crime — I had a thorough talk with Manuel and he made arraingements to have Dowd and Myself fed and got a Mexican that he knew to wait on us.

The Dist. Official was at the Minas Prietas Mine, So I Handcuffed Dowd and My Self together, give the key to Manuel, and he Started for the Mine, going by the place where Daniels and I parted. I was in that Condition for 3 days and 2 nights. We could go outside in the Day but must spend the Night inside.

Just before dark of the 3rd night, Bill Daniels rode up. I can promice you I was surely glad to see him — he had Manuel and Manuel's Brother with him.

Then he gave me the news — He had captured William Delaney at the Minas Prietas Mine and had no trouble and got to Tombstone soon as possible and found that Tex Howard, Red Sample, York Kelly were there in Jail, that about the first man he met was Manuel's Brother who knew that Manuel had gone with Daniels and I. Daniels had a talk with him and he wanted to go with Daniels.

Daniels Knew that he had a good man — and he made arraingements to meet him the next evening at La Morita — a sort of a Mexican Custom House, about one mile across the line in Sonora and near to where Douglas, Arizona now Stands and about 8 miles from Bisbee. They met and then commenced to ride hard for the place where we had parted. They got there the next night just before Sundown but, of course, they did not find any sign — and it was night so they made camp, for they had good grazing for the Horses.

Manuel had rode all day — only stopped long enough to feed his horse about 5 P.M. He said he reached the place about 2 A.M. and he heard a horse Whinney and then he got careful and tied his horse's nose so he could not answer the other horse and then he crawled up on them. He saw the 2 Horses picketed and knew his Brother's horse — which was a Supprise to him. So he gave a signal — an Animal Cry — which was soon Answered and he knew that it was his Brother and he rode in and there found Bill Daniels.

Manuel told Daniels the news and Daniels told him the News from the other End. They wanted to start right then, for they Knew the Condition that I was in — but the horses had to be rested to make the trip and they left at Daylight. They had no trailing to do and Could ride fast. Manuel got a fresh horse at the Place where we first stopped and Also got one for his Brother. The man who had first given us the description of Dowd was there and described Dowd to Daniels and told him he would let him have a fresh horse only a couple of miles further along and did — So the party got to me that same night.

In the morning, we started back, picked up the rested horses, and as we did not have to go to Minas Prietas (for Daniels had made all arraingements there and had a permit to take the man out) we made pretty good time.

I was becoming very uneasy over the loss of time from my own legitimate business for I was at that time just getting a good start with Johnny Barnes in what he was telling me — And I had broken an appointment with him by reason of this trip. So near the Point of the San Jose Mountains, I left the Bunch and they went on to Tombstone — and I struck out for the San Pedro River and down that to Charleston to see J. B. Ayers. When I got there, Ayers said that Johnny was in town and he took me to where he was — and we had a long talk.

The Next day I went into Tombstone. Daniels had told me that Charley Smith had made it back to Tombstone and was there now — We soon got together and he come to my house and gave me all the inside of the workings of the Sheriff's office.

Capt. J. B. Hume, Special Officer for Wells Fargo and Co., was at Deming, New Mexico when the Bisbee holdup took place — and he noticed a man had come into town and acted very suspicious. The Descriptions had gone out by wire and Hume was sure that this man answered the description of one of the men. Tucker, Special Officer for the Southern Pacific R. R., was a Deputy Sheriff of Grant County, New Mexico and a friend of Hume's. Hume went to Tucker and told him about the man and they then watched him a little and thought that they would arrest him, thereby preventing him from getting away. They done this and Hume questioned him and become certain that he was one of the men and Hume wired the Sheriff at Tombstone and Ward Got him — he was York Kelly.

Tex Howard and Red Sample had been captured near Clifton, and when Daniels got in with Jack Dowd, they were all in the Cochise County Jail — Heath, Howard, Sample, Kelly, Delaney, and Dowd.

Heath was the first to be tried and the Trial resulted in a life Sentence for Heath — All that he could be was an accessory before and after the fact.

Sheriff Ward had his Son as Jailer, and Ward had all of his Deputys — the men who would fight — out of town on presumable Sheriff's Business.

I was at that time trying to negotiate the return of Special Officer of Wells Fargo J. B. Hume's two Six Shooters that had been taken from him when a Stage had been held up some time before (I afterward got them.) And Charley Smith and I had been out of town on this business for a couple of days. About 10 o'clock one morning, we could see the town about a

mile and a half. From then on, we rode for we could see that
Something unusual was happening.

When we reached town, the crowd had mostly disperced.
We were coming right up the Charleston road and could see a
man hanging on a Telegraph Pole. The Coroner, Pat Holland, had just reached there and he at once took charge of
Everything and the Body was taken down right away. As soon
as it was down, Smith and I rode up the Street and swung over
to Allen Street And after we had put our Horses away, we
went to Pony Brown's Saloon where there were a good many
of the Mob Celebrating. The man who seemed to be the
leader of this mob was John Shaunessy, the Foreman of the
Grand Central Mine at Tombstone, who was an awful good
friend of mine and when Smith and I went in, they all seemed
to be quieting down. Shaunessy Said, "Hello, Boys," and we
both answered and Said, "Hello, John." And in a minute or
two he said, "Well, you Boys saw the work, what do you think
of it?" I Said, "Yes, we saw the Effects of the work."

"Well what do you think of it?"

From the tone and manner of Shaunessy, I knew right then
that John thought that they had done the right thing and that
Every one else must think the Same way. And I said, "John,
You do not want to know what I think about it."

"Yes we do — what *do you think* of it?"

"Well," I said, "Since you insist on it, I think that you are all
a lot of murdering, Law Breaking Bunch of Damn Scoun-
drells." Then Charley Smith said, "John, that talk goes for
me also."

There was hardly a word spoken by any one and they
Drifted out in pairs and bunches. I will say that my language
in answering Shaunessy was more forcible than polite. And
the answer covers it very well.

Ike Roberts, the Constable, was tending Bar for Brown and

they were both behind the Bar and both of them good friends of both of us. And Ike Roberts told us that Sheriff Ward had planned the whole thing — that there was not a half dozen Pistols on the whole Mob, that they just went down to the Jail and Will Ward opened the Door, and gave the Key to Heath's Cell to the Mob and they just took Heath out of the Jail, went down the Street a little ways and Strung him up to a Telegraph Pole — that there was no resistance at the Jail — And the mob had no trouble at all.

It was an Evident fact that it was all planned by Ward so that the Mob would have Easy access to the Jail — He was going to run for Sheriff again and thought that this would fix it for Him in Bisbee and Tombstone among the Miners.

Charley and I went out of the Saloon and about the first man that we met was Sheriff Ward — He come to us and said a mob went down to the Jail and overpowered Will (his Son) and took Heath out and hanged him. While he was talking I got out my Dep. Sheriff commission and tore it up. And I said, "Yes, I know all about it — And you are an accessory before and after the fact," and slapped the torn up Commission in his face. Smith done the same and we walked off.

John Shaunessy afterwards told me that the Miners would, all to a man, vote against him and that he was a thing of the Past. These Miners wanted a man who could and would enforce the Law. Ward did not even go before the Convention and Bob Hatch was nominated and Elected and Served his tenure of office.

6

THE TARGET OF A

MOONLIGHT MURDER PLOT

Soon after this, Ike Roberts made a proposition to me —
there was going to be a Vacansy in the Constable's Office.
There were 2 Constables Elected by the County. Their jurisdiction Criminally was Equal to that of the Sheriff — but Civ-
illy their jurisdiction was only up to $300. Ike Roberts was
getting along in years and could not attend to the outside
work, Especially the Criminal End of it. He was a man well
liked by nearly Everybody and held the Bulk of Civil business,
and the other Constable was going to resign. The Board of
County Supervisors would receive this resignation and appoint
a successor to him. I had been in the last campain and there
was no doubt but what I could be appointed if I wanted it.

Ike Roberts' proposition was — for me to get the appointment and He and I to go into Partnership and he would do
the inside work and I was to do the outside work which was
principally Criminal. This afforded me a fine cover for my
work — better than the Deputy Sheriff's Commission had
afforded me — So I secured the appointment from the Board
of Supervisors and Ike Roberts and I became Partners.

I done all the riding and Ike done the town work. I felt sure
that he did not know my true Standing and I never told him
— It gave me a fine chance to attend to the getting of the
information that I was always looking for. Charley Smith still
continued to ride with me and I gave him two thirds of the

money that come to me when Ike and I would divide our Fees — It was all on the Fee system and Ike Kept the Accounts. I gave him my mileage and he had the cost on all the Papers that I served and we pooled the whole amounts brought in by both of us.

There were many writs that come into our hands for service — Attachments, Warrants, Subpoenas, etc. — One of these attachments come near to leading me into my final End. Jim Burnett, who had formerly been a Justice of the Peace at Charleston, and a general all arround supporter of Rustlers and bad men generally — and had had to be removed from the Justice of the Peace office for failure to make any returns to the County of Fees and fines received by him — was keeping up a business at Fort Huachuca where he had a Contract to furnish the meat for the Post and he also had the Contract to carry the mail from the Railroad to the Post.

There were several of his Creditors in Tombstone who had to bring suit and attachments were issued levying upon his Property. He also had a Partner in the Butcher business with him, a man named Gene Garlock, who was also a party to these Suits. All of these Papers were placed in our hands for service and I started for Huachuca to make the Levy and Serve the Summons. Of Course, Charley Smith was with me and I took along another man to help bring in what I levyed on Teams, etc. — a man by the name of Andy Ames, a somewhat fearless fellow and I also took along another man to act as Keeper to be left in charge of Live Stock, Cattle, Hogs, etc. by the name of Charley Colwell. When we got close to Huachuca, I left the 3 and went into the Post to See the Commanding Officer who was at that time General Forsythe (Sandy Forsythe), whom I knew quite well, and it was necessary to have the Consent of the Officer in Command to serve any papers on the Military Reservation in order to make the papers Legal. I saw him and got the permission all right and then got the Men that I had with me and proceeded to make the Levy on all property that I could find belonging to the Defendants. The mail was due to arrive about then and I was at the Post Office and when the Mail Driver was in the Post Office, I Levyed on the Team and Wagon. I then went down to the Slaughter House and Levyed on that. I also got some Beef Cattle, Hogs, Sheep, and some Horses.

The Cattle, Hogs, and Sheep I could not move very well — So I put Charley Colwell in Charge as a Keeper to hold all the property that I had under attachment, and Andy Ames, Charley Smith, and I brought the ballance of the outfit to Tombstone.

Jim Burnett was not at Home, but Gene Garlock was there and I got Service on him as a partner. Jim Burnett did not come into Tombstone as we expected he would and replevy the property — but he had to make a Bond in Double the amount of the Attachments and he could not make the Bond.

In two or 3 days, there was a friend of mine from Charleston come to see me and he told me that all the Cattle, Hogs, and Sheep had been run off and all that Charley Colwell had in his possession was the Slaughter House and the Corrals. I talked this over with my Partner, Ike Roberts, and the Parties who had brought the Suits, and Warrants were issued for Jim Burnett and Gene Garlock and placed in my hands for Service. I took Charley Smith with me and also took Andy Ames to put in as Keeper of the Property there and I was going to dispense with the Services of Charley Colwell.

When I got out to Huachuca and got my permission for service of the Papers from Gen. Forsythe, I sent direct to the Slaughter House and Arrested Gene Garlock then fired Charley Colwell. I put Andy Ames in as Keeper and I put Gene Garlock in his Custody. Charley Smith and I then went after the Cattle — for I had been told by my Charleston friend where the Cattle were. We got all of them and took them back to the Slaughter House Pasture and put them in Andy's Charge.

When we got there and I Arrested Gene Garlock, Jim Burnett was not at home, but Gene Said that he would be there that Night and when we got in with the Cattle, Gene told me that Jim was up at the House where he had a Mexican Wife and some children.

When Jim got home, Gene Garlock told him how things stood and told him that I had gone after the Cattle. Jim Burnett then caved arround alot and Swore that he would Kill me if I Come to his House to arrest him. Andy Ames told me all about what Jim had Said and so on — I told Andy and Gene both that I had a Warrant for Jim Burnett and that I was going to Arrest him — and I Started off towards the House, Charley Smith with me. Gene Garlock called me and said that he wanted to see me — Gene was really not a bad fellow but he had got himself hooked up in bad Company. I had sometime before had a chance to do Gene a favor when he needed it, and he sure returned it right then. He told me that he could not see me go up to that House and be Murdered, That Jim Burnett was going to defy me and force me to go into the House after him and that he had a Shot Gun loaded with Buckshot and it was Strapped onto a Log and when I opened the Door, it would pull a String and set both barrels of the Gun off. Gene also told me what he had Said about me which was that I was the first man that had ever got his property tied up and that I could not live till morning, that he was going to kill me, that I was a Blankitty Blank Son of a B and that he had been wanting a Chance to Kill me and he now had the chance and was sure going to Kill me tonight.

I got all the particulars from Gene as to how many rooms

were in the House and which was the Bedroom and all about it so that I had everything down pat. Gene also told me that Jim kept a Double barrel Shot Gun in the room where he Slept also two Six Shooters there, always handy — he told me that the two children Slept in the Kitchen and that the Woman might be there also. I thanked Gene and Started for the House.

When we got up there, I sent Charley Smith to the Back Corner where he could cover the back End and one side, and I took the front and the other End. The moon was full that night and it would Soon be shining on that House — just as soon as it Cleared the Mule Mountains.

I opened the Parley by a "Hello" and it was answered by Jim. I told him that I had a warrant for his Arrest — And what he said to me was not fit for Publication, very forceable, much profanity, etc. I had been sparring for a little time and right then the moon flooded the House with light. I had, during my talk with Jim, located him, also the Woman & children. They were in the Kitchen and Jim was in the Bedroom — this room had a window facing the East. I was close to the Door where the Trap Gun was and I said to Jim, "All right, Jim, I am going to break this Door down and come and Get you," (Just what Jim wanted) but instead I stepped to the window and could see Jim plainly — and I just Shoved my Short Double Barrel Shot Gun right through the Window and I had Jim Covered.

I was then somewhat forceable in my remarks to Jim in which I told him to get his hands up and get them high and the least move in the wrong way meant death to him instantly — Jim obeyed at once. I made him move to the Center of the room and then I called Charley Smith who broke out some more of the window and went in. I kept Jim Covered and Charley put the Handcuffs on him and gathered up the

Guns — 1 Shotgun and 2 Sixshooters — then I went in and Charley and I unstrapped the Shotgun from the Log.

We had 2 Extra Horses Saddled and we were soon on our way to Tombstone which we reached about 4 A.M. We rode right up to the Court House — the Jail was in the Court House and when we stopped, Jim Burnett demanded that he be taken up town so that he could make Bond. He said that he had never been locked up in that town and no S B was going to lock him up now. I told him that he was mistaken and that I was going to Lock him up right then and that it would not be well for him to make any resistance, for I had stood just about all that I was going to stand from him — well, we locked him up allright. I had allready told Gene Garlock that I would see him through in this matter.

Just as soon as we got up town, Charley and I got some Coffee and Changed our Saddles onto fresh Horses and Started right back. We knew that we must beat Jim Burnett to the ballance of the Attached property or else he would have them run over the Line into Sonora, Mexico and we allso knew that when Court opened that Jim Could make Bond.

When we got back to the Slaughter house, we found that Andy Ames had located all of the missing property and by noon we had it all back at the place — Andy Ames had been working on a Mexican that was working arround there and this Mexican told him where all the Property was.

After we had some Dinner and rested our Horses and fed them, we Started back for Tombstone which we reached about Midnight — About 48 hours without Sleep and practically all the time in the Saddle.

We learned that Jim Burnett had made Bond about 11 O'clock that day — for there were plenty of his Kind who could, and some did, qualify for Bondsmen. Jim had asked when he come out, What had become of Dodge and Smith and he was told that we took fresh Horses and had gone right back and he said, "Oh Hell, then it is no use for me to go, for they have got it all by now."

Jim did not try to get Garlock out atall — I and Smith went to Bed at once, but I got up at 8 A.M. and brought Garlock into Court about 10 A.M. and he was released on his own recognizance — I had told the Judge what Garlock had done for me and he readily released him.

About the first man that I saw when I come up the Street was Jim Burnett — but Jim had learned a few and did not care to do as much killing as he had wanted to do the Night before.

Soon after this, Ike Roberts, my Partner, was Killed by a man Named Adams who was lot jumper and always trying to get property by Contesting titles and he had many Papers of different Kinds served on him and was in the Courts much of the time. Ike Roberts was given an Attachment to serve on him. Adams was a man who was a low Sneak but no one ever thought that he would Kill any one — but when Ike Roberts served these Papers on him, it was close to the Courthouse and while Ike Roberts was handing him the Summons in this Suit, Adams jerked out a little Cheap Pistol and Shot Ike and Ike Roberts was a dead man in a few Seconds — I was out of town at the time and did not reach Tombstone untill the following morning.

There was much feeling in town over this murder, and Lynching of Adams was a quiet but very forceful movement and as the miners were, all to a man, friends of Ike Roberts, It was a very serious Condition to face. I surely did not want to be one of the men whose duty it was to protect the Murderer from a mob, but I was a Sworn Officer and I most certainly would have done my duty and tried at least to protect this man who had murdered my Partner and close friend. I had to face it — and I got busy at once. I went among the influential

Leaders of the Miners who were going to be the main ones in this contemplated Lynching. My talk to them was both serious and forceful — and also Sympathetic — but the result was that there was no Lynching. Adams was tried, Convicted, and Sentenced to a life term in the Territorial Prison at Yuma.

The Election was coming on and Bob Hatch was going to need help if he was to win for Sheriff. I had made up my mind not to run and I put in my hard licks for Bob Hatch.

The Election was in November, and after a hot campain, Hatch was Elected — and he took Office Jan. 1st, 1885. Charley Smith, My Riding partner, was appointed Jailor and I was a Deputy but not supposed to be an active one.

Right after the Election while Ward was still in office as Sheriff and I was still Constable, the Mines Shut down. The Miners had been getting $4.00 per day — and the mine owners after a while agreed that they would open up if the miners would agree to work for $3.50 per day but they would not.

Then the Hudson Bank failed to open. The miners Union had their funds there and many others also. The Small Depositors got together and Each one brought Suit on the Justice Court. All these Attachments was placed in my hands, And I at once went to the Bank and took possession and the attachments in my hands were the first served and Superceeded Everything that followed. That P.M. The Sheriff come with a Batch of large Attachments, but all of those had to come after those that I had Served.

So the Prospects for those that I had served stood in a pretty safe position. As the others that followed would have to probably settle with these small attachments before they would be able to realize upon their larger Suits, I put in two Keepers and the Sheriff put in two Keepers. There was some demonstration made by the miners' Union but they were willing to listen to reason and they subsided.

63

It was impossible to tell the amount of the money that was in the Safe which was in a vault. In 2 or 3 days, the Grand Jury Convened and they appointed a Committee from among their members to go to the Bank and Count the Money.

Now at that time, there was only one man in Tombstone who could open that Vault and the Safe — a young man who was the assistant Cashier, a man of unquestioned integrity. The Grand Jury got him and took him to the Bank, he opened the Vault and the Safe and they counted the money.

I was down on the Street when about an hour or more after the Committee had finished the Count, one of this Committee come to me and called me off to where we were in private and told me that the money was Short, that they had made this assistant talk and he had been forced to tell them the amount there at the time the Bank closed — for one of this Committee had been Examining the Books. He did not have time or the right to go into detail about it but he said that the whole of the Committee were unanamous in saying that they knew that I did not know anything about it — but there was going to be a meeting held at the Court house that would be an open meeting and they wanted me to get busy and bring this thing to a head. I told him that I surely would do it, for I knew that I could get the names of those who had taken it.

I knew that the Keeper who I had placed there on the Day watch was as square as a Dye and he would at any time fight for me. The man who was there at night was equally reliable and so was the man that the Sheriff had placed there and those two men would have been Dead if there had been any attempt to get this money at night — So I was sure that it was on the Day Watch and there had been some fine work done to get by my man.

So I went right to the Bank and took him to one side and spread my Cards right out on the Table — he listened and then he Said, "Fred, this is a sure thing and now I know I can tell you what has been done."

The County Officials all had the County money in that Bank. So my man told me that day before yesterday the Sheriff and the Assistant Cashier and two County Officials had come there in the morning and the Sheriff told his man and my man that the Asst. Cashier was going to give one of these men the combination to the vault and Safe for he did not think that it would be Safe for one man only to have this Combination for something might happen to him.

Now all of these men were well Known to my man and also to the Sheriff's man. My Man in telling me, gave the names of all of these men — one of which I thought alot of. The others I knew well and they were straight honest men up to that time as far as I knew; the Sheriff I would not trust atall. He was the same Sheriff (Ward) that I helped to Elect and the same Sheriff that had given up Heath, the Bisbee murderer, to a Mob to be hanged, and the Same Sheriff who I had thrown my Appointment in his face after the Hanging. I did not like him and he did not like me — honors were easy there — and I am not using the names of the others who were there for they had children who perhaps are still alive and I do not want to bring any reflection upon them.

My man told me that after the Sheriff had made his talk about the Combination that they all went to the Vault door and the Asst. Cashier Showed the man the Combination and then they started into the Vault and the Sheriff said, "I do not want to go in there for I do not want to Know anything about the Combination of that Safe and you two may feel the same way, for you have this in charge." And they did feel that they did not want to know anything about the Combination — So they all 3 Stepped aside. They were only in there a very short time learning this man the Combination and then they come out and went away — I told my man to say nothing at all about this to any one, and then I left.

I went straight to the Father of the Asst. Cashier — who was a prominent and a good man — who was in Business there. He was also a good friend of mine. I told him that I wanted to see his Son and himself together. He sent out and had the young man come in and then I went straight from the Shoulder and told him that I wanted the whole thing — who first come to him and what was done and how much was taken. The Father was badly shook up and he told his Son to give me the whole truth and he did — I left there knowing exactly the Whole Story, including the Amnts. taken.

I then went to the County Official whom I thought a lot of up untill that time, and when I had him alone, I again Spread my Cards on the Table and I surely did give it to him Straight. He went all to pieces and come through Clean — He told me that every dollar should and would be returned to the Safe through the Grand Jury Committee. There was a lot of leakage and the news got out and away — but the meeting was coming on.

I had been approached for information but I would not talk to anyone.

When I went in to the meeting I got many black looks. I took my seat just inside the Rail, the meeting was opened and got under way, but I could desern no attempt to bring this matter up. So finally I got up and told them that I had a few words to say in regard to this Bank Closing — as I was the Officer who had put on the first attachments — and then I went into some details. I did not use any names but I certainly had the promice of the return of all of this money — and that I was going to see that it was returned or the balance of the Expose would come. Well, I stood in some different light before that meeting than I did when I come in, and when the Hurra had subsided some, they got order again and one of the Grand Jury Committee made a Statement that since the Meeting had started, the whole amount had been returned to the Grand Jury Committee and the meeting adjourned. When I come into the meeting I was getting black looks and at the adjournment they wanted to carry me out on their Shoulders — if I had let them.

I had a little money in that Bank and when they got through with the Receiver and the whole, after 2 or 3 years, was wound up I got 2 payments of ten per cent making twenty per cent of what I had there — Considerable of a loss to me.

I did not run for the Office of Constable at the Election just Passed, I had about enough — Lost my Partner and had a chance to be accused wrongfully in the Bank matter. And there were other matters that required my attention at Close Range — which was strictly the work for an undercover man. I did not want to be away from Tombstone much of the time — and it all worked out fine.

7

TERRITORY OF ARIZONA vs. BARNEY RIGGS

During the tenure in office of Bob Heath, there was a Bad
Killing. A man by the Name of Hudson from Texas had
aquired a place in the County and had for a neighbor a man
named Bannock Riggs. The Old Man had a Son by the name
of Barney — Old Bannock and Young Barney, as they were
known. Young Barney was married and he become Jealous of
Hudson and not without cause, but Barney was not the open
fighter that he should be. So one Evening, just at dusk, Barney slipped up to a Pen at the Hudson place — where Hudson
was working with a bunch of Horses — And deliberately murdered Hudson. (Barney Shot Hudson while he did not know
that Barney was arround at all.) The other men got busy with
Hudson and Barney made his Escape — he laid out in the
mountains and got his supplys at Home. The Sheriff, Bob
Hatch, could not apprehend him and he run at large for some
weeks.

Charley Smith, the Jailor, and I had many talks about the
matter and one day Charley told Bob Hatch that if he would
let him off, that he would go out and catch Barney Riggs. Bob
Agreed to it — for there was some talk that Bob Hatch either
would not, or could not, catch Barney Riggs. Charley Smith
was well aquainted with Barney and his Wife, So one Night I
left and took the Horses — My Saddle Horse and Charley's
Saddle Horse and one Pack Horse — and went to a place in
the Dragoon Mountains. The next day, Charley Smith, who
had got leave of absence, left on the Stage for a visit to Texas.

At Benson, he took the Eastbound train and left the train at Dragoon Summit where I met him with the Horses, and well before Daylight, we were in a place of good feed and water and perfectly secure from observation and right close to a point that we could see everything going on at the Riggs Ranch — through Field Glasses.

We started in the next day to closely watch this place. In the middle of the Sulphur Spring Valley was a Sort of mound or slight Hill. I was on the early day watch and Just about Daylight, I saw an object moving in right at this Hill — I got a good look and it was a man on Horseback and when he got in closer, I knew that it was Barney Riggs. I called Charley and he had a look and also knew that it was Barney — He evidently was prepaired to stay there for a while, for he unsaddled and put his Horse on a Picket Rope in a low place that was nearly an Arroya where he could not be seen.

A little after Sunrise, we saw at the Ranch — Barney's wife come out and look through a Glass and soon there was a Signal from the Hill. We were pretty sure that they would meet that Night, and a little after Sunset, we saw Mrs. Barney getting ready for a Ride. She was taking along Supplys enough for Several days. It soon got too dark to see much as it was cloudy that Night, which was very much in our favor. We knew a place on that little Hill that was on the opposite side from Barney and where She would come to — our Horses were Saddled and had been all day and we were soon going to our side of the Hill. (This was supposed to be Charley's Catch if we got him and we had all our arraingements made prior to riding that night.) We reached our point very quietly and tied our Horses where they could not make any noise by stamping on Rocks, etc., then we very carefully crept towards where they were. As we reached the place we wanted to get to, Mrs. Barney had just arrived and we found that they were much closer than we had expected them to be, as they had left their horses and had come back afoot, further into the Hill.

We waited untill our chances were good and Charley told Barney to throw up his hands and told him who he was. Barney did as he was told, then Charley went to them and disarmed them — the woman was armed with a Sixshooter, Barney had his Sixshooter and a Rifle. When Charley had them allright and had the Handcuffs on Barney, I slipped away and got to my Horse, and as Charley was giving me plenty of time, I was soon out of any hearing distance and got to our Camp all right.

About Daylight, Charley and his party come in. I was supposed to be there watching for a Horse-thief, who, on his raids, made this Spring where we were camped — it was the only water in Several miles — and they were making it for water and to get their Breakfast. Of course, I was much supprised to see them and we all Breakfasted together, and as I was going to quit Camp that Morning, Charley invited me to ride along with them — which I agreed to do.

After Breakfast and the Horses had had a good rest, Charley Smith told Mrs. Barney that She could go back to the Ranch and tell old man Bannock — She could reach the Ranch easily shortly after noon. We all started, and at the Edge of Tombstone, I turned off to go to my House. Charley took Barney to the Jail and locked him up and Bob Hatch, the Sheriff, was well pleased for his Office had caught Barney Riggs.

Right from the Start, Old Bannock went to work — he was a man who knew what to do, as he was quite familiar with all the workings of a Court room. The Riggs family had had much Experience in Court rooms for they had most of them been tried for from Theft to murder — the whole family of Riggs were Killers and sometimes they did not question the fairness of a Killing. The Hudson Outfit were all more or less aquainted with the Courts also, but this time they were on the side of the Prosecution. The feeling between the outfits was Strong and become very bitter. It looked like there was going to be Another Vindetta in Cochise County, and by the time the Grand Jury had Indited Barney, and Court was in Session, and the town full of Witnesses and their supporters for Everything and from Everywhere, things were getting downright touchy.

Mark A. Smith was the District Attorney and was an able 'd fearless prosecutor. The Defence was represented by Able *q*rneys from Tombstone and also from Tucson — Men who ¹ the tricks of the Trade. The Case was to be tried in *inty* Court before Judge Webster Street — An Able There was a Consultation of Officers which included *,udge*, Dist. Atty., and Officers and The result was any *son* entering the Court Room who was not an Officer was be Disarmed at the Court Room Door — but all knew that *.here* would be Guns smuggled in past the Door. The Sheriff took charge of everything and put his men at the Doors to do the Disarming — and of course had direct charge as Sheriff over Everything and Everybody. I was Selected as Guard for the Person of the Court and to have charge of the Jury. In view of the Circumstances, this was somewhat of a trying and Daingerous position.

So on the date set, the Case of The Territory of Arizona VS Barney Riggs was Called. After the usual preliminaries, both Sides Announced ready for Trial after Several Venires were Exausted, and on the Third day, a Jury was Selected and Accepted and Sworn in to try the Case — And we were off to a hair trigger Start.

We had to take the Jury to their meals which were prepared at the Can Can Resturant where, at one End, there was a Special Table to Seat 14, of which 12 were Jurors and 2 Officers

— I always took along a Deputy Sheriff, one who was the Easyest available — but all of them were good men. The Morning of the third day about 7 A.M., I was taking the Jury to Breakfast (they Lodged at the Court House) and Going up Allen Street just as about the Middle part of the Jury line was passing John Montgomery's O.K. Corral front Entrance, Shooting Commenced right at the Entrance — the Shooters were Bannock Riggs and a friend of his whose name I do not now recall. The Jurors sought Cover at once. I was at the Head of the line and Charley Smith was the Dep. Sheriff with me that morning and he was at the rear End. He collected his men on that E into a Cover and I had done the same for my End — and the I jumped back and throwed down on Old Bannock who sur rendered at once. There were several Officers there in a minute and we sent old Bannock and his friend to Jail and we went on to Breakfast.

The Jurors had been Cautioned by the Court to not talk about the Case among themselves or to any one Else and they all were mum — but thinking. It had been the intention of Old Bannock to Scatter the Jury and thereby make it a misstrial — Then get a change of venue, for it was Evident by the Venires Exausted in securing this Jury, that another Jury could not have been secured in Cochise County. It was pretty sharp work — but we kept that Jury together and they had not been separated. The matter was at once taken up at the opening of Court that morning — and after the Jurors had been questioned, the Attys. for the Defence gave it up and agreed that there was no real or technical Grounds to ask for the Discharge of the Jury.

This was somewhat of a setback for the Riggs interest. Barney was getting restless and fractious — but finally the Evidence was all in and both sides rested and the next morning the Case was Closed and the Argument Commenced. The

Dist. Attorney both opens and closes the Argument and very seldom says more than tell the Jury what the Territory, or State, has proven and ask the Jury to bring in a Verdict warranted by the Evidence, and the Law as set forth in the Charge as given by the Court. And then the Attorneys for the Defense make their Arguments, but the Strongest man is usually the last one to speak, as upon him rests the Responsibility of making an argument that must anticipate the Closing Argument of the Dist. Atty.

My position in the Court room, by reason of being Guard for the Person of the Court, was sitting up beside him near one End of the Court's Desk — which is higher than the floor of the Main Courtroom. His Desk was Slightly on the order of a Cresent, and directly in front and below the Court's Desk was the Table for the Attys. Shaped like the Desk of the Court. Where I sat, I could keep a good outlook over the Prisoner, the Attys., The Jury, and the whole Courtroom. I had my Short Double Barrelled Shot Gun sitting right by me but out of Sight of all but the Judge. We had listened to all the Speeches made by the Attorneys for the Defence and Mark Smith, the Dist. Atty., was making his Closing Argument. Mark was a Personal and close friend of mine and I thought a lot of him. He did not fear anything or anybody and he had flayed the Witnesses for the Defence and had come to where he had taken up Barney Riggs himself. (I seemed to have a hunch that some trouble was coming.) Mark Smith was in his Argument up to the actual Killing, and he was picturing Barney Sneaking up to that Pen like an Apache Indian — "And," (Dramatically) "He did then and there Murder Hudson." Barney was sitting behind Mark Smith and there was a large and heavy Inkstand on the Attys'. table, and Barney jumped to his feet and grabbed that Ink Stand and Shouted, "Yes, You Son of a Bitch and I will

73

murder you." All in a few seconds, I left my chair and jumped. I just touched on the Table and then onto Barney Riggs' Shoulders, crushing him to the floor and taking and throwing aside the Ink Stand, jerking Barney up and throwing him into his Chair. Mark Smith was the quietest man there — he stood still and when I had Barney in his chair, Mark turned to me and said, "Thank you, Fred," and went right on with his Argument. I stayed pretty close to Barney until Mark finished the Argument and the Case was at an End. How I ever made that jump, I cannot tell, even to this day. It was a long jump and was Commented on by many — But I must have helped myself when I touched on the Table and from there on to Barney.

When the Case was finally given to the Jury by the Judge, they retired to the Jury room to arrive at a verdict. Comments were mostly all one way — Hanging — But as the Jury remained out for sometime, Doubt was Expressed. Finally, the Jury announced that they had agreed upon a Verdict. When they were brought into Court, the Foreman announced the fact that they had agreed — And the Verdict was handed to the Clerk and after its perusal by the Judge It was read out aloud by the Clerk. The Verdict was Guilty of Murder in the Second Degree — which carried a Life Sentence.

It was a sure thing that it was a Compromise Verdict. Of course it all come out and it was one man who did it. Each Juror when being Examined was asked, "Have you any conscientious Scruples against affixing the Death Penalty, Should the Evidence in this Case Warrant it?" and the answer from each one had to be "No" else they would have been excused. After the Jury retired to the Jury Room and Elected a Foreman, there was one man who said he had something to say — which was, that at the time he was examined, that he did not have any Scruples what ever about affixing the Death Penalty, but during the trial of this case, he had undergone a change of opinion. He said that in this Case if ever there was a man that deserved Hanging it was Barney Riggs, but he could not sign a verdict that would take a man's life — This man was well Known, and Known to be a man who was thougherly honest in every particular and it had weight. All the Balance of the Jury argued with him, but to no Avail — All the ballance, to a man, were for the Death penalty. So after seeing that there could not be any change made in him they finally agreed on Life — and said among themselfs that a few years Even, at Yuma, was worse than Death. So ended the *trial* of Barney Riggs. But it was not the *End* of Barney Riggs. He was taken to Yuma and was there for some years. He made a good Prisoner — and one day there was an insurrection in the Prison and an outbreak in which Barney distinguished himself by being on the side of and with the Officials and at the Risk of his life, for which, after a year or so, he was given a Pardon.

Now, we were looking forward to another Election — the Present Sheriff was going to run again — and it was quite sure that he would get the Nomination. But there was a strong influence that would be against him, that wanted him to have the Nomination and then be to the Expense of the Campaign, for they wanted to break him financially.

Bob Hatch had a friend in Tombstone who lived next door to where Bob Hatch and his Wife lived and this friend had a very pretty but foolish Wife that was vain and loved flattery. This man had helped Bob Hatch many times financially and otherwise — the two familys were very close friends. Bob finally secured the Confidence of this man's Wife and then Shamefully betrayed this friendship — As usual, the Husband was the last one to hear of anything wrong, but it was well and generally Known by many. Bob Hatch had a Room down town and this Woman used to go there. She spent much time

75

there and finally the Husband heard something, but would not believe this of his friend, but he was told to watch and he would find out — He did. And there, in this house where they had the Room, tryed to Kill Bob Hatch but Hatch Escaped — And Kept out of the way for several days. While mutual friends worked with this Wronged Husband and on the strength of Saving the Woman from public disgrace — which an Encounter between him and Hatch would bring forth. So he finally agreed to not force anything, but he became the bitter and Everlasting Enemy of Bob Hatch. He sent the Woman home to her folks in the East and after a Year or so, he secured a Divorce in California where he had later gone to live — Now this was the influence that would be against Bob Hatch in this Coming Election — Hatch was foolish to Even run at all for any office.

The Convention Come on and Hatch was nominated by the Skin of his teeth. I was wanted by many of the Convention members — but I knew that I could not be Sheriff and Hold my place with the Company and I wanted to Stay in the Service of the Company. I had to come right out and tell them that if they nominated me that I would not run — and even then, Hatch had hard Sleding and when he finally got the Nomination, there was much dissatisfaction and I later knew of Several Members of that Convention that Voted Against Hatch at the General Election. When the Convention was adjourned, I come out by being nominated for Constable which office would have as much jurisdiction criminally. And at the Election I was Elected by a good Majority — Although I did not do any Electioneering and, much against my principals, I Voted for Hatch, as he was the nominee of the Convention. The Democrats put up a man that was a close friend of mine — And I am not saying that I did not change some votes to him. His name was John Slaughter, a Cattle

Man, the owner of the San Bernadino Grant that laid partly in Arizona and partly in Mexico. He was a small man, but game as ever a man was made — And at the Election John Slaughter was Elected by a heavy Majority. We were all to take Office on the first of January 1887, And after Election and before taking office John Slaughter and I had a perfect understanding about our work — And we did work together — and rode together many times. I took Charley Smith as an assistant and Deputy.

8

BANDITS AND BISCUITS

Shortly thereafter, there was a Train Robbery just South of Nogales. The work was done by 3 men — 2 of which was arrested by Rurales under my friend, Colonel Kosterliski, and through this source, I learned the name of the man who had made his escape into Arizona. (The Robbery was in Sonora.) I knew the man well — Bill Taylor was his name. Taylor was in rather bad Standing in Arizona and was in the Dodge from Officers, but he was not much in Dainger from them, for all most Every one was in sympathy with him for what he had done. He was driving a Freight team of 6 mules and there was another team with him of 6 mules belonging to the same man. Taylor had not been paid for a long time and had continually tried to get them to pay him something but was not able to do so. One night, he took both Teams and took them over the Line into Sonora and hid them out, and then sent word to the owners that when they sent him what was oweing to him that he would return the mules — but they thought that they would catch him and send him up, and while all this was pending, Bill Taylor got into this Train Robbery.

I Knew about where he would be hiding out and where he would get his Grub, so I reached there the next day a little past noon. I was closely watching the House where he would get his Grub — it was just inside of the Sonora line and I had no apparent jurisdiction, but I was fixed up all right by my friend, Colonel Kosterliski. As I Neared the place, I caught sight of a man going into an Arroyo just behind the House. I knew this was Taylor, for I would know him as far as I could see him. I knew that Taylor would watch me and I stopped at the House and the man come out — this man that Kept this place was a friend of mine and I could rely on him to truthfully give me any information that he had. I just set on my horse and talked to him — I asked him if Taylor was arround there and he told me that he had just gone up the Arroyo.

I stayed long enough to show Taylor that I was not in a hurry, and then rode along, taking the trail that led through the Arroyo, which was a Saddle trail on a cut off to Fronteras. I had not gone far when I saw Bill standing by a mesquite tree close to the Trail — he had his Winchester, and I sort of halted a little, like I was supprised at seeing him, and started right along, saying, "Hello, Bill. What are you doing here?" And he said to me, "Don't come any Closer, for I am not going to be Arrested." I did not stop my horse any but I kept right on talking, saying, "What is the matter with you? I don't care a thing about those mules, and if you had them here with you, I would go right along on my way — I am going to Fronteras."

By that time, I was up close to where he was. I did not fool myself any, for I Knew that Bill was a sure Shot and that he would be hard to take, if he ever thought that I wanted him for that train Robbery. He had told me to stop several times, and I finally stopped and got right off of my horse, saying, "I am as tired as a Dog for I have ridden a long time." I set right down on the ground and Commenced to make a Cigarette. Bill still stood off by the tree, and he said to me, "Where you from?" I told him that I Stayed with Frank Leslie last night.

I knew that Bill knew the Country and I had to make my rides right — so as he would know that I was right. He then asked me what the news was in Tombstone. (Now, this Train Robbery took place 3 Days before.) I told him that I did not know any, for I had not been in Tombstone for over a week and then I kept right on counting back — I saw that Bill was thinking. He asked me what I was going to Fronteras for and I told him that I was going to try and get Jesus Escalente — that I had a tip about him and thought I could get him. Bill knew about Escalente and that he had shot at me and that I had shot him. And I got quite Confidential about the tip that I had — I just had to keep Bill interested. I was sure I could beat him to it, if I could get a chance. Bill told me I had better look out for myself for Escalente would Kill me if he got the chance.

I made another cigarette, and asked Bill if he wanted one. He said, "Yes, I have no Tobacco and Papers with me." I told him to take mine, for I had some more in my Saddle Pocket and I pitched the Sack and Papers over toward him. He Come to where they were and Set down on his feet like I was setting — and as every one set in those days. When he come to Roll the Cigarette, he had to have two hands and he laid his Winchester acrosst his legs — I Knew that it was my time, and I sure went fast. I had him covered and told him to get his hands up quick, or I would sure have to drill him — he got them up. And then I told him to get up, which he did, and the Winchester then fell to the Ground. I made him step away from it and turn arround and then I had my Gun shoved against his Back. I then took his Six Shooter and then I put the Handcuffs on him which I had in my Pocket, Searched him thougherly, unloaded the Guns, made him Get on my Horse, tied the Handcuffs to the Horn of the Saddle and tied his legs together under the Horse, Got up behind him, and Started for Bisbee about 8 miles away. When I got there, I got a good team, and borrowed a pair of Leg Irons and fastened Bill in the Buggy so that he could not reach me and I drove into Nogales before Sun up.

It would take about 3 months to Extradite a prisoner Either way, and where there was no question as to the Guilt of the Accused, there was a working agreement between the Officers on both sides of the line.

The most prominent Saloon in Nogales was built right on top of the line — part of this Saloon was in Mexico and part of it in Arizona. They Sold Cigars, etc. in Mexico and Liquors in Arizona. Right where the Cigar Stand joined onto the Bar was the Line, and the Line was Marked across the Floor of the Saloon.

I had turned Bill Taylor over to the Officers at Nogales, Arizona. That Evening, Taylor was up town with the Officers to Eat, and then they went into the Saloon, and while there, there was a fist fight Started, and in the *mele* the Officers and Bill Taylor were pushed, while getting out of the way, across the Line. Col. Kosterliski's men were there in the Saloon, and when they Saw Taylor accross the line, they arrested him, and then he was in the hands of the Officers of Mexico and within the Jurisdiction of the State of Sonora, Mexico, where he was wanted for Train Robbery, which Crime was, in that Country, at that time — upon Conviction — Punishable by Death. Two of the men had allready turned State's Evidence and made Confessions — Bill Taylor, later on, also confessed.

Soon after this, I lost my Dep., Charley Smith — he was Shot and never did ride any more. About a year before this there had been a fight between Charley Smith and Charley Cunningham, in which Cunningham was Shot in the Leg. They were both of them my friends, and I got them together, and they had a talk, and then Burried the Hatchet.

There was a man by the name of Lazzard — a 6 footer, and nearly as dark as a Mexican. He did not like Charley Smith or Charley Cunningham — this I knew — but he posed as the friend of Each of them. I had cautioned both of them against

Lazzard, but he kept working on them, carrying his lies from one to the other, untill he finally had them worked up to where it would take very little to Start them going. I had been out considerable of the time, and could not Keep up with them very well, but I Knew what Lazzard would do, for he was as unscrupable as a Snake and as daingerous as a Den of Snakes.

I come in one night near Midnight, and had just put my Horse away, and got back up town. I was at the Oriental Saloon when I heard Shots down Allen Street some where. I soon heard that Cunningham had Shot Smith, and they had taken Charley Smith into Pony Brown's Saloon — I got right down there and they had laid him on a table. One of his Legs was broken and when I got to the Door of the room, there was Lazzard holding the Leg. I Stopped in the Door and Said, "Lazzard, you would-be Murdering Son of a Gun, turn that man's leg loose and get out of here, You Cowardly Cur." My language was not as mild as I have put it here, for at that time, it was strongly Emphasized, and much more forceable than Polite — I was mad and Sore. Lazzard got out, and out of town that Night. He very soon left the Country, and I have never seen him since.

Dr. Goodfellow got there immediately, and he Said that Charley's Hip Bone was shattered all to pieces, And he told me that there was very little hope of saving his life. We got him onto a Stretcher and Carried him home. He lived with Bob Winders and had come to the Country with them, and it had always been home to him. He did not die then, but his Suffering was intense — he was a Cripple and could hardly get arround and a couple of years later Died from the Effects of this wound.

Charley Cunningham left the Country very soon after the Shooting, and I did not meet him for some years, and then met him in the Cripple Creek District where he was running a Saloon and Dance Hall. I had quite a few talks with him and he was truly sorry about the trouble between him and Smith. He had found out all about Lazzard and I think that he would have Killed Lazzard, had he met him — but he had never seen him since the Night of the Shooting.

A Short time before this Shooting between Smith and Cunningham, there had been a Train Robbery at Pantana, on the Southern Pacific, and it was the last case that Charley Smith ever worked on.

We got to the Scene of the Robbery the next day. The messenger was named Smith. I interviewed him and he gave me the Particulars of the Robbery. He said that there was only 2 men in the Robbery and that he did not see any Horses at all. Among other things that he told me was that both of their Sixshooters had black handles, and they looked like they were New.

I Started at the Railroad, and Cut for Sign of a trail. Manuel, the Mexican Yacci Indian that was always with me and a Wizard on a trail, took one side and I took the other, Each to make a half Circle and Meet at a given point on the R.R. near by. I had got nearly half way round when I found the trail of two men afoot, headed towards the Rincon Mountains. I called Manuel, and together we Examined and measured these tracks — we had only one well-defined track at the scene of the holdup and we compared this one with one that we had found on this trail. They were the same, So we Knew that we had the trail of the Robbers. We could see that they were headed towards Mountain Springs, which was right at the foot of the mountain, and on the Old Stage Road — we kept on this trail. There was only 2 men and no Horses — we had about made up our minds that there were only 2 men and that they had left their Horses at the Mountain Springs.

Charley Smith had the balance of the Posse and our two Horses with him and they were Keeping in the background while Manuel and I were working on foot, for it was hard trailing, as the Country was very dry. As we neared the Springs, it was getting Dark so that we Could not trail and be Certain that we were right, So we made a careful examination of one Spring that was a little appart from the Big one — there were no tracks there. So we went into Camp for the Night — Manuel and I both Knew we could pick up the trail the next morning. But that night come a terriffic Rain Storm that was nearly a Cloud burst, and in the Morning, there was no trail. Everything in that Section was washed out and any Cutting for any Sign was Entirely useless.

We rode into Benson where there was a telegraph office and we Could give, and also get, information. About the first one that I heard from was Virgil Earp, who was in Tombstone — Charley Smith and I both wanted to see the Old Boy badly. He come down on the Stage and we met him at Benson. Virgil Earp had been in California Ever since they tried to assassinate him when he was City Marshal in Tombstone.

That Evening, close to dark, we had got word of two men Horseback on the Rincon Mountains, and we were going to leave for there before daylight in the Morning. Virg wanted to go with us, so we got him a good horse and outfit at Benson and we all left before day.

Virg had shown us his Arm and told us all about how it had got along — the Surgeons had taken out the whole Elbow and there was nothing there but flesh. Manuel had been out among the Mexicans, Scouting for information, and had only met Virg a few minutes that night. In the morning, as we were nearing the Rincons, we had an open Mesa to cross and we were Crossing it at a good Stiff Gallop, so that we would be past it before it got light enough to be seen from a distance.

Virg had let his arm dangle and he noticed Manuel observing him closely, So he let his arm flop arround for Virg knew how Supersticious this Class of Indian and Mexican was, and in a very few Minutes, Manuel Come rushing up to me with, "My God, Boss, what is the matter with that man?" I knew Manuel and his suppersticions, and as we were where we Could Ease up or Stop and not be seen, I had to Stop the whole outfit and get Virg to get off of his horse and Show Manuel his arm, and then we told him all about it. He had heard of it, and was very much interested. He felt of the arm, lifted it up, and let it fall, and was much impressed — and he and Virg become great friends. He looked out for Virg on all occasions and took care of Virg's horse for him on the whole trip — Virg was much amused at Manuel.

After we had got the trail of two horsemen, we were climbing up the mountain and were following a Canyon. Manuel took one side and I the other, and they had gone up on my side. Manuel was higher up than I was, and could see the trail in places, so as to make it Easier for me and also save time. As soon as we were sure that they were headed for the Spring that was on top of the Mountain, and Known to Charley Smith, Manuel, and myself, we then took the Easy way and when we got to the top rim, we halted the outfit. Manuel and I cut for Sign and soon found the trail which led to the Spring.

The top of the mountain was a beautiful place of Even ground of about 5 or 6 acres, And a Spring that flowed water sufficient to have Irrigated much more Ground than there was there. The water flowed for about 100 feet and disappeared — it was clear as a Crystall and Cold as Icewater. It was a very interesting Sight for Virg and he was much taken with it.

It was nearly night, and the only place on these Mountains to Camp. We Concluded to Stop for there was good feed for the Horses and As soon as they were Cared for, Manuel and I took a Scout arround before it was too dark to see anything. We found where there had been a Camp, and we also found that there was another horse had joined them there — but we could only find where two men had Camped and it looked like they had spent 2 or 3 nights there. So the sense of the party was that the third horseman had joined them in the Morning and gone on with them, for we found the trail going off of the Mountain and there was 3 horses made the trail. This trail was headed towards the Tanka Verdi, which was opposite from where they had Come on to the Mountain.

We were gone at Daylight and Kept the trail well. Shortly after Noon, we were down on the Mesas where there were a good many Mexicans living, and it seemed that Every family had the Smallpox. Our trail took us into a creek, and we found where they had Come out just below a house that was flying a Yellow Flag, the Sign for Smallpox. We had a Consultation — for it would be a very neat trick for these men, if they were the Train Robbers, to go into this house and hoist a Yellow Flag and a Posse would go by them.

I could not stand it, and I Said that I was going to see anyway, for we could not get the trail past there. I rode up to the door, and when I got off my horse they were all there — Charley Smith and Manuel went to the Door with me. It was not locked, and I pushed it open, and an old Man raised up out of a chair where he had been Dozing and Said to me in good English, "We have the Smallpox here." I said that I only wanted to see what kind they had — he said the Black — there were 2 Daughters, 1 Son, and his Wife that were in that room, all with the Smallpox, and he had had it some years before and was taking Care of them. Just as we were about to mount our horses, he come to the door and said that he did not think that there was any dainger for us, for they had all

86

passed the fever stage. He told me that he had seen one man ride past there about 2 hours before, but he thought there were more with him for he had heard the Horses. There was a Road passed there and we Could not tell any thing by that, and all we could do was to watch for where they left the Road.

I sent Manuel out ahead to see what he could learn from some of the Mexicans. He soon Come back and told me that there were 2 men in Camp up the creek about a mile from the last house. We started right off, and when we got about there, we stopped and Manuel and I went on a Scout. From a point high above the Creek, we could see 2 men and 3 horses — we could not see any third man. We got back, and made a ride for their Camp, and when we rode in, we knew both of them — 2 Cow Boys from a Ranch just below Tres Alemos, on the San Pedro River. They were looking for Stray Cattle, and the Riddle of the third horse on the Rincon Mountain was that they camped there, and left their Pack horse there while they went down arround the Mountain Spring, and then arround the mountain, and Come up from that side. It was on that Side that they were seen and that is the information that we got in Benson and theirs was the trail that we had followed and the Pack horse made the third Horse track from the Camp at the Spring on the Mountain.

We were blowed up and Could not get any trace of any one else, So we Started on our home journey — Virgil Earp left us at Benson to return to California, and it was some years later before I met Virg again.

A Short time after this, there was another Train Robbery at the Same place and the same Messenger — Smith. I felt Sure when I talked to this Messenger, that if Ever he was held up again, that there would be a fight. I Knew Smith quite well and I was sure that he would fight — but here was another holdup and he did not put up a fight. I was supprised and a little hurt, for it looked like I had been Mistaken in the man. The more that I thought about it, the more I felt sure that there was some reason for it. Now, that reason could be attributed to several Causes. Smith, the Messenger, was in Tucson, and when I got to the Scene of the Robbery, which was about Noon, there was a Switch Engine there, and they offered to take me in to Tucson — which was only a few miles away — and bring me back. I had my men rest and feed the Horses at Pantana, And I run into Tucson.

I met Smith at the Depot, and I could see that there was something the matter with him. I questioned him Closely and quite pointedly, and he finally said to me, "There is a reason, and a good one, but you Couldn't drag it out of me with that Borox Team," and I Knew that he would not give it up. But I was very thougherly Convinced that Smith was not implicated in the Robbery in Any way.

There was a Route Agent on that Territory by the Name of Charley Gault. He was not a Stout man at all for he was afflicted with Tubercoloses, and as I left Smith, Gault Come to Me and said, "Fred, Come back with me to Smith and I will tell you all about it." Every one that Knew Gault was his friend, and loved him for his quiet ways and lovable disposition. When He, Smith, and I were together, he said, "Fred, the whole and only reason that there was not a fight at the Robbery was me — I was in the Car coming to Tucson, and I just couldn't Stand it to take any chances in a fight." He said that Smith was going to, and wanted to make a fight, and that he, Gault, just begged him and implored him not to make a fight, as he said he just Knew that he would get Killed — and he finally succeeded in getting Smith to promice not to make any resistance. So that was the reason why Smith did not fight.

Smith described the same two men who had held him up

before, even to the Black handles of their Pistols. I got right back there and got off at the Scene of the Holdup. My men were there and we got the Trail right away, and we run it right to Mountain Springs and Night come on.

During the Afternoon, there was a U.S. Sargent and Six Men Come to me — they were from Fort Huachuca and the Sargent had orders from the Commanding Officer, Col. Sandy Forsythe, to dismount any or all of his men to furnish me Horses. (Our horses were all better that theirs, for theirs were too Fat, and in the Scouting, several become overheated and two of them Died that Night.)

Fred Burke, Chief Special Officer of the S.P.Ry., and John Thacker, a Special Officer for Wells Fargo and Co. Express, — were Coming and would be there in the morning. They had arrainged to have the U. S. Marshal, Meade, to Join them on the Train with a Posse.

We were at Camp, and at Daylight, Manuel and I took the trail. We followed it up the Mountain about half a mile, and it led us to a Cave, and in that Cave we found much Evidence — We found the Rubber handles to the Sixshooters, Showing that they had changed handles on their Guns, we found the Masks and many other things. We also found some remnants of a lunch, and in digging arround, I found a Biscuit. Unobserved, I put that Biscuit in the Bosom of my Shirt, for I Knew that Biscuit, had eaten several like it, and I Knew that there was only one person in that Country that could make Biscuits like it. It was a man and he was named George Wolfork, and he Kept a little Eating house and Corral at Pantana — and I just Knew that George was going to tell who had got that Lunch.

Charley Smith Knew George Wolfork well — Knew him in Texas before he went to Arizona — And was the man to go against Wolfork to get the Information. I got Charley off to one Side and told him what I had, and gave him the Biscuit, which he Knew like I did, and he left for Pantana, less than two miles distant.

We returned down to the Camp, and Manuel, who had gone on a trail that led away from the Cave, was at the Camp — he had trailed them right to Pantana on the old road. It was well that he had done so, for here come the U. S. Marshal and Posse, Fred Burke, and John Thacker. I told them all about the trail that led to the Cave, and the same one that led away from the Cave and to Pantana, but I did not tell them about the Biscuit or Charley Smith's Mission. They had met Charley, and he told them that he was going to Pantana to Send a Message to the Sheriff at Tombstone — and in Case that some one would get inquisitive, he did send the message.

They all wanted to go to the Cave but Some of them were most too Fat to take the Climb — Fred Burke was a very heavy man and lame, having been Shot in the Knee some years before. I had Known Fred Burke since I had been a Boy, and we were friends. Burke could not make that climb, and so stated. I got a chance and told him that I would get him up there, Even if I had to Carry him — which made him laugh. There was in the Soldier Squad, a large, Powerful Sorrell Horse, Capable of carrying Fred Burke anywhere. (Burke weighed over 200 pounds.) I went to the Sargent and told him about this, and he said, "My orders are to help you, but if they were not, I would gladly help you." So we put Fred Burke on the Hurricane Deck of the Sorrell Horse and he made the trip fine, but it seemed that I had Stirred up trouble for myself.

This U.S. Marshal, W. K. Meade, went to the Sargent and wanted a Horse also — for Meade was a fat man himself. The Sargent told him he could not do it. Meade Said to him, "You let this man, Dodge, have the Best horse you have got." The Sargent told him that I could have all the Horses that he had if I wanted them — this did not make Meade feel any better, for he did not like me. And I did not like him, but if he had asked me, I would have got him a horse.

W. K. Meade had posed as a Mining Man, and was one in a way, back in the Tombstone days, during the troubles there, and was one of the Supporters of Sheriff John Behan — and so the feeling between me and Meade was of long standing. He Shot off his Mouth to an Extended extent, untill I had to call him — and while I was about it I called him good and hard — not very polite, but earnestly, vehement, and plain. Fred Burke took a hand and told Meade a few — Meade Knew that Burke had the Southern Pacific Ry. behind him, so Meade subsided much like the Pussyfoot that he was. In his Official position, he later took it up by letter with Col. Forsythe, and the Col. called him down quite hard — for the Col. did not like Meade either. (John Thacker, with water on both Shoulders, Kept out of it.) We all finally Come into Pantana, for it was the Consenses of opinion that the Robbers had come in there and taken a train from there — which way we did not Know.

Charley Smith had done his work, and George Wolfork had told him all he Knew. George W. Said that 2 men that had come there were evidently from a freight train that had gone west the morning before the Train Robbery, and the Conductor of that freight train was named George Green. George W. said that these men Come to his place and had Breakfast, and they had him put up Lunch Enough for 4 Men and had gone down the Track towards where the Robbery took place — This was the first Robbery. George could give no names, but he did give a good discription of both men, for he had seen them both twice. This Train passed through Pantana Early in the Morning, and this same Conductor and Train Crew passed through Pantana going East towards El Paso the Early morning after the Train Robbery. George W. had not seen these men again — untill some time later. This Robbery — the 1st — was on April 27th, 1887.

The next time was on August 10th, 1887. The manner of Stopping the Train was much the same, Only this last time, the Engine turned over but the Engineer and Fireman jumped and were not hurt much. This, of Course, Called out not only the Express Officers, but the Railroad Officers as well. George W. had again seen these two men, the Same ones that he had seen before — they come to his place for Breakfast and had him put up a big lunch. George Baked a Pan of Biscuits and they were used in this Lunch And it was one of these Biscuits that I had found. George could not give any names, but his discription was perfect of the men, and they were the same that had been there at the time of the other Robbery — He was also sure that they had come off of the Early freight train. The Conductor of that Train was the same George Green, and he was the Conductor of the same Train Going East again the morning after.

George Wolfork had exacted a promice from Charley Smith that he would not be bothered any by being taken away from his place any more than it was necessary but he had agreed that he would testify in Court to what he had told Charley Smith.

After Charley Smith had told me all of this, we Conferred together. It was evident that we must tell Thacker and Fred Burke and were lothe to tell W. K. Meade, (for Charley Smith did not like him any more than I did and our dislike was for the same reasons) but as the United States Marshal, he must be included, So I called Thacker, Burke, and Meade off and away from Every one Else, and when the five of us was Entirely alone, I said that there was some information that I had that they must be told, and then I addressed myself directly to W. K. Meade. I said that I was giving this information in his presence, but I wanted it distinctly understood that I was giving this to the United States Marshal and not to the Man, W. K. Meade, who held the appointment. Then I gave them all that I had — how I had found the Biscuit and Knew it, all about Charley Smith's pull with George W., how I had sent Charley in to work on George W., and then all that there was that had been got from George W.

Thacker was full of Foxy Visions, Fred Burke was logical and Careful. It was Evident that a lot of work had yet to be done, For while George W. could identify the men who had come there, The Biscuit I found in the Cave, etc., All would be a link in a chain of Circumstancial Evidence, yet it did not prove that these two men were at the Scene of the Robbery.

There had been taken by the Robbers, $1000.00 in Mexican Silver which might become a Clue.

Fred Burke had to return to San Francisco in a few days, and the whole Case was left in the hands of the Officers and John Thacker. Thacker and I worked together as much as it was possible, but Charley Smith and I worked continuously. We got the time of the running of the trains of which George Green was the Conductor, and it was soon plain to be seen that he was an accomplice. We Also got the names of the two men who George W. had seen and would know. Charley Smith took George W. to El Paso, and without George W. being seen, he saw the two men that we had the names of — they lived in El Paso and their names were Jack Smith and Dick Myers, and George W. identifyed them as the two men who had been to his place twice. They and George Green were friends.

We were working on the Mexican Silver, trying to find where it was Exchanged. Thacker was sure that it was Paso Del Norte, but Charley Smith and I reasoned otherwise, and I finally found the Place where it was Exchanged — it was at

Nogales, Arizona. (This place had two Exchanges — one on the Sonora Side and one on the Arizona side.) Thacker was in Tucson, and I sent to him to meet me in Benson, which he did, and together, we went to Nogales — we got all that we wanted.

We went over our Evidence carefully and was ready to make the Arrests. I sent for Charley Smith to meet us in Benson, which he did. We were all in Benson, waiting for the Eastbound Passenger Train, when Thacker received a Telegram that the Train into El Paso, early that morning, had been held up about 4 or 5 miles East of El Paso by 2 men, and the Messenger, J. Ernest Smith, had killed both the men and they had, that morning, been identifyed as Jack Smith and Dick Myers. Thacker and I went on to El Paso and Charley Smith returned to Tombstone.

When Thacker and I got to El Paso, we found that the two men that we wanted as Principals were dead and that George Green had jumped the Country. (He was later arrested in Fort Worth and brought back to El Paso, where he Pled Guilty and got a sentence of 5 years in the Penetentiary.)

Charley Smith had worked hard on the Case, and it was through him that the first information was obtained, but he did not get one cent of the reward. I was not offered any of it — of Course, I would not, and could not, accept any of it, but Charley Smith was Entitled to Share in it — and it was through the Report and Argument of John Thacker that the whole ammount together with other remunerations were paid to [*Messenger*] Smith, who was known to his fellow workers as "Windy" Smith. Thacker's Manipulations of Reward money was known in Arizona — I do not know whether he received any Cut out of this one or not—

9

ICE WAR ON THE DESERT

On Feb. 25th, '88, The Train on the S.P. was held up at Steins Pass, which is right on the line of Arizona and New Mexico, Both of which at that time were Territorys. The Sheriff of Grant County, New Mexico, of which Silver City was the County Seat, organized a Posse and went to the scene of the Robbery. Steins Pass was a small Abandoned place. There was an Empty Store building and 2 or 3 Empty houses there, also a small Railroad Station, and the Agent was everything — So he was the Telegraph operator also. At that time, there was a small bunch of tough Characters that had been making the place their headquarters — Sort of Camping arround in the Empty buildings — and it was learned by the Sheriff of Grant County, New Mexico, that they were the ones that held up the Train. He started to Arrest them, but they Stood the Sheriff and his Posse off, and forced the Sheriff and Posse to leave. The Sheriff and Posse, for reasons Known only to them selfs, returned to headquarters at Silver City. There was a lot of talk along the Railroad and Stations About the Sheriff and Posse that had been Stood off.

Some days later, I was in Tucson where I received a Message from Sheriff John Slaughter of Cochise County To Come to Tombstone at once. I caught the Train to Benson, then to Fairbank, and Stage into Tombstone. When I got there, I saw a Buggy team and 2 Saddle Horses all ready to go somewhere. I Knew the Horses, One of which was my own favorite Saddle Horse and the other one was John Slaughter's League

Horse. (In old Mexico, they Have Horse races which are matched for 1, 2, or 3 Leagues — a league is 3 miles.) When I got down off the Stage, the Sheriff met me and said, "Let's go. I will tell you all about it as we go." And it was that he was getting news from Steins Pass. The Agent and Telegraph operator there was John Slaughter's Nephew and he was the one who was furnishing him the information, And he had given Slaughter All the Particulars about the Robbery, and the Robbers, and also about the Sheriff of Grant County, N.M. and Posse being Stood off.

Slaughter thought that He and I were all that was needed to Arrest that Bunch — Suited me fine. And as we rode along, the Sheriff told me that he had arrainged with the Railroad Company to furnish him with an Engine and Empty Box Car, and that they were to meet us at Dragoon Summit.

We were traveling in a 2 Seated Carriage from John Montgomery's livery Stable, and had a Driver to take the Team back. There was also along, a Mexican that worked for Slaughter to take care of our Saddle Horses which he was leading behind the Surry. That would Keep them much fresher and less tired than they would be if we had ridden them to the Railroad, and, as we were liable to perhaps have rather a protracted siege ourself, we would also be fresher and less tired.

We got to Dragoon Summit a Short time before the Engine and car reached there, but we only had to wait a few minutes. When they come, we put our Horses into the car and was on our way. We had allready sent the Team back to Tombstone. We had ourselfs and Horses out of Sight when we passed through Wilcox and Fort Bowie — the whole number of men on this Special Train was the Engineer, Fireman, Conductor, the Sheriff, Myself, and the Mexican who looked after the Horses. When we Started, we had a very thorough understanding with this Train Crew who were all three good men and had been selected and instructed by the R.R. Supt.

At San Simon, Slaughter had arrainged to have a message there from his nephew at Steins Pass which would govern our movements going into Steins Pass. (This Operator at San Simon was a close friend of Slaughter's Nephew and we could count on no leak there.) We did not show up ourselfs, but got the Message all right, and it was a little bad. Since the appearance of the New Mexico Sheriff at Steins Pass, this Gang had been going out at night into the Hills to Sleep and riding in in the Morning, and as it was getting pretty close to night, they were leaving for the Hills. The train crew run on aways and went on to a Side track, and we all had a Consultation over the situation, which resulted in our going right along, natural like, passing through Steins Pass, only stopping long Enough for the Conductor to get his Orders from the train Dispatcher, which gave Slaughter time Enough to talk with his Nephew, and we went right along to Lordsburg, New Mexico, and went right on through to the Stock Yards — where we unloaded and fed our Horses for the Night. There was Water in the Pen. Then the Conductor and Fireman went up town and when they got back, we had lots of Grub. We all Eat heartily for we had no Dinner, and then we all Slept in the Car. We were all up very early, took care of the Horses, had our Breakfast, and was ready to go, upon receipt of a Message from Steins Pass. About 7:30 A.M. we got it, and they were coming in, So we Saddled our Horses, and loaded, and was shortly Gone. I Knew all of these men that we wanted and Slaughter Knew them all but one. They were named Dick Hart, Jack Blont, Tom Johnson, and Larry Shehan.

We Rolled up to Steins Pass and the Engineer stopped at a Bank by the side of the track that we had selected the night before. We saw Dick Hart and Tom Johnson near the Depot when we got there — they were afoot. We just jumped our Horses out of the Car, and as they hit the Ground, we hit the

97

Saddles. Hart and Johnson started to run to the old Store building, and we were Close on them. When we all reached it, Slaughter took the Side door and Jumped from his Horse. I took the front door, which was a Double door, and open. I just Swung low and went right into the Building. My Horse stopped at the Word. I was ready for Action. I had, in addition to my Rifle in the Scabard, my Short Double Barrelled Shot Gun. The two men had just reached the End of the Counter when I ordered them to get their hands up — they could see that I had them both in line and Saw what I had in my hands. My Horse was still and I was as steady as though I was on the floor — I Could not miss and they Knew it. They put them up, and Hart Said, as his hands went up, "Slaughter, we have got you, but if we do go on, it is sure death for us from Dodge and that Shot Gun, so we will quit."

Slaughter got the Cuffs on them, and their Guns, and then I got down from my Horse. We took them up to the Car and the Conductor was to Guard them. Just then, we saw Larry Shehan ride arround the point of the Hill — He took in the Situation quickly and settled himself in the Saddle and, hurling vile words at us, headed off into the Animas Valley toward old Mexico. I took my Rifle, and Knowing that a man on a running horse at a long distance was not an Easy Mark, I dropped to one Knee and let him have it. Slaughter was watching the Shot and his Eyes were on the Target when I fired. He said, "Missed the man, but hit the Horse — I say, you hit the Horse." Slaughter had a peculiar way of repeating the last of most of what he said, and always with the words "I say." The man was too far away to waste another Shot on him, and it was in open valley, and we both Knew that that League Horse would soon pick him up. As Slaughter went to Swing into the Saddle, the Lacing String on his Stirrup Strap broke. I jumped right over to fix it. We had time for that

Horse would surely get him, and Said Stirrup might be very important if Larry Shehan put up a fight when he was overtaken. Slaughter, while sitting on his horse waiting, was watching Shehan going and he said, "He's a little wild. I say, he's a little wild." And he was gone, for I had fixed the Strap right then.

I got information that Jack Blont had seen what was going on when he started to Come in, and had turned back into a big Arroya which would lead him arround and out into the Hills towards the mountains. I got on my Horse and made it arround the Hill the other way, and made the Arroya much lower down. I at once left my Horse and Examined the Arroya and seen that no Horse had gone out. Right then I heard a horse, and I run up the Arroya and waited. Jack come along, and I got him without any trouble whatever. I disarmed him, tied his feet under the Horse and Cuffed him to the horn, got up behind him, and called my horse, and was soon at the Car. As I went in, I saw that Slaughter was coming in in about the same way with Larry Shehan — He had to Kill Shehan's Horse as a matter of mercy, for the Horse was badly wounded through the Shoulder and was suffering.

We had these men all four of them chained in the car and loaded ready to go, and we had only been there 45 minutes from the time we jumped our horses out. We had to remain there on a Side track for a while waiting for a Passenger train. When it come, the Conductor had to threaten the passengers that he would go off and leave them — they all wanted to see a real train Robber. We finally got away and we went right through to Tucson, for there was U.S. warrants out for them.

They had friends of their Kind, and they were Soon Supplyed with Attys., given a hearing the second day, and Bail Set, which they made in a day or two, and in about a week after, they were all back at Steins Pass. They had got at this Robbery $700.00 and we got back $400.00, So with the Expense of the Attys. etc. at Tucson, they were all broke — and in a few days, they Staged another Train Robbery at the same place, but they made a Water haul and got nothing. But they entered the Mail Car. This brought out the U.S. Marshal, Meade, and with his Posse, he was soon on the ground. Bob Paul of Tucson was in the Employ of Wells Fargo & Co. and he got there also. The Robbers this time were Dick Hart, Tom Johnson, and Larry Shehan, and they made for old Mexico.

The U.S. Marshal, W. K. Meade, and Posse took after them on a trail 2 days old. This Marshal Meade did not Know anything about the Boundary lines, and the first thing he Knew, He and his Posse were all under arrest and the whole outfit in Jail in Mexico and it took some days to release them.

Bob Paul went by Rail to El Paso and then into Mexico, directly to Chihuahua City. (The State of Chihuahua borders on Arizona and New Mexico.) Bob Paul got busy with the Mexican Officials, with the result that he had a part Company of Soldiers under a Mexican Lieutenant out and into the Section where the Robbers were sure to pass, and the Soldiers intercepted them. The Robbers took refuge in a house on the outskirts of a Small Village. They got all the occupants — men, women, and children — out of the House, and then opened up on them. The Robbers were making a good fight, So the Lieut. had a man go arround the House and set fire to it. So finally they had to Come out, but they Come fighting and all three of them were Killed by the Mexicans — the Mexicans also suffered losses, among which was the Lieutenant in Command, and So Ended the Stein Pass Robbers. Jack Blont jumped the Country and was later Killed in Sonora.

I was away from Tombstone and so was Slaughter at the time of this Robbery, and neither of us knew any thing about it for several days — So neither of us had any thing to do with the Case. Tombstone was getting to be a very dull place.

I was interested for Some time before this in the Stage line, and Wells Fargo & Co.'s Express was delivered by Contract by a local Expressman and the Company was losing a good many Packages. We had a meeting of the owners of the Stage line — who were the Agent, Cashier, Driver, Guard, and myself — and we deemed it advisable to do the delivering of the Express ourselfs. So we got a new light wagon and used one of the Stage Horses and done the Delivering. We also gathered the Baggage and had it at the Office to load on the Stage, which saved running the Stage Team all arround town. This all belonged to the Stage Co., but we were keeping that quiet — and presumably this Delivery outfit belonged to me.

The Constable business had dwindled to allmost nothing and there was not near Enough Work for the Sheriff. I had at that time practically quit the work, and was finishing up the loose Ends of the Company's work in that Country — I was really getting ready to clean up and leave that Country, but there was still much to do.

A Mr. Woods, who owned the Gas Plant and the Ice Plant, made up his mind to Break Wells Fargo & Co. So he put up a large Cold Storage Plant, and filled it with dressed Poultry, Butter, and Eggs, and about all the Cold Storage Commodities that were used in that Town and Community. He then Cut the Prices below what the Stores were getting on Butter, Eggs, Poultry, etc., and in a few days there was not Express enough to pay for the feed of the Stage Teams.

But this Stage Company were allready busy. I made a flying trip to San Francisco to see Mr. Valentine, And the Agent got Instructions to proceed along lines suggested in his letter, which I had the Agent send the day before I left Tombstone. We had a meeting and outlined a plan of proceedure.

One thing was for the Agent to See Woods and tell him that his monopoly of Everything would result in No Express, that it was brought in on Contract by the Stage Company, that they spent their money in Tombstone and it would simply break the Stage Company. Woods was also a Banker and had the only Bank in town.

The Agent met Woods and told him all this in a nice way, and when he had finished, Mr. Woods Said to the Agent, "This is a free Country and we have got to live," and that he — Woods — could see no reason why he should not go right ahead with his business as it was a legitimate one, and he — Woods — could not help it if the Stage Company went broke or even if Wells Fargo went with them. This was just what we wanted him to Say, For he would show no quarter, and it was up to us to meet it and to show quarter or not, just as we pleased. Mr. Woods was getting five cents per pound for Every pound of Ice that he sold — five Dollars per hundred was some price, but there was no other Ice.

When I got back from San Francisco, I had a talk with an Ice man in Benson, and he come to Tombstone the next day — and we made our arraingements with him. (W.F. & Co. was not to be known in this deal for it was presumably the Stage Co.) The man from Benson and I went to Las Vegas, New Mexico and made arraingements for Ice — which was Natural Ice and there never had been any in Tombstone. Our arraingement for this Ice was for one year.

We returned to Tombstone, and the Benson man went to every one of the Consumers of Ice, and on a pledge of Secrecy, he got a Contract from Each one for one year and Ice at two and a half Cents per pound. Two and one half Dollars per hundred — this was Cutting the Price Exactly one half.

There was a very fine Ice house in Tombstone that was built for a Brewery Company that owned the whole Corner and it was about the largest Saloon in town. Instead of turning this into a Brewery, it was turned into a fine Saloon and Gambling House, "The Crystal Palace," and There was no use for the Ice house, so it was Vacant. The night that I returned from San Francisco, I saw the owner of this Ice house and took a two days option on it for twenty dollars, to apply on Rent of twenty five dollars per month if I leased it, and as soon as we had made our arraingement with the Benson Ice Man, I went and took a lease on this Ice house for one year at Twenty five dollars per month — All on a pledge of Secrecy. This place was on Fifth Street, between Allen and Fremont Streets. W. F. & Co.'s office and the Woods Bank were in the Same Block, but about a half Block apart and this Ice house was on the oposite side of the Street, nearly in Front of the Express and Stage Co.'s office.

That night again, we were in Consultation, and the Benson Ice man says, "Here, we have got to have a place for that Ice." The Agent Says, "I just forgot all about that." As a matter of fact, I had about forgotten it myself — I just went to my Drawer in a Desk that was used jointly and handed them the lease. The Benson Ice Man said, "This is the best built Ice house in all the Country."

The day that the Benson Ice man first Come up to see us, we had him go and get a little Place that was mostly a Cellar that had been fixed up for an Ice house. It would only hold about what a two mule Team Could haul and he got Ice from Tucson and sent it in and put it in this place. This was for a blind and it was a good one for it just made Woods laugh. We were allready to go And that Evening about 4:30 P.M., There was some twenty Mule Teams drove in on Fremont Street and turned on 5th St. and Stopped at the Brewery Ice House — it was all ready, and they commenced unloading.

In just a little while, there was a Crowd there, for no one

had ever seen Natural Ice in Tombstone before there was a Carload of Ice brought in and put into that Ice House that Evening. No one knew who the owner was, but the Benson Ice Man Come in on the 6:30 P.M. Stage and He assumed ownership — and that Evening in the Crystal Palace, in front of Many People, (So that the News would Spread) He made a Proposition to me to take charge of the Ice business for him — and I, of course, accepted it.

That night, there was an Ice Wagon reached town — a regular Ice Delivery Wagon which was complete and Ice could be weighed from it and the work done much easier than from a regular Wagon — and being interested in the Stage Company, I used one of the Stage Horses to work in the wagon. I was to have a helper — Manuel — and the next morning, the Delivery Commenced and I was up against it, for it was surely hard work. But we just simply had to win out.

Mr. Woods cut his Ice to two Cents and went right along delivering Ice as usual — All the Heavy Consumers took about the same quantity of Ice Daily and Delivery was made on the Sidewalk. Mr. Woods went right along and left his Ice just the same, and the Consumers just left it there on the Sidewalk and it melted. Mr. Woods Continued this routine for 3 days and then he quit and it run along quietly for the Next 3 or 4 weeks. The handlers of Perishable goods — Meat, Butter, Fish, Oysters, Eggs, Vegetables, Fruit, etc. were getting their Ice so much Cheaper that they could afford to use more Ice, and the Stages were Coming in loaded to the Guards and on Thursdays and Fridays we had to run an Extra Wagon to bring in the Stuff — all by Express.

In the meantime, Mr. Woods' Cold Storage goods was remaining in the Cold Storage Plant and was fast deteriorating. The Handlers of this kind of goods had seen that it was money in their Pockets to not handle any of this Cold Storage

Stuff, and were compelled to keep fresh goods, and they Entered into the War with a Will — on the side of the Company who had brought Prices down one half on the Material (Ice) that it took to keep their Perishables fresh and good.

So one day, Mr. Woods Come to our Agent and said, "You and your associates are about to ruin me, for the goods in my Cold Storage Plant will rot, if we can't get to some sort of an Agreement." The Agent said to Mr. Woods, "This is a free country, and we have got to live," and that he — the Agent — could see no reason why he should not go right ahead with his business, as it was a legitimate one, and he — the Agent — could not help it if the Bank, Ice Plant, Gas Plant, and Cold Storage all went broke. This Agent had used the same language that Woods had used to him, Excepting the windup — Woods was in a rage, but the Agent kept Calm, and Woods went away.

I had overheard all this talk, and I told the Agent that before night, there would be something Come from Woods. I knew that he could not stand the Punishment, as he loved money better than anything in the World.

E. B. Gage was the real leading man in the Tombstone District — And a finer Gentleman never lived. He was the General Superintendent of the Grand Central Mining Company, the largest and Strongest in the District. He was also the Uncle of the Cashier of Wells Fargo & Co., Charley Gage. E. B. Gage thought a lot of his Nephew, Charley, who was also one of the Stage Company and E. B. Gage spent a little time daily at the Express Office. Mr. Woods knew all about the above — and he went up on the Hill to see E. B. Gage in his office.

E. B. was thougherly conversant with the Whole Matter, and had frequently advised with us. That evening after Supper, we were all, as usual, in the backroom of the Express office when E. B. Gage come in, as was his wont, and he said, "Well, you Boys have got Mr. Woods Considerably on the run for he has come to me this P.M. to get me to intercede and fix this thing up."

We had made out a Skeleton form of what we would do — and E. B. took notes from it, after we had gone over it with him and made some additions and some concessions, by his advise. E. B. was a just and square man, and while he did not like Woods at all, he was in favor of some concessions. Mr. Gage saw Woods that same night and gave him the gist of what we would do, and Woods went up in the Air, and he would not do this, and he would not do that. Mr. Gage told him that he was satisfyed that after he had talked to us that we would not change anything, and that he, Mr. Gage, would not have anything further to do with the matter and that he, Woods, would have to do his business with us direct, and left him — E. B. Come to the Office and told us of the result. I told them that I knew Woods, and as soon as he got Cooled down and could do some figuring, that he would Come back with a Counter Proposition. E. B. said, "Fred, I think from what passed, and Woods' attitude, that you are right."

The Next forenoon, Woods went up to see Mr. Gage again. Mr. Gage told him that he would not have anything further to do with it, but Woods just Pled with him, and told him that he would be ruined if there was not something done — Mr. Gage told Woods that he, Woods, was willing to ruin us and that it was serving him right. Woods kept on Pleading to Mr. Gage, and told him that he had a proposition to make to us. Mr. Gage listened to him, and then told him that he would take this proposition to us, but he was satisfyed that we would not agree to it at all.

After Dinner, Mr. Gage Come down to the office and told us of the result, and we just stood pat, and asked Mr. Gage to tell Mr. Woods that we would not discuss the matter any further. Mr. Gage told him what we had said, and also told Woods that we had made many Concessions from our first stand, and that he, Woods, had brought all this upon us and allso upon himself. Mr. Gage then left Woods and went home.

The next morning Woods was up to see Mr. Gage again, and he was all broke up. He asked Mr. Gage to go to us and make the best terms possible, even if it had to be the whole proposition that we had made. Mr. Gage Come, and with a few minor changes, we agreed on our own proposition. Our Skeleton was given to our Attorney to draw up this Contract and Bond — for we required a Bond from Woods for the fullfillment of the Contract.

We required that Woods take over all the Ice Contracts, and at the Expiration of said Contract, the price of Ice must continue at 2½ cents per lb., that the Cold Storage plant was not to be used for that purpose during the time of the existance of the present Stage Company, the taking over of the Lease on the Ice House, and that there was to be no Competition originated through or by him of any of the users of Perishable goods. There was also some minor Safe-guards that were incorporated, And this was all attested to, and Signed, and the War was over. The Consumers were all agreeable, for we had brought the price of Ice down one half, and they were the only real beneficiaries.

Within another week, Tombstone was going to the bad fast, and many were trying to get loose and away — the Stage Company's main income was in outgoing passengers. I had, for some time before this Ice war, been getting loose from all my interests in Tombstone, but now property was dropping daily in Value. My House where I lived was the last thing that I held. The Guard, who was also line Business Manager, wanted to get out. He had a good offer in Los Angeles to go into Business there, and knowing the State of Affairs in Tombstone, he made a Sacrifice proposition to the balance of us, and as we all wanted to help each other, we accepted and he left at once.

Then shortly thereafter, I followed with a proposition for my part — that left only the Agent, Cashier, and Driver. I had a Buyer for my House and lots where I lived, and I tied him up at once — The Boys did not want me to go but I had to, for I knew some things that they did not know. I was under instructions to clean up all matters there and report to my Boss in San Francisco — And the time was drawing near for me to be there. My Proposition to the Boys was that they, themselfs, appraise all the Property owned by the Stage Co. making that appraisel just what they thought that they could get for it, then at that figure, give me my part. This was done and early in 1888, I was loose and with my Family I bid good-bye to Old Tombstone, and it was some years before I ever saw what was left of the Old Town.

Wyatt Earp (seated) in 1876, his first year as marshal of Dodge City, and Bat Masterson (standing), his deputy. Photograph reproduced from a tintype made in Dodge City when Bat was twenty-two and Wyatt twenty-eight, three years before his arrival in Tombstone. Scroll-shaped object on Wyatt's shirt is his marshal's badge.

Morgan Earp, Tombstone, 1881. The only known photograph of him, fortunately for the purposes of this book, taken at the time when his resemblance to Fred Dodge was evidently remarkable.

Tombstone, Cochise County, Arizona, about 1880.

Fremont Street, Tombstone, Cochise County Courthouse, and, on the far left, the office of the Tombstone *Epitaph*.

Page one of the Tombstone *Epitaph* for December 16, 1881, carrying news story of holdup of Benson stage and attempt on the life of editor, John P. Clum. Inset, contemporary photograph of mayor, postmaster, and editor Clum.

Allen Street, Tombstone. At right, Golden Eagle Brewery Building.

Tombstone transportation in mining camp days, the old Modoc stage.

Bob Paul, noted Wells Fargo shotgun messenger and friend of Fred Dodge and Wyatt Earp, in Tombstone.

Bill Tilghman, eminently successful buffalo hunter and a Kansas peace officer, both in the company of Wyatt Earp, later U.S. marshal in Oklahoma.

Pete Spence (real name, Lark Ferguson), notorious outlaw of the Southwest and follower of Curly Bill, who participated in attempt to kill Virgil Earp and in murder of Morgan Earp. Photograph made while Spence was prisoner at Yuma Penitentiary for stage robbery.

Frank Leslie, famous Indian scout, "best bartender in Tombstone," gunman and killer. Shot Billy Claiborn, Tombstone,
1882. Photograph, Yuma State Penitentiary, 1883.

Ruins of old Charleston. All that time has left of the Cochise County outlaws' favorite hangout where bartender, J. B. Ayers, worked as undercover man for Wells Fargo and the Southern Pacific Railroad. He reported the doings of the Clanton gang to Fred Dodge.

Mining camp anarchy — the lynching of John Heath in Toughnut
Street, Tombstone. Sheriff Ward's appearing to condone it caused
Fred Dodge to tear up his sheriff's commission.

After Tombstone's heyday, some of the leading citizens scattered. Here, in 1900, during the Alaska gold rush, three of them meet on the beach at Nome. Left to right: Ed Englestadt, formerly a Tombstone businessman, Wyatt Earp, and John P. Clum, first postmaster, first mayor of Tombstone, and editor of the Tombstone *Epitaph*.

Wyatt Earp in Los Angeles at the time Fred Dodge wrote him the letter included in this book. The old style automobile provides a gauge for his height of 6′ 1″.

Two views of the much-prized watch Wells Fargo presented to Fred Dodge in October 1895 for his work on the Hardin case.

Fred J. Dodge in 1906 when he was living in San Antonio and took possession of his beloved ranch at Boerne, Texas.

Andrew Christeson whom Fred Dodge knew when he came out from under cover and was sent by John Valentine to Texas where Christeson was Wells Fargo superintendent in Houston. At the time of the earthquake and resulting fire in 1906, "Andy" Christeson was in the San Francisco office as general manager, and was responsible for restoring express service to the stricken city. Headquarters was a circus tent until lumber could be obtained to rebuild.

Grover B. Simpson, born in 1858 at Fort Yamhill, Oregon, joined the express business in 1878 as a Wells Fargo messenger on the run between Portland, Oregon, and Tacoma, Washington. Subsequently, he was route agent there and later in San Antonio, Texas. After assignments in Montana and Denver, Colorado, he became superintendent of the Missouri division in 1897, with headquarters in St. Louis. Later, he was general superintendent of Wells Fargo in Chicago.

Amador Andrews, a native to California and a native to Wells Fargo. Born in Jackson, Amador County, California, on July 3, 1854, where his father was a Wells Fargo agent, Amador Andrews joined the company as a young man, serving as a messenger on the frontier and route agent in the Northwest. On one occasion in Idaho, a boat he was in capsized and threw him into an icy river. He narrowly missed death by freezing, but fortunately recovered from the ordeal. His next assignment was route agent in southern California, perhaps to thaw out. Following that tour, he was made superintendent of the Nebraska Division and later promoted again to manager of the Central Department which comprised all lines east of the Rocky Mountains to the Mississippi River, and east of El Paso to New Orleans. His headquarters then was Kansas City, Missouri.

James Bunyan Hume, born in 1823 in New York state's Catskill Mountains, arrived in California in 1850, where he became marshal of Placerville, and later sheriff of El Dorado County. In a short while, he was widely known as a capable officer of the law. The prison in Carson City, Nevada, was badly in need of a new warden to put an end to rampant jailbreaking, and the governor of that state offered the job to Hume who accepted, and almost immediately set out alone, determined to round up the escaped prisoners. Characteristically, he found them all, and then saw he had a desk job, so in 1873, when John Valentine sought his talents for Wells Fargo, Hume was ready to join the company. For thirty-two years, he was head of the Wells Fargo police service. He brought a keen mind and the uncanny ability of a great detective to the job to which he devoted himself until his death in San Francisco on May 18, 1904.

John J. Valentine, born November 12, 1840, in Bowling Green, Kentucky, just two hundred years after his family came to this country from England, joined Wells Fargo in 1862 in Strawberry Valley, El Dorado County, California, transferring shortly after to Virginia City. Before venturing West, he had been in the Employ of the Adams Express Company. Bearded, and towering considerably over six feet, he was the kind of competent and loyal expressman who was congenial in the business and who rose toward the top. J. J. Valentine went all the way, through agent, route agent, cashier, general manager, and vice-president, being made president in 1892, after thirty-two years with the company. It was an office he had held only eight years when he died on December 21, 1901. A widely respected, public-spirited citizen, John Valentine made his home in Oakland, California.

Gerrit A. Taft, longtime friend and Wells Fargo associate of Fred Dodge.

Colt's revolver #1381, .45 caliber, single-action, Frontier Model believed to be the gun with which Frank Stilwell killed Morgan Earp. While impossible to state the foregoing as absolute fact, it is known that Stilwell carried that gun at that time and that it was the weapon taken from Stilwell's body after Wyatt Earp shot him near the Tucson railroad station. The barely visible notch in the handle was there when the gun was taken off Stilwell and may have been cut to record Morgan's murder. Though men who thought anything of themselves did not follow this practice, it is not unreasonable to surmise Stilwell may well have been the kind to notch his gun.

Part II

*Out from Under Cover as
Special Officer, 1890-1895*

10

RESIGNATION REFUSED

I stopped off at Los Angeles and visited with our old Partners and then took my Family to Sacramento to stay a while with my Father and Mother. I went right on to San Francisco, and that night, I reported to Mr. Valentine in Oakland, at his Home.

I had been for so many years under such a Constant strain that I wanted to get away from it alltogether, and I told Mr. Valentine all about it, and told him that I thought I would resign, which some days later I did, and it was not accepted. Mr. V. told me that he would help me all that he could and to just let that resignation go, that there was several things that he wanted attended to that would keep me busy, and in the meantime, I could keep my Eyes open, and that he would send out some quiet inquiries and see what could be done.

I wanted to get hold of a good paying Livery Stable. I had about $17,500 to put into a business and during this time, a friend of mine Come to San Francisco. He had been a Stage man in Arizona, and he wanted to get into the Same Kind of business, and wanted me for a partner. Mr. Valentine had got hold of some information about a place in Fresno, Cala., and this man and I went down there. Result — we bought the Stable, Refitted and bought new Buggys, Carriages, Harness, etc.

We worked fast, for we wanted to Close with the Insurance Co., and on the night of the 15th of the month, the Insurance men were in the office, and all was ready. They were to commence the Inventory the next morning.

That night the Fire Come and wiped us out clean — No Insurance, new Carriages still in the Crate, Stable full of Hay, Harness, and Soforth, 59 Head of Horses, including W. F. & Co.'s whole equipment. (They had closed their Stable and brought the whole outfit to me on the 15th.) I lost, for my part, $16,000 Dollars — 16 days and I was broke, but we did not owe anything. That day, we had all the Carcasses removed, Sold all the Iron from the place, and was through. We had bought out a Transfer Company there, and all of those Horses and Wagons were gone. I felt badly about the burning of the Horses, which was awful.

My Partner and I settled up the Transfer part, and he was going to remain in Fresno, and run the Transfer business, and I was leaving in the morning for San Francisco. I had, that morning, been told by the Express Agent that he had reported the loss to his superintendent, and that he would have a New outfit there tomorrow — My Partner had made arraingements with local Expressmen to get Teams and Wagons from them, and he helped out in the delivery of W. F. & Co. Freight, and so forth, untill their outfit arrived. My Partner had a lot more money than I had, for he had sold out his interest in a good mine in Arizona about a year before, and he was ordering Wagons and Harness allready and looking for and buying Horses. He wanted me to stay and wanted to finance my part. The Hughs Hotel Company wanted me to Stay, and offered to finance me in getting Started again, but I had enough, and that morning I had received a message from Mr. Valentine asking me did I need anything. My resignation had not been accepted, So I wired back, "Don't need anything San Francisco tomorrow night ready to go to work."

This fire was an incendiary fire. The watchman at the Depot was out where he could see the whole Stable building — it was a two Story building and ran through the entire block. He had seen a light like a fuse run up midway of the Building, and right then, there was an Explosion inside, and flames shot up instantly. He gave the Alarm by shooting off his Pistol, but nothing could save it, it went so fast. The whole Block went. All this made me think some. It might be an old Arizona Vindictiveness — or it might be a new Vindictiveness — Some one who did not want to see a new and rival Concern prosper.

Fresno was, at that time, the best Livery town that I ever saw — we did not make a hitch less than $5.00, and Doubles with Surrys $8.00. We put out 2 four Horse teams twice a Week with Parties, and these we had arrainged for during the whole Season, and the Transfer business was also a good one. We had Agents on the Trains to Solicit Baggage, and we Could keep the Teams, etc. at the Stable at very slight cost.

It was tempting to Stay, but I was as well off as I was when I Come into the world — I did not owe anyone, I was where I started. But if I stayed, I would have to owe a lot of money, and if I blew up, then I would be in a hole right — Nothing to do with, and a heavy debt hanging over me. I could see no way to justify my self in taking the chances, and I was in San Francisco on time.

I called on Mr. Valentine, and he told me that he was going to take me out from Undercover, and send me to Texas, with headquarters at Houston, under Supt. Andrew Christeson. He told me that Thacker had done most of the work in Texas, and that he did not like it — it was a 4 days' ride and 4 back. And he thought that if I could show Thacker that I needed a job, and Thacker, knowing much about my work in Arizona, would surely Suggest me for an Appointment to go to Texas — but if he did not that he, Mr. Valentine, would send me anyway.

I knocked arround some, Met Thacker, had Lunch with

him, and told him all about my bad luck, and what I thought of the Fire — and asked him if he knew of anything to do for I had to go to work. Then he told me about Texas, and the trouble that he had there, and the long trips there and back, and that Mr. Braston, one of the Superintendents, had told him the other day that Mr. Valentine had said that he thought that he would put on a man in Texas, for it was taking too much of Thacker's time — This was to ease Thacker down some. Thacker had told me that he had to leave again for Texas in a few days, and he said, "Fred, you are just the man for it, and we will go down to the Office, and I will see Mr. Valentine."

When we got to his office, I met Jim Hume who was glad to see me, and Thacker told Jim about me, etc., and went in to see Mr. Valentine. He soon come out, and with a few words of Advice, he took me — for the first time in my life — into Mr. Valentine's office and introduced me, and said, "This man I am sure can fill the Texas bill."

[*That Fred Dodge was in Wells Fargo's employ at all was known only to Mr. Valentine and himself; thus previous meetings between the two men necessarily had taken place elsewhere.*]

Thacker had to leave soon, and then Mr. Valentine talked to me awhile, and I was to see him that night. Jim Hume Come in, and Mr. Valentine said, "You Know this man, how will he do for Special Officer for Texas and the Southern Division?" Hume smilingly said, "Yes, I Know him and there Could be no better man found." — Dear old Jim, loyal both ways.

[*Of Fred Dodge, Jim Hume once was quoted in the press as*

saying, "He is very very handy, and I don't think anyone could get the drop on him — yes, very handy."]

I saw Mr. Valentine that night, and he went over Texas matters very thougherly with me, the Case that Thacker was on which was at Brownwood, and then he told me that Thacker was going there for the second trial of this case and that he was not entirely satisfyed about it — but I would go with Thacker, and he could tell me all about it EnRoute there — then, as soon as it was finished that there was some very important matters that he wanted me to attend to at Houston. This had to do with the Supt., Mr. Christeson, himself.

Mr. Valentine told me that there was something wrong there, that the Supt. was a good man and a good Expressman, but there was many Complaints about him, and that there was one serious fault with him — that he wrote too severe and harsh letters — which was severely Complained of, and the way things were going there, if not remedied, that he would be compelled to take Mr. Christeson out of the Position and replace him with some one else. But for me to take time Enough to get to the bottom of the whole matter and then let him know just how everything was. (Thacker had reported all these things to Mr. Valentine and had him worked up over it.)

I come out from under Cover, or was supposed to get Employment from Wells Fargo & Co. December 1st, 1890 — So on Dec. 2nd, I went up to Sacramento and there bid goodbye to all my folks. It was hard for me to leave my little Girl. [*Ada*] She was born in Tombstone, and was nearly 3 years old. She was my Partner, and I loved her very much, but I could not take her with me at that time.

I got back to San Francisco Dec. 4th, and the 5th, 6th, and 7th, I was very busy arround the Offices, And at 4 P.M.,

Thacker and I left En Route to Houston, Texas. We Stopped off at El Paso the day and night of Dec. 11th, and Continued our trip next day, and also Dec. 13th, arriving at Houston at 5 P.M. Supt. Christeson had Come on the Train at Rosenberg Junction and met us, and Continued on to Houston with us.

That Night, I got my passes, and we stayed at a Hotel that night, and next morning, Dec. 14th, Thacker and I left for Dallas, Texas. Got there about 7 P.M. That night, I met the Chief of Police, Jim Arnold, and the Chief of Detectives, Bud Curley. The Next day I was in Dallas all day. I got acquainted with the Agent and the Office force, also Route Agents Crowe and Dana, and I got my first tip on what was the matter with Supt. Christeson and his Division.

I left next morning for Greenwood, Miss. on the Walter Jones Case. Jim Hume had tied up $2300.00 in Greenwood that was deposited there in the Bank by Walter Jones. I arrived in Greenwood, La Flore County, Miss. Friday, Dec. 19, 1890. I got up all the Evidence that I could about Walter Jones — this County was his old home — and I arrainged with a prominent Planter there, a man who stood well, to come to the trial at Brownwood. I could not do anything about the Money untill after the Trial of Walter Jones, So I left Greenwood. (I had spent Christmas there at the Hotel.) Than I returned to Brownwood direct. At Temple, I met Thacker and Wm. Capps, an attorney from Fort Worth who had been Employed by Thacker to assist in the Prosecution of Walter Jones. They both Continued on the train with me to Brownwood.

On the trip from San Francisco to Texas, Thacker had told me all that he knew about the Case of Walter Jones. There had been a trial of the case, and it was a hung Jury. I thought the case over, and I made up my mind that there was another man in the case, and that they had not got him. I went into the case thougherly with Thacker, and he would not take to the Idea at all. He said he knew he was right and would not have it any other way.

The Sheriff of Brown County was a fine man and Considerable over average as an officer. I had never given him my side of the Case, So the next day the Dist. Atty., Capps, the Sheriff, Thacker, and I were in Consultation and I gave them my view of the case, Although Thacker said it was only taking up time. All the balance of the party had someway become quite interested in me and wanted me to go ahead — Which I did. I went over the Trial of the Case, and called their attention to points in the Testimony, and then put a flat proposition up to them. There had been a Package of $7000.00 taken at this Robbery. It had come from a Bank in Fort Worth and was to a Bank in Brownwood. Thacker and the Sheriff had dug out the whole Country, and could only find that Walter Jones had used about $3400.00 which included the $2300.00 that Jim Hume had tied up in Greenwood, Miss. I asked them what had become of the balance of the money.

I said to them, "There is another man in this job, and I am going to get him."

The Dist. Attorney had grasped the whole thing and said I was right — Capp also thought that I might be right. The Sheriff, who had been working with Thacker and Shared many of his views, said, "This is a very important development, and I am not going to pass on it untill I think it over, and I will give you what I think in the morning." And he went home. That Night Thacker tried to place himself in an Easier position, for he could see how they all were, and he knew that the Sheriff was a clear thinking man. Thacker was not entirely easy about which way the Sheriff would go in the morning — and in the morning, the Sheriff Said, "Dodge is right and we should have seen this from the start." Then, addressing me, he said, "You say that you are going to get this other man." I said, "Yes," and the Sheriff then said, "I am with you and will do all I can and I want a private talk with you right away." And we had it. We went over all phases of the case, and when we were finished, I told him who I thought was the other man. He thought this over for some time and finally said to me, "This man's Father is one of my very best and old friends — and I am affraid that you are right about this young man. But you need not have any fear of me, for I will do my duty, and I am with you."

Well, we got him, and he made a Confession, and told the Sheriff and myself all about it — this was kept still for the Dist. Atty. was well pleased and So was Capps, and Thacker had to be, and was.

It was a hard and spectacular trial. There were 5 Attys. for the Defense, but when we put our State's Evidence witness on the Stand, it was all off. Walter Jones was found Guilty and Sentenced to 5 years in the Penitentiary. During the trial, I had made a sincere friend out of one of the Attys. for the Defense. He was by far the best Criminal lawyer at that time in all Western Texas. We Continued as close friends through the years that followed, and untill he died.

Thacker made his report to Mr. Valentine, and he took all the Credit of getting the other man and getting up all the Evidence. I made my report to Mr. Christeson, the Supt. at Houston. Soon afterwards, I found out that Mr. Valentine understood the Walter Jones Case thougherly.

During the time preceeding the trial of this case, I had been to Greenwood, Miss. again. We had brought Suit against the Bank there, and on trial of the Case, Wells Fargo & Co. was awarded a judgment against the Bank for the $2300.00 that was attached there — and I was working on Several other Cases — and all the time I was working on what was the matter with Mr. Christeson — and I was sure finding out things.

I was awful busy all the time — I had a big Damage Suit at Overbrook Indian Territory and at Ardmore, I met Dep. U.S. Marshal Heck Thomas. We become friends and he done lots of business for me in that Country. I was cleaning up all of these matters fast. At Dallas, there was a hard case, and it had been worked by Thacker and local men and was ready for trial.

On January 7th, 1891, I met G. A. Taft at Fort Worth. He had been Agent at Fort Worth untill Jany 1st, and was then made a Route Agent. This man Taft and I become close friends, and as the years rolled on we grew closer. He was the truest, closest, and best friend that I ever had and we loved each other like we were close Brothers, and continued so untill his Death. I also met at Fort Worth two more men that were also very close to me — Nick McGinness and S. R. McMullen. McGinness was the man who succeeded G. A. Taft as Agent at Fort Worth, and S. R. McMullen was a Route Agent — These two men were Pardners and very Close to Each other and These two men become awfully good friends of mine.

I was helping Thacker all that I could — The Case was a Case wherein $16,000.00 contained in a Wooden Treasure Box had disapeared from the City Office in Dallas and Everybody was under suspicion. The Negro Porter at the Office, Saul Richardson, had the best opportunity and Thacker soon had Saul under Arrest. He later on made Bond and was released. Soon after, the Empty Box was found on the Bank of the River — And Saul was soon back in Jail, and was there when I got to Texas. (There had been a general Shake up in the Office force at Dallas, a New Agent and Several minor positions had been changed — J. T. M. Connor was the Agent at Dallas when I first arrived there.)

The Richardson case was coming on for trial. The trial

119

commenced on Thursday, Jany. 8th, 1891, and here is where John Thacker over-stepped himself with me. Right after the Box was found, It was noted (by the man who was trying to help Thacker, and was the Manager of the Winsdor Hotel, who had given Saul Richardson work as a waiter in the Hotel so as to keep track of him) that Saul had a button missing from his vest — it looked like it had been torn off — (This was the morning that the empty Box was found.) and at noon it was neatly replaced by a button of the same kind. Thacker Come to me in my room, and he had possessed himself with a Button Exactly like the Balance of the Buttons on Saul's Vest. Thacker wanted me to testify that he and I were searching the place where the Box was found, and found this Button at the place close to the Box. This I refused to do, and told Thacker that I would not have anything more to do with the Case. Thacker then wanted me to promice secrecy about the proposition that he had made to me — and this I would not do — but as a matter of fact, I did not say anything about it, and it was not mentioned again between us.

Right immediately after the Box was turned up, one of the best Criminal lawyers in the State of Texas appeared on the Scene representing Saul Richardson and in the Trial of the Case, this Attorney succeeded in Aquitting Saul and he was a free man. There had been a trial of the Richardson Case before, which resulted in a hung Jury, but now he was Clear, and very soon he went to Oklahoma.

I had during this time been working on what was the matter with Mr. Christeson, and had got it all in Shape, and wrote fully to Mr. Valentine, who wrote to me telling me to go to Mr. Christeson and tell him the whole Story of how my instructions were from Mr. Valentine when I Come to his Division, and on through telling him all that I had found out, and Show Mr. Christeson this letter from Mr. Valentine to me. This was about the first of March 1891.

I went into Mr. Christeson's office and told him that I had some very important matters to talk to him about, and it would take 2 or 3 hours of uninterrupted time. He closed the door and locked it, and I commenced by telling him what my instructions were from Mr. Valentine when I Come to Texas. Then I showed him the letter just received from Mr. Valentine and proceeded to tell him what I had found out. I commenced by telling him about his Harsh letter writing which had given some men the oppertunity to do what they were trying to do — that was to Supplant him as Superintendent. These men were Chief Route Agent C. A. Weatherington, J. T. M. Connor, Agent at Dallas, assisted by J. N. Thacker. Thacker was the man who was to spread the dissatisfaction and drop incendiary news to Mr. Valentine about Mr. Christeson, Weatherington was to be the Superintendent — Suggested by Thacker as the Strongest Expressman in the Division and a man well liked — Connor was to be made Chief Route Agent. Then they could adjust the Division to Suit themselfs. Thacker had become a Subtile Enemy of Mr. Christeson on account of Christeson calling him down on some of his Shady ways —

I gave Mr. Christeson all the ins and outs to the whole thing, for they had come to me believing that I would work in with them, for Thacker had told them I would, and I did not abuse their minds about it — So I got all the inside. I then told Mr. Christeson that as he could see by the letter to me that it was up to him to adjust matters. He then told me all that he had done for Weatherington which showed Weatherington to be an ingrate sure enough. He disposed of both of these men in a way that from that time on they had Nothing to Say. Expressmen were needed at that time badly So he offered Weatherington the Demotion from Chief Route Agent to Agent at Galveston at less than half the Salary and Connor was taken out of the Division.

Mr. Christeson developed into a mighty fine man. He made a fine Superintendent, and when Mr. Valentine was going to change the General Manager at Kansas City, I was with Mr. Valentine at St. Louis and he told me all about it, and knowing that Mr. Christeson and I had become close friends, he done one of the many nice things that he was noted for and said to me, "You can wire Mr. Christeson to meet you in Dallas where you are going and you can tell Mr. Christeson that I am going to Appoint him Gen. Manager at Kansas City and in a few days after you tell him, I will write him Confirming the Appointment." Mr. Christeson developed into a very fine diplomatic letter writer and got on fine with Everybody.

11

THE DALTONS, INDIANS,

AND WHISTLER'S MOTHER

In March 1891, I brought my Family from Sacramento, Cal. to Houston, Tex.

The Saul Richardson Case had been continued several times and was finally tried in May 1901 — virdict not Guilty. I had done a lot of work on this case getting ready for trial — I had been about as busy as two men should have been. I had brought the Suit to recover the Walter Jones money in the Bank at Greenwood and got judgment against them in January 1901, but there were many delays and I had not yet recovered the money. I was settling up old Cases and was getting a lot of new Cases — Office Robberys, Shortages, Robbery in Transit, Etc., Damage Suits which at that time were plentiful.

I had been very lucky with all my work and on May 7, '91, I left for Berwin Indian Territory to investigate a loss at that place. I got there the P.M. of the 9th and went on to Pauls Valley the same night and was ready to leave there for Oklahoma City on the North bound train which went North about 4 A.M. next morning. I was asleep on the Counter in the Office when the Telegraph Operator wakened me about 3 A.M. and told me that the South bound train had been held up at Wharton Cherokee Strip at 10:30 P.M. that night. Saturday, May 9th, A.T. & S.F. Ry.

I got all the information that I could and made the North bound train at 4 o'clock. On that Train I met Dep. U.S.

Marshal George Thornton and aquainted him with all the facts that I had — his Headquarters were in Oklahoma City — and he wired ahead to have his Posseman meet him at the Train with their Saddles and all Equipment necessary — Sam Bartell was the Posseman's name. Geo. Thornton was an Able Officer and a good man. Sam Bartell was at the Depot with all Supplys when we got there — we only had 5 minutes there and I did not get any new particulars.

When we continued on, I was introduced to Sam Bartell — Thornton had told me that Sam was a fearless and good man — and this was the Commencement of a long string of work and Several wild and Daingerous rides that Sam Bartell and I had together. Sam knew the Country and was a very valuable man. Thornton had never been at Wharton but Sam told us that there was very little there and there *was* little there — Depot, one house back on the Hill where the Agent lived and night opperator Boarded.

The Train had been held up about ½ mile South of Wharton where there was a Ry. Bridge over a Creek. We went to work to get men and Horses there — it was Sunday and we could not make much — but finally got men and Horses from Oklahoma City, and they would come on a Special Train. During this time of waiting we had worked out the Scene of the Robbery, found where they had their Horses, and trailed them for about 3 miles afoot. We assertained that there were 3 men in this hold up and they had rode East. This Crime was committed by Bob Dalton, Emmett Dalton, and Charley Bryant — but those names I did not learn for sure so that it Could be proved for some time afterwards. The Loss was $1745.00 So they were pretty well fixed.

We were back at the Depot when the Special Come in with the Posse — Heck Thomas also come on that train. They were all ready and off in a Short time and Geo. Thornton in

Charge, He having Deputized all those who were not officers as members of his Posse. Geo. Thornton, by reason of our work done afoot, was able to start 3 miles from the scene of the Holdup — I did not go with the Posse for there was a lot of work to be done in the way of Evidence, Knowing who the men were etc., and I was going night and day for sometime, starting at the Sac and Fox agency.

[Two separate Algonquian tribes until mid-eighteenth century, the Sac and Fox Indians lived in eastern Michigan, later fleeing hostile tribes and settling for a time in what is now Wisconsin. The Foxes, so called by the French (rénards) and nearly exterminated by them, called themselves Muskwaki, meaning red-earth people, and like the Sacs, were a woodland tribe which built bark houses and cultivated corn and vegetables.

After the war with the French, the survivors of the two tribes joined forces and became known by their present double name. For a time, they lived in Illinois and were victims of a fraudulent treaty which precipitated the famous Black Hawk War in 1832. Following the war, the united tribe moved west to settle in Iowa, Kansas, and Oklahoma where Fred Dodge knew them.

Perhaps the most famous Sac and Fox name in modern times is that of Jim Thorpe (1888–1953), born in Oklahoma and often considered the world's greatest athlete. Named Bright Path by his Sac mother, Thorpe played football for Glenn "Pop" Warner at Carlisle Indian School, Carlisle, Pennsylvania. Thorpe turned in a spectacular performance in the 1912 Olympic Games held in Stockholm, Sweden, and five medals for field events came home with him. A year later however, on the advice of his famous coach, "Pop" Warner, Thorpe returned the medals as it was discovered he had played *semi-professional baseball in North Carolina in 1909–1910.*

Still later, Thorpe played professional football for Canton, Ohio, and for the Cardinals in Chicago, where eventually he became supervisor of recreation for the Chicago parks.

In 1951, he was admitted to the National Football Hall of Fame.]

In a few days, I made temporary Headquarters at the Sac and Fox Agency 55 miles from Guthrie. This was so that I could keep in touch with Everything. All messages and important information would go to Guthrie and the Agent would send on to me at Sac & Fox. I learned in a few days what the Names of the Robbers were — They were Bob Dalton, Emmett Dalton, and Charley Bryant — the two Daltons had Escaped from Jail at Visalia, Cala. where they had been in a train Robbery and Grat Dalton was in Jail for the Same job at this time — Bob and Emmett had made it back to Oklahoma. The Dalton home was near Kingfisher, where their Mother and 3 Sisters lived. The oldest Girl was married to a man named Whipple, The oldest Brother, Ben Dalton, lived at home and run the Farm. Mrs. Whipple was the Brains of the Whipple family but her Husband was by no means an Easy Crook.

There had been a man by the name of Smith, a Special Agent of the Southern Pacific Railroad Co. in the Country, having followed Bob and Emmett from Cala., and he had put out the news that there was a reward of $1,000.00 Each for these men *Dead* or *Alive* — and it was making it hard to catch these men. Bob Dalton had been — before going to California — a Dep. U.S. Marshal and Emmett was his Posseman. They knew the Country perfectly and had lots of friends among the Outlaws, Whiskey Pedlers, and all the Crooked and Short men that were then in the Country.

I had several Dep. U.S. Marshals working with me — some good and some not so good. The best of them was Heck Thomas, and Geo Thornton and Sam Bartell worked with and for me. I had an Indian who was a Sac and Fox by Adoption working for me — his name was Talbot White. I was at Deep Fork and at midnight I got the News that the Semenole Indians had Killed 3 White men and were bringing them into the Sac and Fox Agency. They were supposed to be the Dalton Bunch. I left at once, Talbot White with me, and by a hard ride and Talbot's Knowledge of the Country, we reached Sac and Fox at 10 A.M. Talbot White and many more at the Agency — Geo. Thornton was there also — all knew the Daltons well and these were not the men we wanted but they were Outlaws and Whiskey Pedlers. This killing was the direct result of Agent Smith's "Dead or Alive" reward. This Inquest was held June 2nd, 1891, and on the 8th of June, 3 more men were killed by the Euches Indians — Another Mistake. They needed killing all right, but were not the men we wanted. These two killings of the wrong men had the Efect of calling about all the Indians off from trying to apprehend the Dalton Bunch.

I kept going all the time for there were many Reports that had to be investigated. Most of the time I had some one with me and there was lots of trips that I had to make alone. On Saturday, June 13, I went to Westmoreland's place. I was to meet Heck Thomas and other men that I had out with Heck Thomas. I got to the place about Sunset Sat., June 13th, 1891, and I stayed there all night. I did not like the way things were going. They looked very suspicious and I did not get arround any so that there could be a pot shot taken at me. I was sure that there was a plan on foot to do me and I watched Everything and Everybody.

My Bed was right in front of a window and I took the

Blankets and moved to another part of the room. I was sure that they heard me for the Slightest noise could be heard all over the place. I knew that there were men out at the Shed and Corral. I knew that I could stop any one from coming up the Ladder that come up to this loft — I knew also that there had been a man gone up a Tree that gave him a view of the Bed at the Window. After a while, there was a noise at the foot of the Ladder. (They thought that I was Asleep for I had kept very quiet.)

I had my Short Double Barrell Shot Gun with me and I had seen the family looking at it when I eat supper — I did not take the seat that they assigned to me, but put my back to the Log wall and I laid my Shotgun accross my lap and watched all openings into the room. Later on I was told by the old Lady — who, by the way, was the most villianous looking that I had ever seen in the shape of a woman — that I could go up that ladder there, and there was a Bed up there that I could sleep in. The old man come in and he told the old Lady that the Boys had gone Coonhunting. He and She were out and in.

When I got a good chance I went up the ladder. I saw the bed close to the hole in the floor that I come through and I took the Blankets from the bed and put them in the other end of this low Ceiling room — I was over where the bed was and I was on the floor when the old man and Lady come in. The old Lady called out, "You up there?" and I answered her and my voice come from right where the bed stood, but I soon quietly moved to the other End of the room. In a little while, I heard a horse coming and it stopped at the corral. The old Lady and old Man went out and were out for some time, then the old Lady come in. She very quietly got some food and took it out. They both come in pretty soon and went to Bed. I had seen a Tree right in line and in front of the window. After a while, I thought I heard a sound out there, and I raised up and saw a man going down the Tree — and the Tree and window and bed was all at once Explained to me. The moon was up and shone right on the bed and the man in the tree had seen that I was not in the bed. A Shot from that tree would have been my finish if I had been in that bed.

It was in the latter part of the night that I heard a slight noise at the ladder that come up to the hole in the floor. Pretty soon I could just see the top of a head and it stopped for a few seconds and then commenced to rise. When in full view, I said, "Raise one inch more and I will blow you into Kingdome Come." He fell right back down and I heard him leave the house. Everything was very quiet after that — I was resting but very much awake.

Just as daylight was breaking good, I heard a rush of horses and it seemed like they come from all directions. I heard Voices at the Corral and all most at the same time a voice at the door. The old Lady opened the door and a man said, "We want you and your man." There were two of these men and they come in, and as they come in I heard the other men say, "Look out, there is a hole up there." I thought that I recognised the Voice of the first man but I was not sure. They got the old Man out of Bed and he seemed to take it for granted that it was all off for them. Just then some more men come and said, "We have got all three of the Boys," and the man that I thought I knew his Voice spoke again and then I did know him. He said, "I want to search this Loft up there." I called to him and asked if that was Floyd Wilson. He said, "Yes," and wanted to know who I was and I told him, "Fred Dodge."

I was coming down then and I soon told him of my night's experience and then he told me all about the family of the Westmorelands — they were all murderers but Evidence had been hard to get although they had been working hard. But a short time before, a man accross the Arkansas River had seen on a Moonlight Night some men that he thought were the Westmorelands take something out of a Boat and take it into a sort of Cave in the Bank of the River. This man went into Fort Smith and told Judge Parker, the U.S. Judge, what he had seen and Judge Parker placed the whole matter in Dep. U.S. Marshal Floyd Wilson's hands.

After the arrests were made and we were starting to get Breakfast, another party of men rode up, but they were my outfit under Dep. U.S. Marshal Heck Thomas. He and Floyd Wilson were close friends — they had worked together.

After Bfast, they all went to the place where the Cave was. The water in the River was down and they had no trouble — they got the most of 3 Skeletons. There were 3 Skulls but many Bones were missing from the rest of the Body. They had positive Evidence of 2 more men, Also some Evidence of 4 or 5 more men who had disappeared in that immediate vicinity.

The Wilson Posse started with the Prisoners for Fort Smith where they were all tried and convicted and the 4 men were sentenced to be hanged and they were — the old Lady got a life sentence in the U.S. Penn at Atlanta, Georgia and she died there.

We stayed there the balance of the day and all night — I had been unwell for a week or more and was having a high fever. We made all our plans for future opperation Subject to change at any and all times. In the morning, we all went about our ways. I and Talbot White started for Sac and Fox Agency. I had to have medicine. We got in next day towards noon and I was sick — high fever. Fortunately there was a Doctor from Guthrie there and he gave me some medicine that he said would break up the fever. I was there balance of that day and all the next and I got better. I had been Wet through so many times and laid out in the bottoms at night and was considerable broke up.

I had a lot of traveling to do and I had to go. I went to the Camp we had in Deep Fork Bottom, and then to Sapulpa, to Wichita, Kas. on trains to Guthrie, to Arkansas City, Kas., Columbus, Kas., then to Monett, Mo. I was having fever every other day and I left Monett for Houston, Tex. I arrived there Friday, June 26th, 1891. I had a talk with Mr. Christeson and I saw Dr. Scott, the Co. Doctor. I done very little at the office. On Tuesday, June 30th, I got a message regarding matters connected with the Wharton T.R. which required my presence there. I saw Dr. Scott and he gave me some medicine to take with me and I left that night for the Territory again.

I got to Guthrie July 2nd. Dep. U.S. Marshals Lilly and Ed Short was at the Train, and we went right on to Wharton and then to Stillwater. We were there all night and we found that the whole report about the men we wanted was all wrong and we went back to Guthrie the next day. There I got letters from Mr. Christeson telling me about the setting of several Cases that I had in Texas, So I had to Jump some in getting things in Shape to leave the Dalton Case of Wharton T.R.

I started at once for the Sac and Fox Agency, 55 miles. Got there that night. I worked out of there for two days and got things in as good shape as I could and left Sac & Fox. Got to Galveston at noon July 19 to attend the trial of a man that I had in Jail there for Embezelment — J. C. Murphy. The Case was not reached till Wednesday, the 22 — Defendant found Guilty and sentenced 3 years in Penn.

I returned to Houston that night and trouble started fast and thick — Shortages, Damage Suits, Embezelments all over Texas. I was quite successful and cleaned up pretty fast, only the trials which could not come up till Court met. And Aug. 2nd, I was EnRoute back to the Indian Territory.

The Chief of the Sac and Foxes, Moses Keokuk, was a powerful man in his tribe and he gave me a lot of information about the way that things were conducted there at the Agency. I could not get any help from that source. Chief Keokuk had tried to get his Indians to do some work in the Case, but they were afraid on account of there having been 6 men killed. These were white men — 3 Killed by the Seminoles and 3 Killed by the Euches. These men were supposed to be the Daltons. There was at that time a good many crooked Dep. U.S. Marshals in and through that Country and some of these Marshals tried to make a Case against these Indians and I was able to stop the movement. There had been one Euchie killed and a Seminole badly wounded and all the Indians were scared to do anything. Two of these Indians *far* over the average of Indians become good friends of mine and done me many favors, Long Tom and Little Ax — both Seminoles.

So there was not a chance of doing anything through the Indians and the Daltons had all the renegade Indians on their side for they gave them whiskey, and a little money to get more whiskey, and they also gave it out that they would kill any Indian that gave any information about them. There were also most of the White men — Squaw men and outlaws — who were their friends. It was an up hill job against these odds.

There were also some awfully *good* men in that Country — Heck Thomas, Geo Thornton, Bill Tilghman, Ed Short, Cris Madsen, Floyd Wilson — All of the latter were Dep. U.S. Marshals.

When in Sac & Fox Agency I lived at Chief Keokuk's house. He was married to a White Woman of French decent. I made Headquarters at his Store and through him I had several good friends arround there. Leo Whistler, a full blood Sac & Fox, had a little Store at the other End of the Agency about a half mile from Keokuk's Store. Whistler was the Husband of Keokuk's Stepdaughter and was very loyal to Keokuk and was of much help to me. Whistler had a Brotherinlaw that had a store up on Spiecha Creek and Whistler's Mother lived there. She was a Fullblood Sac & Fox and so was Whistler's Sister and this Brotherinlaw, Kirtly by name, had the Store — he was a White man.

This Store was in an Exposed place about 15 miles from the Sac Agency and they were afraid that if they gave any information that the Daltons would kill them and this was probably true. Whistler could not and did not trust his Mother so we had to be Careful there. I could go there and stop there for it was well known that anyone could stay there, and I did at times. Kirtly was not altogether trustworthy So I was in rather close quarters all the time.

Charlie Kountz, the Chief Special Agent of the Atchison, Topeka & Santa Fe Ry., was a man who I had known well and he helped me all that he could, but he was a man that could not get out into the interior. He had suggested that we get a man into the Country and let him get with the Daltons and then tip us off. I did not think it could be done for I did not think that Bob Dalton would allow any stranger to join his outfit, but we tried it for Kountz had a good man — Jim Matthews — of Las Animas, Colo. fame some years earlier, and a friend of mine.

I had to have some of my men know him and I picked them out and made a meeting at Sapulpa with Matthews. The man that kept the little Hotel there was a Crook and the friend of all criminals. I had the men who I wanted to see Matthews get close to and in Sapulpa. Matthews was on time and he started right in to work. Heck Thomas and Floyd Wilson got on the train together at Red Fork 3 miles from Sapulpa. Matthews was on that train. He saw they were Marshals and he asked the Conductor about them and was told that they were U.S. Marshals. Matthews got ready and as the train was going arround a Hill slowly (This was on May the 26, '91) he jumped off and took to the Brush. The Conductor told Thomas and Wilson about Matthews asking the questions and then jumping off the train. They were right at the yard at Sapulpa and it was Dark.

Matthews come in that night after this play. He got to the Hotel and saw the Proprietor to whom he had a letter from a mutual friend at Dodge City. The Proprietor, Ford by name, was ready and willing to do all he could for Matthews and he put him away. I got to see Matthews for a minute and made the appointment to meet him next night.

Next day, Matthews got this man Ford to buy him a good Horse, Saddle, and Rifle and he did. This Horse was a Dun in Color and Jim Matthews had him get a slicker which was yellow. I met him the next night with the 3 men that I had there, for Talbot White was with me and he was the one to get the word to a selected few of the Indians.

I got back to Sac & Fox and the next night about Sundown, Jim Matthews come riding in — I wanted Thornton and Sam Bartell to see him and they did. I met Jim that night and we had a very full talk. I knew that the Stable man was Drunk and I went and got his keys and let Jim out the Backdoor of the Stable. (They were half doors and the Lower half was locked Every night.) In the morning the Stranger was gone, the Barn was locked as usual, and there was much conjecture as to how he had got his Horse out of the Stable, and they made up their minds that he had jumped him out the back way.

That night the mail come in, and there were 2 or 3 Postal cards for the Officers and the Indian Agent giving an accurate discription of Matthews, and he was supposed to have killed the City Marshal (a very close friend of Jim Matthews) at La Junta, Colo. This was surely the man that rode in there the night before and had got his Horse out of the Stable and gone.

I heard of Jim throughout, but took no chances on meeting him for it was too daingerous. He had certainly taken a very Daingerous job on his hands for he was subject to be Shot at or arrested by any, only the few who were on the inside of the matter. This went on untill July 11th when I met Matthews again at Orlando, Okla.

We had a long talk. Jim had got to the Daltons, and had been with them a few days but Bob would not allow him to join them. Bob said that there was Enough of them then and more men would only be a menace to their safety. Bob told him of several places that he could go and he would find friends that he could trust. Bob also said the he would help him in any way that he could, get him fresh Horses if they run him too hard, and be of any and all kinds of help that he could, but that they had an agreement that no one could join them. Jim was resourceful but he could not press anything as it would make Bob suspicious, and they shook hands and parted.

Jim was of the opinion that I was at first, that Bob was too Foxy to let anyone join them, and we called it all off.

Jim pulled out for parts unknown, after he had got the Crook at Orlando who he was staying with to sell his outfit, and left word with this crook that he was going to make it to South America. Jim was soon after with his friend, the City Marshal at La Junta, the man he was supposed to have killed before he left there.

At Guthrie, I got a letter from Mr. Christeson telling me

about the Trials that were now approaching. I had to make some arraingements to leave that Country, So I made a drive to the Sac & Fox Agency and got out to several places from there. During this time I was handicapped by rains and high water in Creeks, etc.

I left Sac & Fox on the 17th of July 1891, and made Guthrie at 10 P.M. that night. Made the Train at 11 P.M. for Houston, got to Houston at 5:30 A.M. Sunday, the 19th, had long talk with Mr. Christeson and left Houston at 2 P.M. for Galveston.

I found out at Houston that we had a lot of little cases to look after. I was ready, for the Murphy case was tried on the 22nd, (Convicted and Sentenced to 3 Years in the Penn) and went to Houston that night. I worked hard and fast and cleaned up a lot of small cases arround over Texas and left Houston night of Aug. 2nd for the Indian Territory again. Reached Guthrie and got busy at once. Left next morning for Iowa country. Stayed at Iowa village with the Missionary who looked after the Iowas, a good man, and the only place where anyone could get anything to Eat between Guthrie and the Sac & Fox Agency. The Missionary's Wife was a fine Cook and She made as fine Biscuits as I ever ate.

That night I learned of the Perfidious work of a U.S. Marshal who wanted to make fees — at any cost. This U.S.M. used that road a lot and always stopped to Eat at the Missionarys' and he owed them for meals for over a year and the amount was over $20.00. (They only charged 25 cts. a meal which barely paid for the food.) He passed through there and Stopped to Eat and he told them where there was a Bee tree — It was an old stump that the Tree had been burned and it was above the Road and all that passed there could see it. This U.S.M. told them to cut the Tree and get the Honey and put him up a can of it. So next day, the Missionary and his Son cut

136

the old stump and got the Honey. This U.S.M. come along again and stopped for Dinner and they had a nice can of Honey for him to take along and send to his folks that lived in Wichita, Kas., and they had hot Biscuits. He set and gorged himself with hot Biscuits and Honey, and took his Honey and went on his way. He went into Guthrie and before a Commissioner of the same Stripe as himself, he swore out warrants and sent back and arrested the Missionary and his Son for Cutting Timber on Government land, brought them in, and took them to Wichita to Jail there where all U.S. Prisoners were kept. (there being no Jail in Okla. at that time) Then they were brought back for examination, they were then held for Grand Jury, then they were taken back to Wichita and thus U.S.M. was making his mileage and fees all the time.

Finally the Missionary and boy got out on Bail and were at trial aquitted, and it had cost the Missionary everything that they had including his Team and 3 Milch Cows. There were many kind of these tricks that were worked in order to make Fees and the U.S. Government was surely being robbed by these kind of men.

I went on next day to Sac & Fox. There were several places that I had to keep up with — and Several Indians that I could go to. In Tulsa I had a friend named Burrell Cox who was a close friend of Heck Thomas. Burrell was married to a Creek Indian Woman who could go out for a day or two and get more news than we could get in a week — And she was sure square. Of course, She never did tell anyone anything, only Burrell. I also had friends in Muskogee and McAlester. They were all just wide places in the road. Tulsa had 3 Houses, the Depot, a little sort of a store, Gen Merchandise, and the House that Burrell Cox lived in. But I worked all over the Country. In the Creek Nation I could stay at Cezar Jack's a Creek Indian of influence, and it was handy and on the road between Sac & Fox and Sapulpa. I had places to go besides, and was on the go hard all the time trying to get a line on the men we wanted, and get the men that I had out on a good trail. I was on the go all the time.

There was going to be an Indian Stomp dance on Euchie Creek and I made my arraingements to cover that and on Monday, Aug. 24, I was on Euchie Creek and vicinity. I was at Doces Place where the dance was to be and I was ready for what ever might come up. All the men that I had working with me were at Strategic points — Heck Thomas and Burrell Cox — Geo Thornton and Sam Bartell — Talbot White with me — and had out some Indians who could be trusted. These were selected by Moses Keokuk, Chief of the Sac & Fox. They were supposed to be attending the dance and were mixing and getting information from other Indians.

About daylight, I went to Keokuk's new Store on Euchie Creek and a runner from the Sac Agency come in shortly and brought me a message that on Sunday, Aug. 23rd, Ed Short, Dep. U.S.M., had killed Charley Bryant and Charley Bryant had killed Ed Short On the Rock Island train north of El Reno. I got back to Doces and get the men together and Burrell Cox come in and told us that Bob and Emmett Dalton had gone up Stillwater Creek and that he, Burrell, had sent his Indian right back so as to have the trail for us. I told the Boys about Short and Bryant, and there was some strong feeling there for Ed Short had several awfully good friends in that Bunch, which included myself.

We left at once, and got to the Creek and went up it, and Burrell Cox found his Indian at the mouth of Tiger Creek. We followed the trail and it was then heading towards the Creek Nation. We followed it till It took us to Henry Miller's. It was then Dark and we had to stop. We camped at Miller's and learned that Bob and Emmett had passed there 3 hours before we got there.

At Daylight, we were on the trail again and followed it all day, and at Dark again we were in 2 or 3 miles of the Sac Agency. The Boys camped on the Trail, and Talbot White and I went into Sac & Fox. I wrote some letters and we got back to camp nearly Daylight and at Daylight we were again on the Trail. It took us past Cezar Jack's place. It had commenced to rain when we got there and there was a regular downpour for over an hour and then we had no trail at all. We got Dinner and spread out trying to pick up the trail or some information, agreeing to meet at Jane Owens' by Sundown.

Jane Owens and her whole outfit was the friend of any Criminal and Outlaw on Earth, and we all knew that the Daltons were being helped by Her and her *whole* family. We camped near there that night. We had had Spies arround there — renegade White men and Indians — but nothing had ever come of it. Jane always had Whiskey and She got away with all that she ever tried to do for Whiskey will go further in an Indian Country than the money of a white man if the white man is after a Criminal.

We tried to pick up something next day, but no use. We stopped at Nigger Hamilton's that night. Next day we broke up, Thornton and Bartell going West, Heck Thomas and Burrell Cox Swing more North to meet Talbot White and I at Red Fork. That Night we all met there. In the next A.M., Heck and Burrell went to Tulsa and I went to Sapulpa, while Talbot White had gone in the A.M. We were in Sapulpa that night and next day, we made our way back to the place of Nigger Hamilton's and then into Sac & Fox, where I was to meet Thornton.

At Sac & Fox I saw Thornton and a man named Koonce who, with a man named Lee West and a man named Jacobs, had a scheme that they were working on to Catch the Daltons. They were known to Thornton and Bartell, and I was the only other man that was supposed to know anything about them. Koonce was at Sac & Fox and was sure that the men wanted were in the Euchie Country along the line of the Creek Nation.

I did not take much Stock in these men, they were from Oklahoma City and Thornton wanted to go into that part and see about it. They went out that night, and for the next week, we all done some riding. I went all arround the vicinity in question — was at the Euchie Creek, Kirtley's, Miller's, Hamilton's, Old Man Mayes', Keokuk's new Store.

I was sick and could hardly make it. I was taking Quinine all the time but it did not seem to do me any good and on Sept 15th I come into Sac & Fox too sick to ride. I was there for a week but I could not get out — the Iowa, Seminole, Potowatomee, Pawnee, Sac & Fox, and Creek Nations were all about to be opened, and I could not get any kind of Conveyance to get out with — Everything was in use ready for the Opening. On Sept. 22nd, I got out with Leo Whistler to the new place where they were going to locate the Town of Chandler. The Surveys were not completed by the Military for this Townsite. There was a Company of Soldiers there, Capt. Hays in Command, and as all else was ready and the Run to start, they just let them, at the appointed time, make the run for the town lots and then moved them all off for a few days till the Survey was made, and on an appointed day, let them make the run over again. I saw Capt. Hays about getting help into Guthrie (this was about half way between Sac & Fox to Guthrie) but he could not do anything for me as he needed every man that he had, but he told me that as soon as the next run was over that he would be glad to help me and would send me on in then. There was nothing to do only wait. I got back to Sac & Fox that night with Whistler's team and Stayed there Sick with this fever that I was having and I stayed there for six days more.

I was completely broke down. The rainy season had been right along with me. I had been wet and dryed out same clothes, laid out at night sometimes no Bed, only my Saddle Blanket and Slicker, wet and cold. I had my Horse Shot and me Shot at, Bullet going through my clothes — Close Call. But this was not done by the Daltons. I was mistaken for another party, but at any time this might occur for Serious Mistakes were happening in that Country all the time. I found out about this mistake so that I was sure about it, and it was at a later date.

While at Sac & Fox I got the true facts about the killing of Ed Short and Charley Bryant. Bryant was at a friend's House in El Reno. Short found it out and went Singlehanded and arrested Bryant and guarded him over night. (All U.S. Prisoners were kept at Wichita, Kas. where they had a large and good Jail.) The next morning, Sunday, Aug. 23, '91, Short started to take Bryant to Wichita.

The Rock Island Ry. run through El Reno and was opperated by the United States Express Company. Short had done many favors for them and got permission to ride in Company with his prisoner in the Express Car. The Express Messenger was also in the Car. Short had received news that at a point North of El Reno that there would be an attempt made to take Bryant away from him. As they neared this point, Short told the Messenger to Guard Bryant while he, Short, went onto the front platform to see if there was anything that looked Suspicious. (This place was only a siding and the Train did not stop there.)

When Short went out the front door, the messenger was doing something and laid his Pistol on the Desk. Bryant was right there and Grabbed up the Pistol and turned it on the Messenger and made him turn towards the wall and keep his hands up. Bryant was handcuffed but he took the Pistol in his two hands and went to the door and opened it. Short had not discovered anything and was about to re-enter the Car as Bryant opened the Door. As he did, he Shot Ed Short but Short got his Gun and Shot Bryant. The Messenger could see it all and it was fast. They Each shot a couple of times and both men died right there.

So ended the life of a bad outlaw, and also ended the life of a Brave, Efficient, and good Officer, and on Monday, the 28th, I got out again to what was to be Chandler — Whistler helped me again.

When I got to Chandler, Capt. Hays took me to his Tent and the Doctor made me comfortable. I lay there and saw the Run made for the lots. By night the military had got everything quiet and disputants easy and Capt. Hays, true to his word, sent me on into Guthrie that night, reaching there at nearly daylight. I was very Sick and was at Guthrie all day and left that night for Houston at little after midnight Wednesday, Sept. 30, '91. In the Early A.M. of Oct. 1st, we got to a little below Purcell where there had been a Washout and we had to make Transfer by Wagons. The Porter had helped me out and I was partly lying in a pile of Ties. The Conductor had told me to wait for him and he would take me over personnally. Route Agent G. A. Taft showed up there and he passed me and did not know me. He passed me several times. Finally the Conductor had told him and then he come to me and he and the Conductor took me over and I got to Bed in the Sleeper. Taft went through to Houston with me and we reached Houston the next day, Oct. 2nd, and Dr. Scott went right to work on me.

12

OF A BITING HORSE, A CARELESS AGENT,

AND A SELF-STYLED DETECTIVE

On Sept. 2nd, '91, there was a Train Robbery at Samuels Siding on the Galveston, Houston & San Antonio Ry. (Southern Pacific) and the Raingers under Capt. Jones were keeping up a Chase of these men who were 4 in number. This case was needing attention badly. Although still very weak, I was much better and on the Night of Oct. 12th, I left Houston on this Train Robbery Case. (I was far from being Entirely well, but Dr. Scott at Houston had put me on a Quinine schedule and I was keeping up with it and It was late in December before I stopped the Quinine.) On Oct. 22nd, '91, I got a message telling of the Capture of three and the killing of one of the Samuels Train Robbers by the Raingers, under Capt. Jones. These men would all be taken into El Paso And on Oct. 26th, I left Houston for El Paso, arriving there night of the 27th. I met Capt. Jones and he went over the whole case with me. One of the Robbers had made a partial Confession to Capt. Jones.

I had now Started on this Case at El Paso. It was in the United States Court, and I was destined to be kept in the South for some months and all I could do in the Indian Territory was by mail and Telegrams.

For sometime after this Case at El Paso, W.F. & Co. had all kinds of Cases in Texas, and I still had the money to recover from the Bank at Greenwood, Miss. in the Walter Jones Case, and Life was certainly one ———— thing after another.

The Next day, Oct. 28th, Capt. Jones and I worked on Langsford — he had come clean in his talk to Capt. Jones and he did not come entirely clean this day in his talk to us. He did agree to take the Stand and testify on behalf of the Prosecution — in other words — he was willing to turn State's Evidence. (A State's Evidence Witness is strong testimony, but it must be corroborated in detail and then it becomes strong Evidence.)

The Loss at this Robbery was $3,600.00, Ammount Recovered was $1,400.00, and that left a Net Loss of $2,200.00. Langsford accounted for this loss in a fire that had occured in a Canebrake on the Rio Grande River. Capt. Jones told me that they had thought that they had the Robbers surrounded in this canebrake and had finally set fire to it to make the robbers come out, but they were not there. Langsford said that they were in camp and were dividing up the money when the lookout reported Raingers and that there was a fast Scramble. They hid the most of the money that had not been divided, and from the Hills they saw the Raingers and the Fire, and after the Raingers left, they come back and found that the currency had all burned and the Silver was discolored. This was Corroborated by Capt. Jones and by the amount recovered from the Robbers. There had been originally $1000.00 in Silver and the most of that was with the Robbers when they captured them and some of this was discolored.

The Raingers did not get their Trail again for some time afterwards but when they did overtake, the Robbers had just begun to Eat Breakfast. There was a fight and one of the Robbers was killed. The one killed was named Tom Flint, the others were Jack Wellington, Tom Fields, and Jas. Langsford — the one that was confessing was the latter one.

On Nov. 1st, I received a message from Mr. Christeson telling me of a loss at Honey Grove, Texas, nearly a thousand miles away. The Loss was $3,000.00 and I left for there, passed through Houston, and Mr. Christeson went with me to Honey Grove where we arrived in the Evening of the 3rd. G. A. Taft was allready there and we was up nearly all night. I interviewed all the Employees and next day we were getting a line on things. G. A. Taft was a helpful man for he was a natural Detective. I worked on that case for a week — it was a question between the messenger on the train and the Negro Porter at the Station. It was sometime after that we got at the bottom of the Case — It was the Negro that had taken the Pkg. He got rid of most of the money, Gambling and Women. (These Gambling places among the Negros was hard to get at for they Shoot Craps mostly and the Games are Scattered among the Negro Quarters. The ballance of the money was recovered on the Bond of the messenger and the Agent at Honey Grove — both of them were culpabley negligent and they should have never let the Negro handle that Package.

Also at this time we had a Damage Suit trial at Waco of long Standing — one of the Company's Horses had bit a Boy, and his Father and the Attorneys wanted $30,000.00 Damages. I was back and forth for a week between Waco and Galveston — I had had a case at Galveston of Embezelment, J. C. Murphy defendant. We had convicted him and he was sentenced to the Penn for 3 years but when the Judge went to Sentence him, which was 10 days after the trial, the Judge had discovered a flaw in the Indictment and the Dist. Atty. was Compelled to ask for a new trial which was Granted and I had this trial on hand and on Nov. 20th, '91, we had that trial. Murphy stood true to his promice and made his confession on the Witness Stand but the Jury Said he was a liar and brought in a Virdict of "Not Guilty". We were well satisfyed with the result — Murphy had been in Jail for over a year and he had been punished sufficiently.

The Fee of the Attorney had been paid by an older Brother

of Murphy's and this Jury had been Paid and Selected by this Atty. Everything arround the Courts at that time was simply rotten.

This Jury had all gone down the Street a little ahead of us. Murphy and I and this Atty. went downtown together and at a Corner Saloon we come up with the Jury. One of them was going to buy the Drinks and the Atty., Murphy, and I was invited in to drink with them but I refused, and I was asked what I thought of the Virdict. I told them that they did not want my Opinion of the Virdict or Jury that brought in the Virdict but then they insisted on me telling them — So I said to them, "No, I don't think you want to know," and then they insisted again — So I said, "well, since you insist I will tell you." (I had taken a position at the Start so that no one could get behind me.) And I said, "I think that you are Twelve of the most damnabel Perjurers that it has ever been my misfortune to meet." I was anticipating something to happen but nothing did. They never said a word but went on into the Saloon. I did not go in, and Murphy stayed with me, and presently we went down the street together.

Back at Waco, the Attorneys for the Company was advising a Settlement be made for the horse bite if we could make one that was reasonable, and on Nov. 27th, I succeeded in getting an Agreement from the Plaintiff in the Case — they Agreed to settle for $3000.00. The Attorneys for the Company and Mr. Christeson were jubilent, for the Attys. had recomended a much larger Amount. It was a very daingerous Case, for there was no doubt but what they could prove that the Horse that Bit the Boy was a Vicious Animal. We had to keep that Horse there untill the case was settled one way or another, and every day we were taking chances with him. We settled in Court, they agreeing to take an Agreed judgment for $3000.00. We wound up the Case, and that night sent the

146

Horse to Houston where he did not leave the Stable, but commenced to get rapidly worse and they had him Killed. The Vetenary who examined his Brain Pronounced the Horse Insane.

I left Houston for points East, on Dec. 19th, '91. I had a case at Crowley, Louisiana where there was a loss of $1000.00 in Silver, and I wanted to recover that money. The Agent was clearly responsible for this loss for it was culpibal negligence on his part. I only had a couple of days to spare on this matter for I had to get on to Greenwood. I wanted to wind up that Case that I had there against the Bank for $2300.00. I was at Crowley a day and a half and at New Orleans on the Crowley Case, and I left the night of Dec. 23rd for Greenwood. I got there on the P.M. of Dec. 24th — I had spent Christmas the year before at Greenwood and it was surely for me to spend another one there which I did.

I had to give a Bond to the Bank and our Atty. and I got up the Bond which I could not make in Mississippi account of no representative in that State, but they agreed to a Bond made in New Orleans. On Dec. 28th, I wired for Mr. Christeson to meet me next A.M. in New Orleans and I left for there that day. I met Mr. Christeson the next A.M., made the Bond and left again that night for Greenwood — there at 5 A.M. next A.M.

I was quite uneasy about this money and it was noon before I got it. I had found out that there was no money in the Bank and they were getting in some money to pay me. I agreed to wait untill Noon. I knew that I could get the money out of the Fixtures and Safes, So I got out an Execution ready to levy and had the Sheriff ready to make the Levy and take possession. I told the President of the Bank that I was ready to make this Levy and that I would make it at 12:05 o'clock noon. At 11:30, they sent word to me that they were ready to make the Payment. I went there and it was in the private office of the President that I got the Money — it was in all kinds of Denominations, and the last of it Come in the Back door while we were Counting — it was $500.00 in Silver.

Well, finally I had the money and I can assure you that I lost no time in getting it into the hands of the Southern Express Co. there. I shipped it to Mr. Christeson from My Self, got my receipts, and then I was ready to go. As far as I was concerned, it could be for all time — and it was, for I have never been in Greenwood since that day. (In Confidence, while in the Office of the President at the Bank, I was told that there was only $20.00 left in the Bank when I got the Walter Jones money, but the Directors were to meet at 1 P.M. and they were all to put in more money so the Bank would be Solid — and they did so.)

While En Route for Ft. Worth Jan. 5 1892, I got a message from Mr. Christeson telling me of the Houston Depot Office Robbery the night before, Jan. 5th, 1892. I continued right on to Houston and arrived at 5:30 A.M. Jan. 7th, '92. I got the particulars and went to work and right here commenced a very trying and Intricate case which brought on many complications. The Sheriff, Geo. Ellis, was a square and Efficient Man, The Chief of Police was also a good man.

The night man did not Lock his Safe when he went out to work a Train. This was his habit and it was known to an Ex-Driver by the name of Archer, And He and confederates Entered the Office while this Night Man was working the Train and got away with this Package.

In 2 or 3 days, I knew all the men who were in this Robbery — their names were Archer, Hobson, Austin George, and a Gambler, whose name I will not Make public for his family was an old prominent and respectable family of good standing. I had several pretty good friends among the Gamblers in

Houston — men whom I had known in the Tombstone days Among whom was Billy Thompson, Brother of Ben Thompson, and from Billy I got my first tip. I at once got 2 other Gamblers busy getting information for me. Austin George was a Gambler, Archer and Hobson were Gamblers but not professional Gamblers. All of this money was lost over Faro Tables the first and Second Night after the Robbery, and all of this Bunch was broke. A couple of days after this John Thacker come. He had been East and Stopped off for a while. He got there on night of Jan 11th and There was not much left to do as it was a case of Dig, Dig for Evidence and was going to take some time. Thacker left for San Francisco Jan. 19th.

During the time that he was there, and through his recommendation, there was a reward offered of $1,000. This was a Mistake for it Caused several *would be* Detectives to get into the case for the reward, Among them one man named Tinsley who caused us a lot of trouble. I had a talk with him in the presence of Supt. Christeson — and Explained to him and also requested that there be no arrest made without first Consulting with me or Supt. Christeson — which he agreed to. Tinsley said that he had reason to believe that Archer and Hobson were in it and he suspicioned that the man whose name is not given and Austin George were connected with it. But Tinsley absolutely did not have one Scintilla of Evidence against any one of these men.

The Sheriff and the Chief of Police did not have any Confidence in Tinsley atall. He was a man that was into Everything that he could get his hands into — He Monkeyed with Commissions on real Estate deals, tried to be a Collector, etc. and whenever he got Hold of any money he Gambled, and of course was broke most of the time.

There had been a watch taken in this Depot Robbery and

on Feb. 3rd, '92, It was Pawned at Galveston. I got word same night and went down there the next morning. It was the watch all right and the discription fitted the nameless man in this Robbery, but the Pawnbroker would not Identify the man. The Chief of Police and I were fully satisfyed as to who the man was and we also knew that the Pawnbroker was afraid to make any identification at all for this man was a hard man and very daingerous when Drinking. He had killed one man in Galveston and another man in Houston, and was fast and sure with a Gun. We did not want to make any arrests at that time.

Late in the Evening of Feb. 11th, I heard that there had been a Warrant issued for Archer. I saw the Sheriff and the Chief of Police and there had been no warrant reached them. The Sheriff and I went to the Residence of the Justice that we heard had issued a warrant and he told us that there had been a complaint made and Sworn to by this man Tinsley and a warrant was issued upon the Complaint and Tinsley said that there would be no arrest made unless Archer tried to leave Town.

We were fully advised as to what Archer was doing and we knew that he was going to move with his family to another town — and that is just what I wanted, for I could keep close track of him and he would be away from the influence of the other men and would be much easier to handle. The next day Archer got a Box Car and loaded all his Effects into it and he and his family were going on a Passenger train later in the day. After the Car of Household effects was loaded, Tinsley got out a Search Warrant for the Car and took it and the warrant for his arrest to the Sheriff, who was Compelled to Execute them. The Sheriff sent me word and then Arrested Archer and also Searched the Car — without results. I went to see Archer in Jail but he was Sullen and would not talk to me at

all. His Examining trial was set for the next P.M. and On Slim
Evidence he was bound over to the Grand Jury and Bail set at
$1,000.00 which the Bunch soon made, but there was no name
on the Bond that was in the Robbery.

Tinsley also had a warrant issued charging Archer with assault on the Depot Agent and this was set for the 17th of Feb.
At this time the case was Called, and Tinsley put on all the
Evidence that he had which included that of the preceding
trial. At the termination of this Examination, the Court released the Bond in the former case and Discharged the De-
fendent and also Discharged him in the present Case.

That Evening I had a long talk with Austin George.
George was a man far over the average of his Kind and I had
made up my mind that if there was any fall down at all that
my help would be in Austin George. In this talk I learned a
lot about the nameless man and I learned that the whole town
was afraid of him — and I could see that George also had the
fear in himself. But George was getting Sick of the Gang.
George told me that it would be a very daingerous thing for
me to do if I went to this unnamed man and tried to talk to
him about this Robbery, but I had my own Ideas about that.

Mr. J. J. Valentine, President, W.F. & Co., come and
stopped off for one day and Night and I gave him a complete
history of the Case. We were in Consultation untill far into
the Night. He Cautioned me about taking too many chances
and told me that he would rather loose the case Entirely than
for me to get hurt.

I made my arraingements to get to see the unknown man
and I was introduced to him by the Proprietor of the Strongest
Gambling House in Houston. He brought him into his private office where I was, and after the introduction he said to
the unknown man, "I have known this man Dodge for a long
time and I want to tell you that he is a man that will keep his

word regardless of what may happen If he once gives it to you. And if there is any passing of Confidences or his word given to you, I will be responsible for Dodge in the keeping of his word." Then we were left alone and this man said to me, "I have known him Closely and a long time and I have never known him to go so far before. He certainly must know you, or else he would not stand good for you.

We visited for a while, and then I come right out and talked straight from the Shoulder. We did not get very far as to any information that I wanted — but as we were about to part he said to me, "I have not given you much information and I will not either — But I am and will be your friend for I like the way that you Come right out with what you have to say."

I did get a lot of information from him later on, and soon after this I lost Austin George. There was a big fire in Houston. It was a Convent, and in Saving two of the Sisters, Austin George was so badly burned that he died that day.

I had a lot of other work piling up on me and I had to keep up with it. Later on, the unknown man matched himself a Gun fight with another fast and sure Gunman who was wounded badly but succeeded in Killing the unknown man.

Later I learned that Archer brought a Damage Suit against Wells Fargo & Co. for $30,000.00 for Arrest and False Imprisonment, result of Tinsley's having him arrested in the Case of Depot Office Robbery of January 5th, 1892. The Company was in no way responsible for the Acts of this man Tinsley. (He was a private Detective) But Wells Fargo & Co. had money and Tinsley had no money. Hence, Suit against Wells Fargo & Co. While there was no liability on the Part of the Company, still, it was important that we did not allow a Judgment against the Company.

The Case was called at Galveston November 4th, 1892, and we went to trial, and when the Plaintiff (Archer) had finished their testimony, they Rested and we at once submitted the Case on their own Testimony. Result — instructed Virdict in favor of Wells Fargo & Co.

I had to go to El Paso to get ready for the Trial of Samuel siding Train Robbers, and I left Houston April 2nd for El Paso, and untill May 1st I was at El Paso — it took a month of awful hard work. The Defense Quashed the Indictment. This case was in the United States Court and Judge Maxey, a very able man, made an order to convene a U.S. Grand Jury which was done and they reindicted all the Defendants.

There was an array of the best attorneys that could be had for the Defence and one Old Man that was counted the most foxy and Trickey man in Texas. The Reason of this Hard fight for the Defense was because the Family of Tom Flint were of good standing and they tried to show that Tom Flint had been out on a Cattle buying trip and had just run into the Robbers' camp while they were at Breakfast and Eat with them.

It was while they were Eating Breakfast that the Raingers rode on to them and in the fight that Ensued, Tom Flint was killed. Flint had the Silver Coin with him when he was killed — it was one Thousand Dollars and they tried to Show that this money was for the purpose of buying Cattle, but we positively identifyed him with this Bunch for 2 weeks before the Robbery and all the way with them after the Robbery. The old Atty. reffered to above caused some delay by some crooked work but I will not touch on that for his Son is an honored Citizen of El Paso and has a large family. We went into the trial of that case April 4th, 1892 to May 1st, same year, and I left El Paso for Houston on the date last named.

On the 15th May, I had to go to Dallas where I had a Forgery Case coming up for trial. Case come on for trial on date set. On the 19th, Mr. Amador Andrews, General Manager at Kansas City, arrived in Dallas and with him a clerk who was studying law in the Gen. Atty.'s office at Omaha. This firm represented the Company at that point. This clerk Kohler attended Court the next day, and he thought that it was an Easy case. I had a Confession from this Defendant and he Admitted its truth on the Stand. He was Defended by, at that time, the best Criminal Lawyer in Texas, but he could not see any way out for his client and he told me so and we discussed the case fully. I was quite willing to take a light sentence for I had recovered the money which was made good by his relatives.

Mr. Christeson had come to meet Mr. Andrews at Dallas and we were having a Conference that night at which Kohler was present, and he wanted to get into the case and make an argument. Mr. Christeson and I both advised against it and told him that his argument would not be well received, that the Jury would take an adverse view of any argument made by a Stranger, and that the Atty. for the Defense would call it Persication instead of Prosecution, that while the Dist. Atty. would probably consent to allow him to make his argument, that it would not set well and that all the Attys. would resent it, but in the morning at Breakfast, the manager determined to let him try it. I positively refused to have anything to do with it and told him that he must make his own arraingements which he did. His Argument was ridiculed by the Atty. for the Defence and not atall relished by the Prosecution. Result — Jury in 15 minutes brought in a verdict of Not Guilty, and it suited me to death.

The Jury after being dismissed congratulated me on having a good case but they just simply had to rebuke this man and they done this to perfection. He left there that night and he did not get any where with the Company — I have never seen him since his return to Omaha.

After this case, I went to Houston and caught up the loose Ends and next morning I left for Cuero.

There was a Strike on On the San Antonio and Aransas Pass and trains were running when they could. It was an Engineers' Strike and I left Cuero with a Thrashing Machine Engineer. We met a wreck and that put us 5 hours late and then we run into 2 Cars of Lumber on the Main Line. The Fireman was so badly hurt that he died a few minutes after we got him out and there were a number of Passengers hurt among which was my Self. This Collision was right at Eagle Lake. I worked pretty hard getting the Fireman out as the hot water was reaching him and he was in misery.

Then I commenced to know that my foot was hurting me considerably. There were several Doctors there and I had sit down on some Lumber and I guess my Complexion was a little white, for a Doctor come up to me and said, "Say, look here, you are hurt some your self." I told him that my foot was paining me some.

We had to cut off my Boot and we found that a large Sliver from the Lumber had run down clear through my Foot just missing the Instep bone. The Doctor fixed me up and when I got the chance, I come on to Houston after a hard night. I got into Houston in the morning about 16 hours late. There, I got Medical Attention and my foot was put in as good shape as it could be at that time. I remained in Houston 4 Days and my Foot was well taken care of and was doing as well as could be Expected.

Tuesday, May 31, '92, I left for Wichita, Kansas. The man, Crawford, that was the one that left his Safe open and was robbed Jan. 5th, '92, was then living at Wichita. There had been a mixup about collecting on his Bond and I took his Brother, the Chief Clerk for Mr. Christeson, with me. On our way up there we were on the north bound Santa Fe and the South bound Santa Fe was held up and Robbed at Red Rock Cherokee Strip. I was advised of this and I stopped off at Red Rock.

This Robbery was at 11 P.M. June 1st, '92, and I arrived there the A.M. of June 2nd, '92. I organised a Posse to get out after these Robbers. There was nothing at Red Rock, only the Station and a Section House. That night, I went to Arkansas City to meet Supt. Stockton — Red Rock was in his Division. I met him the next A.M. (I was using a cane on account of my foot and this foot was bothering me some, for I had to use it too much at Red Rock.) We went back to Red Rock on same train that he was on and returned to Arkansas City that night.

Next A.M. I went to Wichita and Supt. Stockton went to Kansas City, And on June 4th, I arrainged the Bond Matter of Ex-Agent Crawford and had to see a Doctor about my Foot. The Doctor cut it open and then fixed it up so that I could keep going. The next A.M. Got a Message from Stockton to meet him and Supt. Simpson who was from Omaha at train to go to Guthrie. They had Arrested a man there Claiming he was Bob Dalton so we went on to Guthrie and we also went to Oklahoma City to see partners located there — no good. There were men being arrested all over the Country.

That Evening I went back to Arkansas City to meet the Ry. Supt., Resique. I then went to Wichita to see about a man there then come back to Arkansas City to meet U. S. Marshal Swain and Posse. (this is the outfit that I sent out) Supt. Stockton returned on this same Train and he and Marshal Swain went to Oklahoma City. They Returned and Supt. Stockton and I started for Las Vegas, New Mexico to see about a man under Arrest there. No good. At Las Vegas, we met Supt. Dyer of that Division of the Santa Fe and we returned at once to go to Englewood to meet U.S. Marshal Swain and Posse. We got to Englewood June 17th and met U.S.M. Swain and Posse. They done no good, and Stockton and I thought best to send them on home which we done.

That Night we employed a man who knew the Country and was a Straight and fearless man — Fred Edwards — and we left Englewood the next morning to cut through the Country and see if the Robbers had gone West. We got a good Team and were well equipped and the next morning we started. Going down through No Man's Land, we worked through that Country for Several days and finally got over towards the West End of No Man's Land, and went to Beaver City. Met Frank Healy — the Sheriff and many others.

I made some good friends in that Section that done me a lot of good later on, and in that Section I found out that it was the Dalton Gang that had Robbed the Train at Red Rock, June 1st, '92. I had worked this Country thougherly and knew for a Certainty that it was that Gang that we wanted.

Next the Post Office was Robbed at Wanamaker which was only a few miles N.E. of Kingfisher. The Daltons lived on a Farm close to Kingfisher. We got good Discription at Wanamaker and it was undoubtedly Bob and Emmett Dalton, who had been at their home for a couple of days. We followed them through to the Santa Fe and then they went East to where they had many friends. We drove into Orlando which was close by and the first Town in Oklahoma. We went on the Train to Guthrie and there I got a Telegram from Dep. U.S. Marshal Sam Bartell at Oklahoma City. I went right on down there and met Bartell, and we started for the Sac and Fox Agency at once, and that was the Commencement of a wild Ride.

Bartell had a good Team and Buggy. These Horses were Exceptionally good. They worked in Harness *and* were both good Saddle Horses and he had the Saddles in the Buggy — The Sac & Fox Agency is 55 miles N.E. of Oklahoma City. We got out 4 or 5 miles and we Cited a Horseman who did not seem to be wanting anyone to see him. He rode on faster

and was leaving us behind — we were not pressing the Team
for it was a long drive.

We finally come to a place where there was a Squaw man
living who was a friend of Sam Bartell's and we got him out
and his Wife was getting us some Supper and this man called
Bartell outside and told him about the Horseman — who had
also stopped there and Watered his Horse. He told Bartell
that the man was Grat Dalton. (Bartell told this man that I
was all right and to come in and do his talking which he did.)
It was surely a Supprise to me for the last that I had heard
which was about 10 days before, Grat Dalton was in Jail at
Visalia, Calafornia for a Train Robbery there from which Bob
and Emmett Dalton Escaped. I could hardly believe this
news, but I knew that this man knew all the Daltons — men
and Women — and could not be mistaken, and that Explained the Trip home of Bob and Emmett a few days Earlier.

We soon started and then we were surely traveling. We
finally got sight of the man and Again he speeded up. We
were sure that he would leave the Road when he got to Deep
Fork Bottoms and we done our best to Overtake him before
he got there, but he was ahead of us beyond Rifle Shot. When
we got there, we changed and put our Saddles on and went in
after him but we never got sight of him that night any more.

We then went into Sac and Fox where we got Fresh Horses
and met the man we were to meet — Geo Thornton, Under
whom Sam Bartell was a Dep. U.S. Marshal. Geo. Thornton
was a U.S. Marshal and was quartered at Oklahoma City.
We all 3 rode all day. Grat Dalton had 2 Horses and he
changed several times during the night before. We were not
Able to get any news at all of him and he was then in a Country where he and his Brothers had friends.

13

THE DALTON GANG

DEAD OR ALIVE — OR BOTH

There was a Movement on foot for all the Companys who had Suffered from the depridations of the Dalton Gang to go together and all Share alike in the Expense of fitting out an outfit to go after this Gang and Stay in the field untill they were Killed, Captured, or driven out of the Country. This was a big undertaking and it took a whole lot of preliminary work to make all these Arraingements. I stayed in Houston till the night of July 25, '92, And left for the Indian Territory. I stopped a day at Dallas and a day at Gainsville seeing partys on this work. I got to Guthrie the morning of July 28, '92, and was there all day in Consultation with the U.S. Marshal and Deputy U.S. Marshal.

That Night I was woke up and they had news at the Marshal's office of a man who answered the discription of one of the Gang who was wounded — The Marshal and I left at once. It took all day and night and then the next day and we got back to Guthrie at 2 O'Clock at night, making 48 hours. This was a trip that profited nothing — when we found the man, he was the wrong man and this was a fair Sample of most of the information that one could get in that Country.

The next day, I went to Newton, Kas. to meet Supt. Stockton and we returned to Kas. City En Route to St. Louis to meet mngr. Andrews and Supt. G. B. Simpson. (Wells Fargo & Co. had succeeded the Pacific Express Co. on the St. Louis and San Francisco Railway and Supt. Simpson had been moved from Omaha to St. Louis to become Superintendent of the Missouri Division.) I was in St. Louis Aug. 4, 5, and 6, Looking over the new men that we had taken over from the Pacific Express.

On the P.M. of the 6th, the Superintendent of the St. Louis and San Francisco Ry. come over to the office of Mr. Simpson, the new Supt. of Wells Fargo, and he had a Message from the Railroad Agent at Winslow, Ark. and one from the Agent at Ft. Smith Advising that there were 9 men heavily Armed that had been seen close to the Tracks. The night watchman at the Tunnell at Winslow had seen these men and they had had their Horses tied in a little Canyon close to the West End of the Tunnell and they were Evidently looking over the Ground to see the best place to make the holdup. This Supt. of the Ry. was soon joined by the Gen. Manager of the Ry. and the 2 of them gave us all the information that they had and was willing to cooperate in any way that we wanted to handle the situation. The Gen. Manager and 2 Supts. of Wells Fargo & Co. were also there with me and it was I who had full charge of a Situation like this one. I at once told them that I would leave on the first train for Ft. Smith and take charge of the matter as we found it.

Wells Fargo & Co. were new to them. Only by Reputation were we Known to these Officials and we wanted them to know just how Wells Fargo & Co. would react to a Situation like the present.

I left St. Louis at 8:25 P.M. for the Scene. I reached Ft. Smith at 2 P.M. and at once had a Conference with the Ry. Supt. at Ft. Smith and we went to see the U.S. Marshal there who was Marshal for that District, Mr. Yoes, and we made our arraingements to get into the Section in the morning and run this outfit down. Floyd Wilson was given charge for the Marshal with such men as he wanted to go. I was out with him in the fore part of the night talking with men who could give us some information about the Situation and selecting the men to go in the Morning. At 11:30 P.M. — I went to Bed.

At 1:30 A.M. I was woke up with the news that the Tunnell Watchman had seen these men and that their Horses were tied near the West End of the Tunnell. Floyd Wilson was on hand and had 2 men with him, Payton Talbot and Bud Ledbetter. The 4 of us, — 2 awfully good men whom I afterward Employed to run as Guards for Wells Fargo — we all got in the Express Car and rode it through to the next station North of Winslow where we met the South bound train and rode *it* through to Ft. Smith where I again Consulted with the Ry. Supt. who was a very Efficient and cooperative man and also we had the U.S. Marshal, Yoes. We determined that if these men wanted to Rob a train that we wanted them first.

So we got horses and a couple more men and loaded them into a Box Car, had some Breakfast, and left with a Special Engine at 7 A.M. and returned to Winslow where we unloaded and was ready for the Trail. We got word of these men who had been seen a few miles away. We went to the place, and in Searching arround we found a camp. We could not find any Horse tracks and in Circling the camp to hunt for these tracks, we run on 1 man and from him we got the whole thing. He was a merchant in Fort Smith and was well known to Floyd Wilson, Talbot, and Ledbetter. We all went back to their camp and this man told us all about it. Counting the Cook there were 10 men in the party, and they all Commenced coming in, 1 and 2 at a time. It was a hunting party and they had been out several days and everyone of them was Known to all or some of the Posse. I had a talk with Floyd Wilson and it was Evident that the Watchman at the Tunnell had lied about the whole matter. We were invited to have Dinner with the Hunters and we did.

161

Then we went into Winslow and went and woke the Watchman up and I took him in hand. He told his Story again, and we went to where he said the Horses were tied, but there was no Horse Tracks there. Then I took him in hand myself with only Floyd Wilson as a Witness — I finally brought him through. He had got up this Story thinking he would make something of a Hero out of himself and it was all a lie. We loaded up our Horses and returned to Fort Smith with nothing but a Story, but Wells Fargo & Co. had fully demonstrated to the Ry. People that we were not only Eficient but ready to go to the front at any time and on Short Notice. — I had personally made quite a number of friends there which were later on of much value to me.

I left Ft. Smith for Tulsa to take up again the Persuit of the Dalton Gang arraingements — which were of some Complications. I arrived there the next day at 8 P.M. and I met by appointment Heck Thomas and Burrell Cox. (Burrell Cox was married to a Creek Woman and He had many friends among that Tribe.) We went out into the Country and met a man that we wanted to do a part in this arraingement that would require much ingenuity and also much Courage. We made a very Satisfactory trip and returned to Tulsa in time for me to take the Train for St. Louis — we made all other arraingements as far as we could go.

I arrived in St. Louis the next A.M., Aug. 13th, 1892. I was there a Couple of days working with the Railway People on the Arraingements to go after the Dalton Gang. I went to Kansas City — arrived there Aug. 15th and met our Gen. Manager, Mr. Andrews. We were working on this business mostly by wire. Our President, J. J. Valentine, was in San Francisco, and he not only represented Wells Fargo & Co. but also the Southern Pacific Railway. We finished the work with him and was told to go ahead — this was the night of Aug

16th. The next day, Mr. Andrews and I went to Topeka to see the head Officials of the Atchison, Topeka, and Santa Fe Railway, and all was finished there which finished the Arraingements with all Concerned.

I wired Heck Thomas to Come to Kansas City, and during the day, Mr. Chas. Foulks, Chief Special Agent of the A.T. & S.F. Ry., received a Wire from the sheriff at Norton, Kansas that he was sure that he had the Daltons Spotted there. I agreed to go and investigate this matter and Mr. Andrews and I returned to Kansas City for the night. The next morning Heck Thomas arrived and He and I left that A.M. for Norton. We got there at 11:30 P.M. and had a talk with the Sheriff and his Chief Deputy. It all looked wrong to me. So the next forenoon, we got a look at the men whom they had spotted and they were not the Daltons at all — So that was that.

We returned to Kas. City that night and the next day Heck Thomas and I were getting the outfit ready. We ordered the Rifles from the Factory for we wanted all our outfit to have the same kind of Guns which would preclude any mixup of amunition, which was very important. We bought Saddles — Riding and also pack Saddles. We had also ordered the amunition from the Factory. This took us all day of the 20th & 21st of Aug. and that day we got news of a Train Holdup at Augusta, Kansas. We left Kas. City that night for Arkansas City where we were going to buy Horses and Finish fitting out. (Augusta, Kas. was in Supt. Simpson's Division and he was going to Augusta.) Supt. Stockton went with us as far as Winfield, Kas. and from there he went to Augusta — Heck and I continued on to Arkansas City. The next day we were Buying Horses. We bought our Saddle Horses and Pack Horses in and arround Ark. City. We also got other Supplys there that we would need, Such as Provisions, Raincoats, and such other clothing as was required. Burrell Cox joined Heck and I at Arkansas City. Saturday, Aug. 27th, we finished up ready to go, and on Sunday, Aug. 28th, 1892, we got out of Town.

Burrell Cox had got the Horses Concentrated the Night before At a friend's House a couple of miles below town. We had all of our Supplys in the Office of Wells Fargo & Co. The Wagons used to load in a closed yard in the rear of the Office. There was a train due there about noon and the Wagons used to meet it. We had all of our stuff loaded into a Closed Wagon, and the Driver knew where to go, and he pulled out. Burrell was with the Horses and Heck and I separated and went on foot to a point about a mile from there where we met and Continued on to where the Horses and the Supplys were now at. When we got there, we had some Dinner with the friend of Burrell's and then Sorted and fitted our Saddles and the Packs and now we were ready to Ride. Which we did.

There were 5 Railroads and 3 Express Companys which were to divide the Expenses and the Rewards that were paid — These Rewards were for $1000 Each, Dead or Alive. All of these Companys had insisted that I was to have charge of Everything and pay all Expenses and Rewards and I done so. The Names of these Railways and Express Companys were Atchison, Topeka, and Santa Fe, St Louis and San Francisco, Missouri, Kansas, and Texas (Katy), Rock Island Railway, and Southern Pacific. The Express Co.'s were United States Express Co., Pacific Express Co., and Wells Fargo and Company Express.

We started and traveled South and East till Dark and made Camp on the Arkansas River. We were up and off early the next morning, traveled all day, and camped close to Gray Horse Osage Nation. (This, the 29th of August 1892, was my Birthday I am today 38 years old.) We kept traveling all of next day and Camped on Salt Fork the next night. The next night, Aug. 31st, we got near to Tulsa where we were to stay for a few days.

We left the outfit with Burrell Cox, and Heck Thomas and I went into Tulsa and left there the next morning for Ft. Smith. Got there late at night. Next A.M. we met U.S. Marshal Yoes and Dep. U.S.M. Floyd Wilson, and we all went to see United States Judge Isaac Parker who was a power in that Country. (At the time of his death some years later he had sentenced 100 men to death by Hanging.) We met Him and as time and years rolled along, I knew that in that day I had made a great Friend.

After meeting him and the preliminarys were over, He asked us what he could do for us and they designated me as the Spokesman. Yoes and Wilson were good friends of the Judge, and Heck Thomas was an old and good friend of the Judge also, and had worked out of his Court for a long time. (Heck Thomas was a Dep. U.S. Marshal for Oklahoma and a man that was known to always get his man — Sometimes dead but he got him. Heck was a man who believed in arresting his man and then reading his warrant to him and it was known that he always read the Warrant to them — alive or dead.)

I had been Sizing up the Judge, and with what I saw and what Heck had told me, I made up my mind about him and I just plainly and briefly spread all my Cards on the Table. The Judge looked at me closely all the time and did not overlook a point. He Said to me, "I have known about you for some time, and quite recently I have known how you handle matters in an Emergency and it Suits me." (I knew that he had heard from Yoes and Wilson about the farce of the Contemplated hold up on the Frisco Ry.) "And I am ready to do my part in the Extermination of the Class of people that you are after and I also know of the handicaps that you will be subjected to." He then made Heck Thomas and I Special Deputy Officers of his Court.

We knew that the greatest block to our plans would be the friends of these Outlaws, So he told us to arrest Every man, Woman, and Child that were furnishing information to the Criminals, to Concentrate them, and Guard them, and Send after a Dep. U.S. Marshal who would come and bring them into Ft. Smith, and that he (Judge Parker) would see that they did not bother us any more untill we were finished with our work. We spent a pleasant Evening at Judge Parker's House and I got more thougherly aquainted with him. Heck and I left Ft. Smith at midnight and reached Tulsa the next night late. Supt. Simpson joined us at Monett and Come to Vineta with us.

There were in the Outlaw Bunch 8 men that the Companys had a reward on Dead or Alive of $1,000 Each and they were Bob Dalton, Emmett Dalton, Grat Dalton, Bill Powers, Dick Broadwell, Bill Doolin, Slaughter Kid, and Will Blake, (alias Tulsa Jack). We had to put fear into the supporters of these Outlaws and we knew quite a number of them and started in making arrests and sent them into Ft. Smith to Judge Parker. Our outfit and men were close to Tulsa. (At that time, Tulsa was not the City that it now is. There was a Small Depot at the R.R. Track, and a little ways from there, there was a Store that said "General Merchandize," and across the Creek was the House where Burrell Cox lived and that was Tulsa.) Our Horses and men were 3 miles from there where there was feed for the Animals and a place for the men. Heck Thomas and I joined the outfit.

We had 12 men on the Pay Roll. 2 of these men did not come near the outfit atall. They lived some distance apart and just rode the Country and got any news that was moving and would send one of their Kids with the News — these men were both Squaw men and were not Outlaws. Neither were they Straight men. Their Connection with us was not known by any one, Only Heck Thomas, Burrell Cox, and My Self. These men were very friendly to Heck Thomas and Burrell Cox, and by reason of this friendship we could depend on them.

We had 2 Scouts for the main bunch, and when traveling, Heck Thomas and I rode ahead and well out to Each Side. Some men had their own Horses and were, take it all in all, a mixed bunch but all were men that had been selected and could be depended upon. With Heck and My self riding out and the 2 Scouts gone, we had 6 men left in the main Bunch. 4 of these men rode scattered out and 2 men back in the rear with the Pack Horses — these 6 men were in the immediate Controll of Burrell Cox. Owing to the Standing of some of these men with the Law, it is not advisable Even at this late date [*probably about* 1935] to give the names of this Posse, and I am naming 4 of these men — Heck Thomas, Burrell Cox, Talbot White, F. J. Dodge. Talbot White was a Sac and Fox Indian and Educated. He was a staunch friend of mine and usually rode with me when I left the Party to send Dispatches and receive News from Headquarters. I had an Arraingement with Mr. Delaney, Agent for Wells Fargo and Co. at Guthrie, where and when to send any thing to me, and he surely kept right on the job. We put in that day at the Main Starting place.

We had an Agreement, on account of the men who were with us that it was advisable to keep in the back ground, That we would not allow any one to Come to the Posse, and only twice did we have to make that Agreement good. Once a Dep. U.S.M. and his Posse man wanted to make camp with us. We sent him on his way and then we saw a party coming towards us. We bunched, and putting the Horses where they would not be seen, we got to an Advantageous place and when they come up, we halted them and told them they would have to ride around us. Heck and I both knew the U.S. Marshal and he had 5 Posse men with him. They finally made up their minds to do as we requested and they did. We afterwards heard of both of these U.S. Marshals who reported that they had run on to the Daltons and that there were 14 of them and the odds were too great to risk a fight with them and we were soon classed with the Wild Bunch.

We were arresting, at different places, Men who were friends and who were assisting the Wild Bunch at any time they could. We sent them all in to Ft. Smith to Judge Parker And things were becoming Considerably mixed. Everybody was becoming afraid to help the Dalton outfit for fear of Arrest, and we were Circulating reports all the time, that we were getting information from their friends — and they were getting afraid to trust anybody.

All the best people in that Country were doing all they could for us. We got word from a Cattle man that we Knew was our friend that he and Some More wanted to See Heck and I. We Knew from runners and our Scouts that we were pretty Close to the Daltons, but after dark, Heck and I left our camp and went to the place we were to meet these Cattle Men. We got there all right and met them. They told us that the Daltons had been seen by one of the men that Evening at a point that was between where we were then and our Camp. (These Cattle men told us to take any or all of their Horses if we needed them and to kill a Beef any time we wanted to.) We started back but we rode carefully and finally reached Camp all right.

The next day we Called at a Squaw Man's house and he told us the Boys had been there Early that Morning and Bob

Dalton told him to tell Heck Thomas and Fred Dodge that they had been close enough to us the night before to Cut the Buttons off of our Vests. Emmett Dalton told me later on that it was true and that Grat wanted to Kill us but Bob would not let him.

It was hard to do any trailing for it rained every day or night. We rode hard and worked hard on all kinds of Clews and trails. We Knew their friends and where they were Strong in little towns, and by the use of Spies, we kept a good lookout on them. We were Camped in a very secure place, and from a high hill allmost over our Camp, we could see any one going into or leaving Ingalls. We used powerful Glasses in the day-time and posted men on the Roads so we could work at night. We had a man in Ingalls who would Show a light at night if the Bunch come in there.

We stood regular Watches, and the 1st night there was a funny thing happened to me. Heck Thomas was on from 9 to 12, Burrell Cox followed him 12 to 3, and I followed Burrell — he called me at 3 and I went up allmost over the Camp. The Boys had Spread down a Blanket and a Slicker right at the foot of a big tree where we could see by day and see the light in town at Night. I had set down at the foot of this Tree, and I set there for some time watching for the light in town, and as I looked arround, I saw a man Standing close to the Edge of the Hill, close to where we come up and went down. He was beconing some one behind him — and I was mad and disgusted at my self for Ever letting this man get up there for probably the whole bunch was there.

We had an Agreement for a Signal in Case anything hap-pened and any one got close to us, and quickly I made up my mind that I was going to make that Signal Count. I had my Short Wells Fargo Double barrell Shot Gun with me and I knew that I could not miss, So I slid down and partly rolled

169

over so as to give my self a better oppertunity to shoot. I was
all fixed and had slid my Gun arround to where I could handle
it fast, So I took a look at the man and was at the same time
getting my Gun sighted on him.

As I looked, I could see that this Arm that he was beconing
with was at least a foot from the man's Body. I knew then
that I was mistaken and that it was no man at all. I got up
and went over to it. It was a Black Stump about as high as a
man's head and the Arm that done the beconing was a Limb
of a Bush about 3 feet from the Stump and the wind was sway-
ing the Branch. I went back to the Tree and put myself in my
first position and there was the man and he was beconing.

I was surely glad that I had not Shot for I would have had
the Bunch up there at once, and they would surely give me the
laugh. Needless to say that I did not say anything about it
when my relief Come up to take my place. It was light then
and the Sun was rising. While we were getting our Breakfast,
one of our Scouts rode in and he had had a talk with our man
who was the light man in the little Town. He brought information that put us going right away.

That afternoon, I was riding ahead and off to one Side and
Burrell Cox rode out to me and after a while he said, "Say,
Fred, did you see anything up there at the Guard Station last
night that was unusual?" and I said, "Yes," and when we had
talked it over, Burrell had had the same experience that I had.
We then agreed to not say anything about it for it was likely
that Heck Thomas was in the same Boat, but it was the next
day before Heck fessed up. He had the same experience that I
and Burrell had. Then we told the whole Bunch that night in
Camp and they all enjoyed it.

We had got news that the Wild Bunch were going to try
the Train at Wharton again, and we were trying to Cut them
off and Mix it a little with them, and were camped near

Wharton, which at that time had only 2 houses beside the little Depot. I got into Wharton and got the Agent and he done the Telegraphing. We got the Agent at Guthrie and he got Delaney. I got all the news that he had and had him send some Supplys on the Early Morning Train to me at Wharton. I got back to Camp which was Well hidden. In the morning we sent Burrell and Talbot White into Orlando to get some Horses Shod. The Agent got our Supplys out to us during the day.

Near night, Burrell and Talbot come in and they reported some men had Shot at them about 6 miles out. We got out there and made a Dry camp till morning for we could not see to trail till Daylight. Heck and I got as close to the trail as we could, and when day did come, we found the trail of 2 men and about a ½ mile from there we found trail of 2 more men who joined and all 4 kept on together. We knew then that our Party had been tipped off or else seen.

We kept the trail till Middle of the Afternoon When there Come another of those hard Rains that seemed to be a general downpour. We got to an old abandoned Squatter's place and went into Camp. The Rain Continued Untill well after Dark, and in the morning we had no trail at all and although we cut for the Trail Several Miles out we could not get it. We got news — some good and some no good. It Rained on us and we would loose the Trail then had to Scout arround to find any Trail. We had been on the Arkansas River and had to Cross several times — Men and Horses down in the Quicksand.

On Sunday, Oct. 2nd, we had reliable news for the Wild Bunch had been in camp at our informant's House and he told us that they were going to make one more good clean up and then quit the Country and all of them were going to South America. The full party was present at this man's House — the Wild Bunch were camped near this man's

House. He could not tell where they were going to Strike. (Bill Doolin was opposed to doing as Bob Dalton wanted to do whatever it was and we also learned that Bill Doolin was a Sick man for he had the Dengue fever.)

We all started for the House of this man who had come to us with this information — we could depend on him for reliability as he was a Brother of one of the men who was with us and a close friend of 3 others of our Party. We got to his place and Camped in a Secluded place but not where the Wild Bunch had camped. The only thing that we had was that Bill Doolin had told Bob Dalton that it was a Death Trap and that was not much for us to tell where they were going.

So we went into executive Session and I sent a man to the Rail Road for we had made up our minds that they had not been lucky on the Railroads and might try a Bank. We were about equally Distant from Muscogee, Vineta, and Coffeyville, Kas. This man that I sent to the Railroad carried Messages to Wells Fargo & Co. Agents at Muscogee, Vineta, and Coffeyville. Then we had a rain for a change. We finally picked up a trail — Sometimes we had it and then we would not have it on Account of the Rain. This Trail headed towards the Santa Fe Ry. and we thought that they were going to Strike on the Santa Fe.

Oct. 6, we were camped about 25 miles from Sac and Fox Agency and I wanted to Notify the Officers and Santa Fe to be on the lookout. We had lost the trail late in the Afternoon before — Rain Again — and while the Boys were Scouting to get it again, I took Talbot White and went into Sac & Fox and as I rode in one End of the Agency, there was a man riding in at the other End who had a Message from Agent Delaney at Guthrie telling me that Bob and Grat Dalton, Bill Powers, and Dick Broadwell were Killed and Emmett Dalton badly wounded at Coffeyville the day before, Oct. 5th, 1892.

I at once returned to our Camp. We were then sure that Bill Doolin, Slaughter Kid, (alias Bitter Creek) and Will Blake (alias Tulsa Jack) had split off from Bob Dalton.

I split up our Party, part going on one trail and the Balance on the other, but to come together near Wharton, and Heck Thomas and I Started for Coffeyville Via Guthrie. We changed Horses at Sac and Fox and at Chandler. We rode all night and got into Guthrie at Sunrise making our Ride Something over 100 miles. We had to wait untill night to get a Train that would make Connection for Coffeyville, and during the day I confered with the U.S. Marshal's Office and with Sheriff Hixson, and they sent out men to try and intercept the Outlaws.

Heck and I left on our Train and we got to Coffeyville on the 8th, 5 hours late. There we met Supt. Simpson and Supt. Stockton. Coffeyville was in Supt. Simpson's Division. They had Everything in good Shape and in the morning, I got busy and Interviewed Every body that I could. I put down Stakes where the Bodies were and where Emmett was wounded, for I was satisfyed that there would be much Contention as to who done the Killing. We had to pay Rewards on all these men of $1,000.00 Each, and there were 5 of them — Bob Dalton, Grat Dalton, Bill Powers, and Dick Broadwell Dead, and Emmett Dalton wounded, and I was the one that had to Satisfy all of the Claimants.

I talked to those who had any claims at all to the Reward, and I could see that we were not going to be able to Satisfy all of these Claimants. I talked to one man — John Klauer — who the newsPapers had Published widely as John Spears and he, according to the Papers, Killed about all of them. They did not get his name right or much Else about him, and he was pretty sore, He told me, and went and showed me where he rested his Gun and said that he had only killed one man and that was Grat Dalton. He said that he sighted for his Head but Undershot a little for he hit him in the Neck right on his Adam's Apple and it Broke his Neck. Klauer felt badly about the Noteriety for he thought that his Neighbors would think that he was trying to Hog it all. He kept a Livery Stable and was a Crack shot and he was industriously undoing the work that the NewsPapers had done. The Papers all made Corrections and it wore out.

I could see where I was at in any attempt at Settling these Rewards and I done some tall thinking for we wanted all of these People Satisfyed. And I again went into Executive Session with Supts. Simpson and Stockton and told them that I had a plan that might work out and have them all satisfyed. My plan was this — to Call a Meeting of the Citizens that afternoon and have them appoint a Committee of 5 of their representative Business men to head the Claims of the Claimants and to make such adjustment as they deemed necessary and agreed upon. There was a lot of feeling and Excitement there for there was several of their Citizens had been Killed and Wounded — some were *badly* wounded. A Banker by the name of Ayers was Shot in the face and it was problimatical whether he would Survive, (He did get well but badly scarred.) And I did not see how we could ever pay these rewards Satisfactorily. Both Supts. Agreed that it was a good plan, if we could get it through.

We got out at once and got things going And the meeting was called. During this time we were all busy telling Everybody that we wanted to make these Rewards good and have everybody satisfyed. There had been Papers that Stated that the Citizens of Coffeyville had seemed to be partly prepared which was true. Wells Fargo & Co.'s Agent at Coffeyville, Mr. Brooks, had got the Message that I had sent into Coffeyville that morning that the Daltons Come in, and he was busy

174

Notifying Everybody when they come. Mr. Brooks was a man who stood well in the Community and he was a power in getting this meeting together and in getting the Committee appointed to make the Adjustments of the Reward.

The Meeting was attended by nearly Everybody in town. Supt. Simpson made a talk after they were organized in which he stated what we wanted to do and to have this Committee appointed by them of their own Citizens and whatever they done in this adjustment would be final and would be lived up to by the Companys, that we did not want to have any Voice in this adjustment what Ever. The meeting agreed that this was a Fair and just proposition and there were 5 of their Citizens, all Business men in the Town, appointed, and the whole matter of Adjustment of Rewards were in their hands. There could not be any appeal from the findings of the Committee. What they done would be final and we would place the money in their hands for said Adjustment.

This was surely a load off my Shoulders — No Complaints to Come to us, No Damage Suits, No Comebacks at all. We prepared our Releases for the money and Gave them to the Committee. I was through as far as the Rewards were concerned. Supt. Simpson was to remain there for a few days with them and help what he Could.

Emmett Dalton was to be taken to Jail at Springfield, Kas. I saw him several times and he talked to me quite freely. Bill Dalton was there and so was the Sister, Mrs. Whipple, really the Foxiest one of the Dalton family. Bill had been a Politician in California, and at one time was a member of the Legislature there. These two would bear Watching.

The Sheriff from Springfield was there and I had several talks with him. I offered to put 2 men at the Jail to be paid by me — both of these men were familiar with the workings of Criminals — but he, the Sheriff, said that he was sure that they would not be needed. I told him all about how they would send in saws, Etc. in Cakes and Pies, And told him all about Bill Dalton who I was sure was going to join the Wild Bunch, and also told him how Mrs. Whipple would work among the Women at Springfield. And I finally told him that it would not be 30 days before they were sending Emmett Dinners and good things to Eat. The Sheriff said to me, "No, Mr. Dodge, We have not got that kind of women in our Town." I told him that I did not want to Cast any reflections on the Women there, but that I would bet him a Box of Cigars that they would be sending in to Emmett things to eat inside of 30 days and he took the Bet. At Houston, Tex., Oct. 26th, I got a message from this Sheriff saying, "They are doing it now" — and Shortly the Cigars Come along.

I learned Shortly afterwards that he had really got hard boiled and would not let a woman Come into the Courthouse Yard only on Business, and then She must be acompanyed by Some one Known to the Officer in Charge. Later on I had many talks with this Sheriff and they had just run Bill Dalton and Mrs. Whipple out of town for they become Satisfyed that they were trying to get Emmett out, and that they were daingerous.

Heck Thomas and I left Coffeyville the night of the 10 of Oct. '92 to rejoin our men. We were with them on the 12th. Then we got news that there was a new Bunch forming to try and rescue Emmett. This was true, but later on they Abandoned the plan. We had our whole Party and when we got a trail, it rained on it and we lost it. We were then near the Arkansas River, opposite the mouth of the Cimarron River, and on Sunday, the 16th of Oct., I made up my mind to take the Party in and Disband. The Wild Bunch, what was left, were badly split up and I knew that meant that we would likely have a still hunt for the men that we wanted. The

176

Rainey Season was upon us and we could not keep any trail because the Rain would wash it out, So on Monday, Oct. 17th, 1892, we were in Tulsa having ridden in in the night. I settled up all the Bills, Inventoryed the Equipment, and Shipped Everything into Kansas City Except the Horses, and we put them on Pasture at Gourmaz's in charge of Burrell Cox. I left Tulsa the next morning for Kansas City and the next morning I was there, and that day and the next I was busy with Gen. Manager Andrews Settling up the whole matter as far as my Expenses were Concerned.

[It was several months, during which he was nursed and encouraged by his old sweetheart, Julia Johnson, before Emmett's injuries permitted him to stand trial for his part in the Coffeyville bank raid. At 21, he was sentenced to life in the Kansas Pen at Lansing, after pleading guilty to second degree murder.

In prison, he not only learned the tailor's trade, working on prisoners' black and whites and guards' uniforms, but he found a philosophy which guided him well as long as he lived. In 1907, the governor of Kansas pardoned him and Emmett emerged a man of wisdom with the courage to reform. As she had promised, his patient Julia had waited for him. They were married and for the remainder of his life, Emmett worked arduously to show the world from firsthand knowledge, that crime never has and never will pay.

Eventually, he and Julia moved to Los Angeles, where in addition to dealing in real estate, Emmett collaborated on writing his memoirs, and worked occasionally on motion pictures, both writing and taking small parts. After his release from Lansing, he lived thirty years making a greater than ordinary contribution as a decent citizen, thereby showing that a man with a strong will can recast his original dye.]

14

TRAIN ROBBERIES — COLEMAN Y,

CIMARRON, ST. JAMES, MOUND VALLEY

Morning of May 25, 1893, we got a Message which told us that the Train had been held up and Robbed on the Coleman Y, right Close to the Depot. We all left for there in the morning. This Train had been Robbed May 24th, 1893, at 11:30 P.M. I arrived at Coleman at Midnight May 26th, '93, Asst. Supt. G. A. Taft with me. Mr. Christeson went on to Ballinger.

I had wired ahead and had the Messenger, whose name was Barry, at Coleman. He met us at the Depot and he was able to give me a minute and very acurate discription of the two men that held up the Train. We worked with him till nearly morning.

By noon, I Knew who one man was and had seen him. I told G. A. Taft but we did not say anything to Messenger Barry about who he was and After Dinner I said to Barry, "This is Saturday and there are a good many People coming into town and it would be well for you to get arround town some and see if there is anyone who looks like the Robber. If there is, you can tell me and it will help me to get a more perfect likeness in my mind."

I Knew where the Robber was at that time. Barry went down town and Taft and I remained at the Hotel. In about 15 minutes, Barry Come back under much subdued Excitement. I quieted him down and he told us that one of the men who had held him up was right here in town now and was the one that Come in his Car and the one who he could and did describe to us. I questioned him carefully and also asked him if he could Swear positively to this man as being the Robber and he said that he could without any doubt of it. So we went down Town and he pointed out the man — which was the right one.

The Sheriff was named Kingsbury, but the man who done most of the outside work was the under Sheriff named Jim Saunders — a good man and not afraid of anything. (He was afterwards Sheriff of the County.) I had a warrant issued and the man was arrested at once. His Name was Will Teague. His Bond was set at $5,000.00 and Noah Armstrong made the Bond and Teague was released.

G. A. Taft and I both looked for trouble as Teague was a hard man and was counted a Killer. Noah Armstrong come from a hard family of Killers. His Brother was Sheriff of Bell County and was under Indictment with others at that time for the Murder of Sheriff Olive of Cliburne County, which was a foul murder. Will Teague was there at the time. Sheriff Olive was Shot as he left the Train at Belton (County Seat of Bell County) and the man who Shot him was under the platform. We knew later on that Will Teague was the man under the Platform. Noah Armstrong seemed to be determined to make me believe that Will Teague was innocent of this Train Robbery. The way that he followed me about caused some attention, and during the process of this Case — I told him many times that if he did not quit fooling arround this Case that I would surely put him in the Penn. I always made these talks when there was 2 or 3 men of good Standing present in the Crowd to hear me. I knew at the time that Noah Armstrong had planned and directed this Robbery, but I also knew that Noah was not present at the Scene of the Robbery.

The Teague Case was originally set for June 1st and on that

date the Case was Continued untill June 7th. Taft and I were working like Beavers, As there was a Competent and Energetic array of Talent Against us. There was one man, a staunch friend of all the Armstrongs, Steve Killmen, a Gambler who was a fixer. He had Engeneered the Alibys and Crooked testimony in the Armstrong Cases at Belton of which Noah Armstrong was one. Steve was a longheaded Smart fellow and a hard worker, but he was no Killer and he kept right after Noah to stay away from me. Steve knew Noah was in it and told him many times to stay away from me or I would surely put him in the Penn. I knew that Noah was Guilty, but I also Knew that I must have positive Evidence of that Guilt or Else I could not Convict him in that Community. And Another thing, I did not have the other man in that Robbery as he was on the outside and the Messenger never saw him. So I played Noah Armstrong for all I could.

The Teague Examination Come on on time and he was Held over to the Grand Jury on the 12th of June. May 29th, 1893, the Bondsman Surrendered Will Teague and a few days later made another Bond.

I was working hard on Noah to get a Start on the Second Man and by close hard work I got it, and also learned that he lived in Hunt County. His Name was Minton Alexander — Alias Kid Alexander — and we put things in Shape to get him. This was the man that we wanted for the fall down so we could get Noah Armstrong Sure.

I worked with the Attys on the 5th getting ready for the Examining trial of Will Teague, for I Expected to get much information from this Examination. (And we did) Jim Evans was Spec. Agent for the Santa Fe Ry. and he helped us all he could. Our Attys. were Tom Crossin, District Atty. and Simms and Snodgrass to assist the Dist. Atty. — All very able men.

We went to Trial on Wed., June 7th, 1893. Atty. Snodgrass had been selected for the Examination of Witnesses as he was by far the Most Able Atty. in that Vicinity. I sit right beside him and suggested Any Question that I wanted and also the same proceedure in the Cross Examening of the Witnesses for the Defendant, and we were Able to bring out much testimony that had been in the Background. I had talked with Snodgrass about some points that were very valuable to us in the way of getting a Starter on the 2nd man. So when Noah Armstrong took the Stand and had testifyed — which was nearly all an Aliby for Teague — we were ready for him and we got from him the Name of the 2nd man who was Minton "Kid" Alexander And at once I got messages off that would result in his Capture. He was only 15 years Old.

Teague's Examination Ended on June 12th, 1893, and he was held over to appear at the next Grand Jury. A few days later, he was taken before Judge Jessie Woodward, the Dist. Judge for that District, who lived (and still does) at Coleman and his Bond was set at $6,000.00. This had Noah going some.

I then arrainged with Asst. Supt. Taft for the work to Continue for we that knew we would catch Kid Alexander — it was only a matter of time. Made all Arraingements with the Sheriff's Office, for it was necessary for me to leave this Case for a while for there was many cases that required my attention elsewhere.

We had had a Train Robbery and our Messenger, E. E. Whitlessy had been Shot and Seriously wounded at Cimarron, Kansas on the A. T. & S. Fe Ry. on June 10th, 1893, and I was due there several days ago. On Tuesday, June 13th, I left Coleman to take up the Train Robbery Case. (Noah Armstrong went as far as Belton with me and I got quite a bit from him about Kid Alexander — Noah talks too much for his own good.)

Sheriff Frank Healy had a fight with the Cimarron Train Robbers when they passed through his County. He was alone and he saw them in Camp. He could hardly tackle 4 men but he had a chance to see them, and at once made a ride to get a Posse together. There were only Nesters [*a term applied by Southwestern cattlemen to first homesteaders, later by cowboys to other cowboys who had married and taken up farming*] in that Vicinity but he got 6 of them quickly and then (knowing the Country) he Cut in ahead of them (the Robbers) and rode on to them. The Robbers opened fire at once, and the whole Posse of Nesters quit him then and there, and he was alone to fight 4 men. He jumped from Tree to Tree, Shooting when he could. He was afoot, as they downed his Horse the first round of firing. He soon had to quit for they were getting away from him.

He knew that he had Hit one man, a Tall Man, which was Bill Doolin, The most daingerous man in the Bunch. He trailed along after them and found Blood on the Trail And he had seen the man jump and hold his leg. He got back to where 3 of these Nesters lived, And after telling them what he thought of them for being a bunch of Cowardly Curs, He got a Horse and got back to Beaver City. I had made Arraingements with him to meet him soon as I could.

I left Guthrie Early next morning for Interior to get positive information as to Identity of the Train Robbers. I was out 4 days and got much good Data. I had felt sure as to who these men were from remarks made by them at the Scene of the holdup and Sheriff Healy was sure that the man he Shot was Bill Doolin, as he had seen him a Couple of years before.

I had a friend who lived 3 miles from a town called Ingalls and this was a town known to all officers as a Heaven of Safety for all Criminals. I finally got to this friend's house at night and had a talk with him and I stayed under Cover near his

House while he went into Ingalls. Late that night he returned home and a lot of good Information he brought. He found out that about a week before the Train Robbery that Bill Dalton, Bill Doolin, Slaughter Kid, and Will Blake had been in Ingalls.

I had been to see the Wounded Messenger, Whitlessy, and I had him tell me all that he could about what they Said. I had been Satisfyed that Bill Dalton was going to the Wild Bunch and I felt sure that Bill Dalton had been in this Robbery. Language that he used there and Expressions that he used made me know that Bill Dalton was there.

There had been a horse Captured by Healy in the fight and I wired him to take off the Shoes on this Horse and keep them for me. This Horse-Shoer in Ingalls was a good one — the very best in the Country. I had sent horses in to him and had them Shod and I knew his work.

And now Commenced a hard job. I must have proof of these men going to, and coming from Cimarron. I proposed to do this on one trip and I did. I went to Kingfisher and started from there and I was soon on the Trail. I went into Cantonement and got good Identification there from Some Indian Scouts (white men) who had seen them going and coming. I then Struck into the Country that was known to Frank Healy. I had wired him from Kingfisher to meet me at the scene of the fight for I knew that I would find that. I had also learned at Ingalls that Bill Doolin had been Shot by Healy and Healy hit him in the Heel and it broke Bill's ankle. He was treated for it by a Doctor at Ingalls.

I made it to the fight grounds and met Healy who was a full day ahead of me. We camped and then next A.M. we Commenced to see the men who could be any good in the way of Evidence. There was a Cattle Man who had a large bunch of cattle and had a number of men working for him and we went to see him. His name was Taintor. We stayed there 2 days with him waiting for a couple of his riders who had seen the Robbers going and coming. Taintor had seen the men going. He Knew Bill Doolin and the Slaughter Kid. (Doolin and the Kid were both of them good Cow men and used to be Square and honest.) The 2 Riders come in the Second day. They both Saw the men going and coming and both of them knew Doolin, the Kid, and Blake, and one of these Riders was in Coffeyville at the time of the Killing. He told me that the man that was a Stranger was in Coffeyville at that time, and he said to me, "You know this man for I saw you talking to him." He told me the time and just where I was at and he said, "You talked with him a long time, at least half an hour." I recognized the time and the place and I told him that the man was Bill Dalton.

We made all necessary arraingements with Taintor and his 2 Riders so that we could get them at any time and we left there the next A.M. on our way towards Cimaron and we Encountered one of those Hot Winds accompanyed by Dust. It is useless to try and Explain what it was like — only one who has been in one could understand it. We went through Beaver City and Healy gave me the Horse Shoes — the Horse was badly wounded and Died shortly after I was there. Healy kept on with me and we seen some more men and one Woman who had seen these men.

The Woman, the Wife of a Settler there, gave us a good discription of all of the men. They had come to their house about 10 O'Clock in the morning and wanted to get her to fix Breakfast for them and offering to pay her for her trouble and the Meals. Her Husband was away and these men seemed to be all right so She got Breakfast for them. She surely did not Miss anything that was said or done — and her memory was good. (Healy knew this man and his wife and they were allright.) She told us all about them and said that the Stocky man was certainly a talker. She gave a good discription of all of them and said that She would know all of them if She ever saw them again. I told her about Bill Dalton and that at one time he had been a member of the California Legislature and was quite a Politician in and arround Visalia, Cala.

We went on and Frank Healy and I parted at the County line. I went on alone, the wind and Dust still bad up to about 10 miles from Cimarron. I got in there finally and had a long talk with the Sheriff, and he had a man there by the name of Lilly who could identify all of the men in the Robbery.

Next I was back on the Teague Case. I got a Message from G. A. Taft telling me that Kid Alexander had been captured. We saw the Kid that Evening but he had nothing to say. We worked on the Kid some — Mr. Christeson, the Supt. and G. A. Taft, asst. Supt., were there and remained there. We used all ligitimate ways to Break the Kid down for a week — but not a word out of him. All that he would say was, "I wern't there."

I was doing some thinking for I was sure he could be reached. I had wired to Coleman for a Dep. Sheriff to come to Dallas and there was 2 of them come — Goodfellow and Saunders. I was during this time working with the Officers in East Texas, and as I Knew there was an Indictment out for an Uncle of the Kid who was a Hog Thief, (his name was J. P. Stafford and he and the Kid were very Close) I had been working with Sheriff Dupree on this line. Stafford was out on Bond. Aug. 1st, 1893, we took the Kid to Coleman. The 2nd, he was brought out and his Examination Set For the 8th. This gave me plenty of time and we were both of us very busy — G. A. Taft and Myself. I succeeded in arrainging for the Kid's Uncle Stafford to come to Coleman on my wire through Sheriff Dupree.

On the 8th, the Examination commenced. (I had wired to Sheriff Dupree to Start Stafford and he arrived at midnight the 8th and I had a long talk with him that night.) Noah Armstrong was of course a witness and he was asked such questions that he had to Answer only one way for I was trying to prove to Kid Alexander that Noah Armstrong was giving him the Double Cross. Examination closed that Evening and in the morning, the Kid sent for Noah. I was ready for him by having G. A. Taft in a wardrobe in the Room. I let it Slip — so Steve Killman could hear it — that I was going to get it all for I had Taft in the wardrobe. I was thougherly satisfyed that if Noah done the Square thing with the Kid that the Kid would stand pat. I knew that Noah had not given the Kid a square deal for he had not given him his part, and by the Wardrobe work I could prevent Noah from making any promice to the Kid. Steve Killman got to Noah before he went to see the Kid and that was Enough.

Stafford had had a talk with Noah and Noah would not do anything for them in any way. I had promiced the Kid immunity if he would let go and give up the works. I had told Stafford the same thing. The Kid sent for his Uncle Stafford. I was also ready for them, but no tip to an outsider this time, and the Wardrobe worked again. The Kid told his Uncle all that he could get out of Noah and then the Uncle told the Kid of his talk with Noah. He then asked the Kid if I had promiced to let him off if he told everything. The Kid said, "Yes." Then Stafford Advised him to do it for Noah was Double Crossing him. The Kid said, "Send and get Dodge and I will tell him everything."

I was handy and was soon there with Tom Crossin, the Dist. Atty., and we both made a talk to the Kid and Tom Crossin told him that as Dist. Atty., he would promice him immunity if he would turn State's Evidence and the Kid said he would. We then got a Statement from him in writing tell-ing all from the Start to the finish — we made it complete and in Detail. When it was finished, we called in a Notary Public and then Minton Alexander signed it and Swore to it.

On the 10th, I had Noah Armstrong arrested and had Will Teague rearrested for there was a deficiency in his Bond. On the 11th, Teague was brought before Judge Woodward and his Bond raised to $6,000. He did not make it — Steve Killman was busy getting up a Bond for Noah Armstrong.

The Kid had told me about another man who was at Noah's House and was the man that the Kid Come from East Texas with. His name was Randall Waits, A Horsethief by occupa-tion and a man who did not Show up very much in the day-time. He had the Kid's and his part of the Money which was not a full cut by several hundred dollars. Waits was in Jail at Greenville and Sheriff Dupree had what money that they got off of him.

On the 12th, Saturday, I left Coleman for Greenville and Mt. Vernon — East Texas. I had Dep. Sheriff Jim Saunders and the Kid with me — Saunders had the Custody of the Kid. We stopped in Greenville and had a talk with Randall Waits. I was not promicing him *Anything*. He told us that Sheriff Dupree had got him at his Brother's, Joe Waits, and got what money there was. We went on that night to Mt. Vernon and saw Sheriff Dupree. He turned the money over to me and then we went out to see Joe Waits — but he was of little Value to me as he was a Petty Larceny Thief and his reputa-tion was very bad. We Come back to Greenville, and Randall Waits agreed to testify as to his being at Noah Armstrong's with Kid Alexander, and after the Robbery that Noah gave them what they Supposed to be their part of the money taken at the Robbery and there was where Noah made his mistake.

No one knew the Amount except Teague and Noah, and

if Noah had been square with the Kid he would never have weakened. When the Kid sent for Noah after we reached Coleman, he had another chance So the Kid thought, but my manipulation of that interview precluded Noah from saying anything to the Kid at all. The Sheriff at Greenville let me take Randall Waits to Coleman next night. I had done some hard thinking on this case and I had a plan that I believed to be good. I had submitted it to G. A. Taft and he was against it, but a night's Study made a difference and he was with me in the morning. I then took it to the Attys.

I wanted to place Everybody Under the Rule and to put Noah Armstrong on the stand first, and then before he could get a chance to talk with his Wife, to put her on the Stand and She would testify just as she had been taught. I would not have taken these chances only I knew that Noah was smart and well versed in court proceedure. It would be a Supprise to his Attys. and to him and he was going to be very careful about what he Said and the Strength of our case was in the way that Noah was questioned. The Dist. Atty., Tom Crossin was the 1st to come to my side of the Case. I had laid Everything before them, all the benefits and all the Daingerous parts. We discussed the Question of my plan making Noah our Witness.

The Examination was to Commence in the morning and we were going to Use Randall Waits. We would Kill the whole day with him and at the Same time Scare Noah up some. My hope in this proceedure was to get a flat-footed Contradiction between Noah and his Wife and it was a sure thing that we could. All testimony had to be taken in writing and the Witness would sign it and Swear to it and this would keep them from changing their testimony in any particular. I Knew that Sims and Snodgrass were very level headed men. Sims was a deep thinker and the closest and hardest Examiner in the

188

Country. These 2 men said they wanted to sleep on it and would give their Answer in the morning — before Court met at 10 O'Clock.

Randall Waits was a Witness for the Prosecution and it was the logical thing to Start with him. These witnesses were all put in a room and after testifying, they were put in another room and it precluded any talk between them untill after their testimony had been signed and Sworn to. And then they could not change it.

All the Attys. and Taft and I were at the Office of Sims and Snodgrass Early, and they had studied the matter till late and while considering the dainger of making these Witnesses our Witnesses, they both agreed that it was a master Stroke, Considering the fact that Noah Armstrong was a Smart fellow. Snodgrass was selected to Examine and Cross examine all witnesses. We went into the Examination and used up the day with Randall Waits. They could *not be* Satisfyed by what Waits had testifyed to, and that night they were surely going to Strengthen themselfs.

When Court opened the next morning, I had Everything ready and good Officers handling the witnesses. It was surely a Supprise to the Attorneys for Armstrong when we called him as our second Witness and there was no chance for any Consultation. It put Noah to thinking and the questioning by Snodgrass put Noah up a Tree. Finally he was through and Signed and Swore to his testimony and on the whole he had made a pretty fair Witness for us — only he denyed of course any Knowledge of Money.

He was taken out and Mrs. Armstrong was brought right in and She did say her little piece just as She had agreed upon and She did Contradict Noah in all of her Testimony. She signed and Swore to her Testimony, and She was taken out and then we brought in a Boy that was living with the Armstrongs and he was all that was there according to Noah's testimony and also that of his Wife. His name was Mort Something I don't remember. The balance of testimony was all in on Saturday, Aug. 19th, 1893, and Noah Armstrong was held to the Grand Jury and his Bond set at $6,000.

I then made arraingements for work in the future. The Attys. were all very much pleased at the result of my plan.

These cases came to trial in September — the Case of Noah Armstrong was called Monday, Sept. 18, 1893. We were in trial of that Case untill Thursday, Sept. 21st, and then the Case went to the Jury. The Will Teague Case was then called and a Jury got the first day. The Armstrong Jury on Sept. 22 brought in a virdict of Guilty and gave Armstrong 6 Years in the Penn. The Evidence in the Will Teague Case was all in on Saturday, Sept. 23, 1893, and Will Teague withdrew his plea of Not Guilty and Plead Guilty. The Jury rather Supprised the Attorneys and Teague for they thought that by pleading Guilty he would get a light Sentence, but the Jury gave him 25 years in the Penn.

This Case had been a very daingerous case from the Start. The Armstrongs were all Killers and so was Teague and there was a movement on foot to take Noah Armstrong and Will Teague away from the Officers during the trial and allow them to Escape. But they did not Count right. The Sheriffs Association of Texas had failed to Convict these two men when they Killed Sheriff Olive and they were not going to See anything go wrong in this trial. They had on hand men who were known to be go getters and they all come to Me and Taft and told us they were there to help us. These men were Jeff Mason, J. Dupree, Bascom Sherman, G. W. Arington, Jim Saunders, and Bob Goodfellow. Taft and I had some friends there that lived in Coleman and they surely would not do for any of the Armstrong Crowd to fool with. These Convictions had been secured and at any time during these trials, the slightest thing would have started the Ball to roll but it looked too desperate for the Armstrongs to go against. Minton Alexander was given his Liberty for turning State's Evidence and testifying for the State.

Meanwhile on the night of Aug. 28, '93, I had left for St. Louis to work on the St. James Train Robbery. That afternoon I went out to Cuba and then to St. James at midnight. Next day, I Started Early with a Team to go through the Country. I had a fine man with me, Route Agent Bradway. About 2 P.M. we got to a Farm House and were then Hungry. The Husband and Wife were sitting on the Porch when we Drove up. We talked with them a while and I asked if they could give us something to Eat and the Lady Said, "We haven't got anything but new homemade Bread & Butter and Milk." I told her that it was too good for us. We sit down to a table that was in a cool place and we had a Big Pitcher of Milk, fine Bread, and fine Butter, and to flank this, She put on the Table a Big Dish of Honey in the Comb, and to say that we stuffed our Selfs was drawing it Mild. When we had finished I asked, "How much is this?" and they both Said at once, "Nothing." But I left a Dollar Bill on the table for the Lady. We had surely Enjoyed our selfs.

We Stayed all night at the County Seat, Rolla, and interviewed the Sheriff. Next A.M. we started again and went to the South side of the R.R. so we could make a complete Circle of St. James.

About 9 A.M. I heard some one in the Distance Shouting. I stopped and got out and saw a man on Horseback waiving for us to stop. When he come up he had a message for me — The East bound train into St. Louis had been held up at Mound Valley, Kansas and messenger Chapman murdered. This Case of course took precidence over all others for the time being.

I got right back into Rolla and was then ahead of the Train

that had been Robbed — the Train had been held up about 11 P.M. the night before. (Mound Valley Rob. and Murder, September 2nd, 1893) I made this train and rode on it towards St. Louis. I interviewed Everybody that Knew anything among the Passengers, then the train Crew who were the most important of all, Conductor, Engineer, Fireman, and Brakeman. I got all that could be had from any of them.

I left that train at Pacific, Mo. and then Started right back on the train that I should have made at St. Louis, and would put me at the Scene of the Robbery that night. On that Train I met the Supt. G. B. Simpson and at Rolla we picked up Bradway. The Supt. was highly pleased that I had gotten all these statements and Data from the Train that had been Robbed for it saved us much time and travel.

We reached Mound Valley at 11:30 P.M. that night and the next morning we were at work. I had gotten the description of the Robbers from the Train Crew and we had been at Work all day that we were coming to Mound Valley and had the Country pretty well covered.

It was a most baffeling case to get any Starter. We got out ourselfs and the Sheriff, Mr. Cook, and his Deputys got out also. (Mound Valley was a small Station and was in Oswego Co. and Oswego was the County Seat.) We scoured the Country Round About but failed to get any clew. No one had seen them come or go. There were only 3 men but we did not get any clews at all. Supt. Simpson who was a deep thinker could not Even start a trail. We were all bothered some by the Railway Supt., Mr. Button — His headquarters were at Neodesha. He was a Theorist and he had a Theory about 3 men and all he had in the way of Evidence was that they all 3 of them were mean Enough to do it. I guess they were mean enough all right but it would not Convict anyone of the Charge of Murder. So it was rather unpleasant to try and work with him at all.

On the night of Sept. 5th, 1893, there was another Train Robbery on this same Line — the St. Louis and San Francisco Ry. This was close to St. Louis and was handled from there. They were coming too fast and thick for one man to work them all so I stayed on the most important one.

I Cut the Country arround Mound Valley for any Signs at all of the Robbers. I kept on Digging for a Starter. I went to Coffeyville, Kas. for there was most always some clue there for any body. I was there 2 days and finally got a Starter on a man named Bill Chadborn who was an outlaw and wanted for many Crimes. He had been in Coffeyville several times always at night and alone.

Bill usually played a lone hand. He was a young man and was well known in that part of the Country. I kept Digging on him and finally had Enough on him to warrant an arrest. I made arraingements with Sheriff Cook at Oswego to attend to this for me and he put the machinery to work to arrest him. Bill was a hard one to Catch and we Expected a long siege.

Oct. 10th, I just grabbed up my Family and left for Chicago Worlds 1893 Fair. Supt. Simpson and Family and a few more of us and their Familys had agreed to meet in Chicago Wednesday, Oct. 11th and we were all there. Of course we had the Best of it in Every way for the Company had men there whose business was just to look out for Expressmen, etc. and they did. They Guided and Saved them many dollars. We Saw Everything that there was to see and our Guides saved us miles of Walking.

We went to see Buffalo Bill's Wild West Show. I have seen the Show several times since then but it never has been as good as then. I knew Buffalo Bill and I knew Nate Salsbury, the financial backer of the Show. There was plenty of Fakes in it but it was the greatest Show on Earth.

One Evening we were doing the Midway and we were taking turns in paying the Entrance fee — we saved a lot of time that way. It was my turn and we were at the Turkish Village. The Entrance fee for our Party was $7.50. I put down a $20.00 Bill and right then and there I done something that I had *never* done before or *since*. The first thing that this Turk who was selling Tickets did was to give me $7.50 worth of Tickets. Then he commenced counting out Silver. This Silver made a load and I said to him, "Is this the best you can do?" And Say, he went right at it then. He told me it *was* the best he could do, and told me what I could do if I did not like it. He said a plenty but we had women and children with us and I kept still. All this time he was counting out Silver and he pushed over to me $18.75. I had the Tickets and I said to him, "Well, this is the best that I can do," took the money and went on our way. I then had Tickets $7.50 and Cash $18.75 = Total $26.25. Supt. Simpson was right behind me and as we turned away he said to me, "If you had not taken that change, I was going to see how hard I could Smash you." This Turk seemed to think that we were a very inferior race and only put there to be *done* — If I had not had Women and Children with Me, I would surely have mixed it with him. I have had many chances to take the best of it before and since then but I have never done it.

We put in the time at the Fair till Sunday, Oct. 15th, and we all left for our homes at 8:30 P.M. I arrived Kas. City at Noon and left for Oswego at 9:30 P.M. to attend to the Mound Valley T. R. Case. Chadborn Examination Set for 17th. It was waived.

These Robbers and Murderers did not get anything from the Express Car So they went through the Train and Robbed the Passengers and they were not Masked. I got a Mrs. Manning and Daughter at Pittsburg and took them to Oswego to see if they could identify Chadborn. I had the Engineer and Fireman at Oswego also. Chadborn was the only man on the Engine. They all four positively identifyed him — they Picked him out from 8 other men. Then I knew that I had Chadborn sure and then had something to trade upon with his Attorney, Mr. McBryan. The next day I had 2 more to See him, Mr. and Mrs. Bartram, and they both were positive in their identifycation of Chadborn.

At 1:30 A.M. next morning, I left for Kansas City. All this time I had to Keep up and work on the Brown Paper $35,000.00 Case and I was not well. I was very busy for a week and then went under the Doctor's care for Bladder trouble which took several days. On Nov. 3, '93, Sheriff Cook from Oswego called on me and we went over the case of Chadborn very thougherly and the next night I left for Oswego, where I was to meet Mrs. Wm. Chadborn, Mother of Bill Chadborn. I had wired Supt. Simpson to meet me there also. They all come and also Mrs. Chadborn's Atty., McBryan, who was a close and old friend of the Chadborn family, having known Bill Chadborn all his life. Mrs. Chadborn was keeping a Boarding House on the St.L. & S.F. Ry. at the End of the Train Crew run. Messenger Chapman boarded with Mrs. Chadborn at that End of the run and She knew him and liked him. (Everybody who knew Chapman liked him.) Both She and Atty. McBryan Saw that our terms on the trade for Chadborn's Confession was a good trade — 10 years and a day (this meant the full 10 years.) and they agreed to it.

Bill had a head of his own and we quickly saw that there was an Agreement or promice that had been made and we knew that we had that to overcome. We worked on Bill for 2 days. His mother seemed to have more influence with him, but for all the legal End, Bill looked to Atty. McBryan. McBryan Showed Bill that any promice or agreement made after entering into a Conspiracy was just as unlegal as the Conspiracy itself. We had worked on Bill for two whole days and the

Night of the second, Bill told McBryan that he would think it over during the Night — And I knew then that we had Bill allright. The next Morning, Bill Chadborn Said that he would come through — and it took us all day till 10 O'Clock that night to get this Statement in Shape and Sworn to before a Notary Public. We had been careful and the Statement was in Detail and Legal and right here I want to say that in all my Experience of 50 years I had never before or since had a condition such as this confront me. It was that Bill Chadborn was about 5 O'Clock in the Evening close to Coffeyville in a Brushy Bottom, hiding out waiting for night to come so he could go into Coffeyville in Safety and get to a place there where he could get some Supplys, and there at that place two men come on to him. They told him that they also were hiding out and that they were Escaped men from a County Jail and had only known each other while in that Jail and that they both had Escaped . . .

[That is Fred Dodge's last word on the Mound Valley Robbery and Murder, as the six surviving journals end right there. However, with the aid of the very brief diary Fred Dodge kept for the year 1893 — he kept one each year for about forty years, usually mentioning only his comings and goings which were many, and which case he was on, with little or no detail — we can sketch some of the remainder of the Mound Valley Case.

On November 8, according to the diary, they "throwed Bill down" and he made a "full confession." November 9 Bill's picture was taken. Until November 24 Dodge was in St. Louis, Little Rock, and Pine Bluff on the Mound Valley Case. He mentioned getting a ring of the Bartrams' which evidently was of some importance.

Chadborn was not mentioned again until the entry for

196

December 16 when Dodge visited him in the Lansing Penitentiary "about pictures" — possibly referring to those taken November 9.

December 18 found him at Guthrie to "see Kelly about Hydrick." December 21 mentioned a reward on Chadborn and December 26, Hydrick and Shephard were captured in Jackson, Mississippi. Dodge got a requisition for them December 27 in Topeka and left for Jackson to get them; they were let out of the penitentiary there after the governor gave Dodge an order on the Warden of the Pen. Dodge got his men as usual, and they took the 5 P.M. train December 29 for Oswego. There was a holdover in St. Louis to work on Hydrick and Shephard for a confession. They left January 2, 1894, for Oswego, arriving there the next day. Dodge paid W. A. Clay $1000 reward and Hydrick confessed in the afternoon. It was January 7, 1894, before Shephard gave in and confessed. They came to trial Monday, February 5. Both pleaded guilty to the murder of Messenger Chapman and were sentenced to be hanged. February 6, Dodge and the Sheriff left with the prisoners to return them to Lansing Penitentiary, delivering them the following day, February 7, when Dodge mentioned seeing Chadborn. Though the diaries run until 1918, this is the last reference I found to the Mound Valley Case.]

15

$35,000 BROWN PAPER CASE

I was in Brownwood, Texas on Wednesday, November 30th, 1892, settling up some old Cases — And in the P.M. I received a Message from Mr. A. Christeson, Supt. at Houston, telling me that there were two Packages of Money from New York to Galveston Said to Contain $35,000 all of which was Short at Galveston. Here Starts a Case that took 2½ Years and is a Book of itself. Case Started Nov. 26, 1892 and was finished April 25th, 1895.

At that time there was only one train each way from Brownwood and I could not leave Brownwood untill Early next morning which I did and arrived at midnight. Mr. Christeson met me at the Depot and gave me all the information that he had. We could not do anything that night, and Mr. Christeson and I left at 7 A.M. for Galveston the next morning. At Galveston, I talked to the Bank People, got the Packages, and got the Way Bill from our Agent and soon was satisfyed that there was no Colusion between the Banks and that night I left for New Orleans. Mr. Christeson went with me.

These two Packages were received by Wells Fargo & Co. from 2 Banks. 1 Package Contained $25,000 Consigned to Ball Hutchings & Co.'s Bank in Galveston, Texas and 1 Package Contained $10,000 Consigned to Island City Savings Bank, Galveston, Tex. They both Come from two different Banks and going to two different Banks precluded Colusion of Banks at Each End. This Money left New York on Saturday, November 26th, 1892, and reached Galveston Tuesday, November 29th, 1892. This was what was called Cotton Money, for the purpose of handling Cotton, and it was necessarry for the money to make the best time that was possible.

Wells Fargo & Co. Received this money and carried it to Cincinnatti, Ohio. This money was carried in a through Safe and the Messenger did not have the Combination of that Safe and could not get into it. It was opened at Cincinnatti, Ohio, and there transferred to the Adams Express Co. and by them Carried in an open (Messenger's) Safe to Nashville, Tenn. and a quick and direct transfer made, Messenger to Messenger, on same train to the Southern Express Co., and by them Carried in an open Safe (Messenger's Safe) to New Orleans. There, it was a direct transfer just across a Narrow Platform and again transferred to Wells Fargo & Co. and put into a through Safe locked by the Depot Agent, and carried by them to Houston, where the Safe was opened by the Depot Agent and then transfered to the Galveston Messenger, who carried it in an open (Messenger) Safe to Galveston and by him delivered to the Depot Agent at Galveston.

This Agent at once delivered the two Shipments to the money delivery man who took the two Packages to the two different Banks. Ball & Hutchings & Co. was the first. The Receiving Teller there placed his Package on his Shelf in his Cage. The next delivery was to the Island City Savings Bank. They needed some small money and had ordered small money from New York and they at once opened the $10,000 Package and instead of Currency they found Brown Paper Cut to the Size of Bills. (This was before the Government had reduced the Size of the Bills.) The Money Delivery man at once went right back to Ball Hutchings & Co. and told them about the Package that he had just delivered. They had not opened their Package yet, but at once proceeded to do so and they also found their Package of $25,000 to Contain only Brown Paper Cut to the size of Bills.

Wells Fargo & Co. Both Received and Delivered this money. The loss was theirs, and in 3 days the money was paid to the two different Banks in Galveston, Texas.

Mr. Christeson and I reached New Orleans at 7 A.M. Saturday, December 3rd, 1892. The two Packages carried the Seals of the two New York Banks and that they had been opened was Evident by the discovery of the "Brown Paper." Some of the Seals had been substituted and only the word "Bank" was there. At New Orleans, Mr. Christeson and I met Gen. Supt. O'Brien and Division Supt. Fisher. At New Orleans, Wells Fargo and Co. were joint with the Southern Express Co. That is, one Agent, Mr. Pardue, and the Employees were all also joint — the two Companys had been rather close for several years.

I got right busy for I wanted to know where that Seal was made, and there I made a very close Examination of Each and Every one of those pieces of "Brown Paper." I discovered that they had been cut 5 at a time and on the lower side I could see that they were bent over a little and on that Side there was a line, which caused me much thought. I knew that somewhere, at some place, I had seen a simaler line. I had these two Packages Photographed and we brought out all the Points that were there. I had them Photographed from all the Ends and all the Sides, and when we were through we were going to put Paper between the Photos, which was a couple of days later. It took several Sheets of Paper and they had to be all of one size and he said to me, "I can make this all right," so he took some Paper and we went into a back room where all of his tools and Paraphanalia were, and he took 5 Sheets of this paper and marked it off and then went to his machine that he used for Cutting Tintypes — which was a Solid plate that had a Knife lever that he could bring down and cut the Paper — right then I knew where I had seen this worked before. I was having a lot of small pictures made to put on Circulars describing a man. It was at Fort Worth, Texas, and when he cut the paper I looked at it and there was my line. I asked him all about this machine and he gave me much information.

There was just the word "bank" on the Seals that had been substituted. I had a set of instruments to measure the letters in any Seal that I was working on, and by close measurement I found that the letter "A" in the work Bank was a trifle higher in the wax than the Balance of the letters. This could not be seen by the Naked Eye so it gave me a sure thing on my Identifycation of the Seal, if I ever got to where it was made. (This was also a fine identifycation as Evidence at a trial — if I ever found the Seal Maker.) This I kept strictly to My Self.

I had learned all I knew about Seals from Capt. Jim Hume, then Chief of Wells Fargo & Co.'s Detectives. I knew that he was coming. Jim Hume was without doubt the most expert Seal man that was in existance at that time and now, 50 years later, I have never seen the man who was his equal. So I had an Expert as a Tutor.

Jim Hume arrived in New Orleans December 7th, 1892, and we went into Consultation at once. I had worked hard and I had much to tell Capt. Hume. I had seen all the Seal Makers in New Orleans, also all the Paper men (for this was a Paper that could readily be found at most Paper Co.'s — it was what was then Known as "Butcher Paper") and they would be likely to know and note any unusual Sale of the Particular Paper. I had also interviewed all the men who had handled that Shipment but had not as yet taken their Statements with a Stenographer as I wanted Hume there then.

I told Capt. Hume all that I had got, and also the Measurement of the letter "A" in "Bank" and he was sure tickled. It was surely a very valuable piece of Evidence for there was several ways that you could use it. Capt. Hume had been very much interested in my use of the instruments in the past for it was Capt. Hume who had made me a present of these Instruments. He agreed with me that the part referring to the measurement and the letter "A" being higher than the rest of the letters should be kept to our selfs.

We then had a Consultation with the Officials of the Southern Express Co. On the 8th, Mr. Christeson left for Houston at 5 P.M. and I left for Montgomery, Ala. at 7:50 P.M. — I had, and so had Hume, the right given us by the Officials of the Southern Express Co. to interview any or all of their men. Capt. Hume remained in New Orleans that night and next day. I arrived in Montgomery, Ala. at 6:15 A.M. next morning. I worked all day seeing all Seal Makers and Paper men. I also made a careful investigation of Messenger Tomalson — he was the Messenger that carried the Shipment from Montgomery, Ala. to New Orleans. I had interviewed Messenger Tomalson at New Orleans and I did not get anything detrimental against him in Montgomery.

The next A.M., Saturday, Dec. 10th, 1892 at 6:15 A.M. I met Capt. Hume and Supt. Fisher at the Depot and continued on the train with them to Nashville, Tenn. arriving there at 8:30 P.M. Dec. 11th and 12th, Sunday and Monday, I was in Nashville, Hume and I in Consultation with representatives of the Southern Express Co. The next Morning Capt. Hume left at 6:30 A.M. for Cincinnatti — I remained at Nashville. We had interviewed Messenger Harwood who carried the Shipment from Nashville to Montgomery on the 11th, and on the 12th I interviewed Sam Burchill who was the Baggageman and run in the same car with Messenger Harwood, but I did not get anything of Value from Burchill. I saw all the Sealmakers and Paper men in Nashville but I did not get any information. I left at 8:10 P.M. for Cincinnatti.

Tuesday, Dec. 13th, 1892, arrived at Cincinnatti — there

all day. Met Hume. We Employed a Stenographer and then we interviewed some of the Adams Express Co.'s People, Weston, Bonner, and Miller — This Shipment passed through their Hands. I left Cincinnatti that night and went to Louisville, Ky. — there at 1 A.M., there bal. of Night. There the 14th, Making some arraingements to get a line on Charlie Hardin. This had to be done very quietly to keep him from knowing that we were suspecting him — And we were surely doing just that. I also saw some of the Seal men, and at 1 P.M. I left for Cincinnatti — there at 5 P.M. and there the balance of the night. The 15th, Capt. Hume left for New York, and I was in Cincinnatti 16, 17, and 18. During this time I had been busy. I had seen the Seal and Paper men there. I had also seen and interviewed Messenger Dowell, a W.F. & Co. Messenger who brought the Shipment from Salamanca, N.Y. to Cincinnatti.

I had also met Chas. Hardin, the Adams Messenger, who took the Shipment from Cincinnatti to Nashville, Tenn. I was in his Company all that I could be. We went to the Depot where he went and come in — I also interviewed him closely and took a statement from him. (But I did not believe it to be true at all) He was going out and coming in on his Run as usual —

I had several very close and Confidential talks with Bonner and Miller. Bonner was the man who received this Shipment from W.F. & Co.'s Money Transfer man and he positively and emphatically said that the two Packages were not now in the same Condition that they were when he received them from W.F. & Co. and positively said that if they had been in that condition, that he would never have received them. Miller, the man who checked them out into Messenger Hardin's hands, said that if there had been anything wrong with the Packages that he would never have received them from Bonner and Messenger Hardin said the same, that if there had been anything wrong with the Packages that he would never have received them from Miller. So we could show that both Packages were in good condition when they went into the hands of the Adams Express Co. at Cincinnatti. This transfer had been made on Sunday, the 27th of November 1892, and they all had plenty of time to scrutinize all the Seals Carefully, which they did. These Statements of Bonner and Miller had been made when the matter was fresh in their minds, and they were both Sworn to.

Capt. Hume returned from New York Sunday, December 18, 1892. I had much to talk over with Capt. Jim. We had both met Col. L. C. Weir, the Gen. Manager at that Point and Capt. Jim and I talked untill late at night. Next day, we had a long and very full talk with Col. Weir and Capt. Hume and I left for Louisville at 7:30 P.M., there at 11:30 P.M. and there the balance of the night. Col. Weir had given us Letters of introduction to the Officials of the Adams Express Co. in Louisville. On the 20th of Dec. we met the Supt., Graham, the Gen. Agent, Maj. Owens, and that night Mr. Brachy, the Route Agent, come. We had talked to Supt. Graham and Maj. Owens very fully. Maj. Owens could and did give us a lot of information, but Supt. Graham did not *want* to talk much. We met Route Agent Brachy at the train and took him to Supper with us and then we went to our Rooms and Brachy gave us a full history of Hardin. Hardin had been recomended by Charlton Elrod, a Photographer, and he had stated to Brachy that Hardin had worked for him a long time and that the Confinement was too much for him and he wanted some outside work, messenger work or something like that, that could be more in the air. There was a Strike on at that time among the Adams Express Employees and Brachy put him to work and made several trips with him and looked on him as the making of a good man in the Express business. We got all there was to get from Brachy that night and we agreed to meet in the morning and make a thougher canvass of the Seal makers.

We met in the A.M. and we called on Elrod whose picture Gallery was just a few doors from the Adams Express Office. I did not want to alarm Elrod for it would surely go to Hardin. I made an excuse and got a Box that Dry Plates are shipped in, but I did while getting that Box see the Tin Type Cutter that had cut the Paper that was in the Packages.

Then we started on the Seal makers and about the 3rd one we come to was the place where the Seal had been made. I had the Photos of the Seal and that is what I showed the man. He looked at the Photo for a while and said that he believed that they had made the Seal and that they always made an Extra one or two that was thrown in a Box that they kept for that purpose and we commenced to look in that Box. After a while we found it and he let me have it. I was certain that it was the right one.

We knew that Capt. Hume was at the Hotel and we went there and found him. This Seal Maker was one of the firm, and his Wife was the other one of the firm but She was not there when I got the duplicate of the Seal. (The firm name was Chas. Brenner and Wife.) Brenner had told me when he was describing the man that had got the Seal that his Wife could give me a more perfect description of the man than he could and that She would be there that afternoon. Capt. Hume and I both was sure that it was Hardin, and we also felt sure that Hardin would *not* be identifyed by the Brenners, as we felt sure also that Hardin would not be so foolish as to get the Seal himself for it was on his Run and he could not afford to get it himself.

We Consulted with Supt. Graham and Gen. Agent Owens.

We then left for Cincinnatti and took Route Agent Brachy with us. We wired to Col. Weir that it was important that we see him at his Office that night. When we got in, Col. Weir met us and we went direct to his Office and then Capt. Hume and I both spread all of our Cards on the table, and went over the whole thing from the Banks in Galveston right back to Cincinnatti and all the Handling of the Shipment from New York to Cincinnatti and the delivery of said Shipment to the Adams Express Co. there, which Col. Weir was thougherly Aquainted with. Col. Weir then went over the whole Case and was most positive that it was Hardin that had made the substitution and had taken the Money.

Hardin was supposed to be in Louisville and in the Morning, Brachy and I went to Louisville, but we could not find Hardin. We got a message from Col. Weir that Hardin was in Cincinnatti. Brachy and I returned at once to Cincinnatti, but while waiting for a train I interviewed another Elrod, Walter Elrod, who was a Photographer also, and was running a Photo Gallery in Louisville. He was a Brother of Charlton Elrod — but was no friend of his — and Walter Elrod told me that Hardin's name was Ketchum — Charlie Ketchum — that he was always a Wild, bad Boy, that the Elrods and the Ketchums were all raised in Louisville, and that Ketchum's Father had been in business there (in the Carpet Business) and here was a very peculiar Condition — Ketchum's partner's name was Cheatam and the firm name was "Ketchum and Cheatam." Walter said that Charlton Elrod and Charlie Ketchum had always been friends from childhood. Walter said that Charlton had run a Photograph Gallery in St. Louis for several years and about a year before, Charlton returned to Louisville, that Charlie Ketchum showed up there and worked for Charlton Elrod but he was Sick when he come to Charlton's and that Walter saw him there when he first come, that he looked Sick and was very pale and waxy. Charlton Elrod and Walter Elrod were brothers but they were Enemys, and I had to be careful about taking what Walter said without investigating it thougherly. Brachy had been raised in Louisville and remembered the Firm of Ketchum and Cheatam but could not remember for sure whether there was a Ketchum Boy.

When we got to Cincinnatti we met Col. Weir, Capt. Hume, and Hardin. They had investigated the Place where Hardin roomed and Hume found out that there was a Woman that had been there with Hardin and She had told the Landlady that she was the Wife of Hardin. She was gone and Hardin would not claim the Woman as his Wife. Said it was his Girl. Brachy, Hardin, and I went back to Louisville. Supt. Graham come to the room and Maj. Owens was with him. Maj. Owens, the Gen. Agent, was trying to do all that he could for us, but Supt. Graham, who was a cold blooded proposition, was doing all that he could to thwart us. He was taking the Stand that if we did not convict Hardin that the Adams Co. was not responsible for the money.

In the morning, we went to see the Brenners. I had during this time met Mrs. Brenner. They failed to identify Hardin, and I felt Good for Hardin would surely have proved an Alibi. I got back there as soon as I could and Mrs. Brenner Said that Hardin was a much larger man, was much taller and heavier than the man who had Ordered and Got the Seal, and that his Hair was much lighter and so was his Eyes. I was quite sure that I could find the man whom she described, for I had seen him sitting in Charlton Elrod's Gallery both times that I had been in there, and he was missing the next day when I went there.

I went to see Supt. Graham and laid the whole matter before him about the identifycation and I told him that if they would take Hardin into Custody that they had a good chance to get most of the money back. I supposed that they were going to do it. My opinion was based on the way that Supt. Graham talked.

That Evening after Supper, I had a long talk with Walter Elrod and he told me much about Charlton Elrod and his Picture Gallery at St. Louis and all about the time that Hardin Showed up at St. Louis. He told me that Hardin did not look Sick but that he was awfully White, bleached out. He also told me about the People who worked in the Gallery, and Especially about a Young Lady that worked there. He said that She was very beautiful and that She was supposed to be Engaged to Hardin, but about the time that Charlton Elrod busted up there, that there was a break between Hardin and this Young Lady. He did not know her name or anything more about her, and that Hardin, Elrod, and most of the help come on to Louisville where Charlton had a Small Gallery that he had kept running all the time that he was in St. Louis.

I left for Cincinnatti that night at 12 midnight and was in Cincinnatti Next Morning at 7 A.M. At Cincinnatti, I met Capt. Hume and I give him all that I had learned and Especially about what Walter Elrod had told me. Capt. Hume and I agreed that we should see Col. Weir and lay the whole matter before him, the same as I had done with Supt. Graham. This we did that same day and Col. Weir agreed that the Adams Express Co. was liable for the whole ammount and that they would start right in — Col. Weir wanted me to remain in the Case, and Hume and I agreed to that. The Pinkerton Agency had always done their work. Billy Pinkerton was a close friend of mine and I was glad that they were to Come into the Case. Col. Weir told us that the last man that they had for this work was Supt. Frank Murray of the Chicago Office and he sent a long Wire to the Agency and Murray answered it and said that he would be in Cincinnatti the next morning. Then Col. Weir went home. Hume and I Called on the Chief of Police, Chief Deitrect, and met several of the Officers. Next Morning, Thursday, December 27th, 1892, Hume and I met Capt. Murray. We went over the whole Case with Murray and Showed him the two Packages. He now had all that we could tell him.

The Next Morning, Hardin could not be found in Louisville or Cincinnatti. They had Called Col. Weir on the Phone at his House and He Called us all and we met him at his Office. He took hold of the Situation in a masterfully way. He just pulled down some maps that were in his Office and Sent Messages to all points outside of where Hardin Could reach from Cincinnatti or Louisville by that time in the Morning. It just looked to me like it was a long and steady hunt that was now ahead of us.

Capt. Hume and I did not agree on Col. Weir. Hume was sure that Weir was a Square Man — while I was not so sure of it. I had got hold of Enough from Walter Elrod to make me suspicious of the whole bunch. I did not trust Supt. Graham at all and the whole Combination did not fit me at all.

That Evening's train brought a letter to Col. Weir from Dr. Stoddard of Brookville, Indiana that he had some sure information, So at 5 P.M. I left Cincinnatti for Brookville. There next A.M. at 7:30. Went right to See Dr. Stoddard. What he had did not fit, or help our Case any — I Phoned Col. Weir and gave him all that there was. I was in Cincinnatti next A.M. at 10 O'Clock. Capt. Hume had Come in from Lima, Ohio, and it all looked to Everybody that St. Louis was the place to get a start, So I made all arraingements to leave for St. Louis in the A.M.

Capt. Hume and I left for St. Louis in the Morning. He was going on to San Francisco and leaving me in charge of the

whole works — he had written to Mr. Valentine that I was
fully Competent to handle the whole thing. I had made several reports on the Case and Capt. Hume had a Copy of all of
them and we had much to talk over during the day. We
reached St. Louis that Night, Sunday, Jan. 1st, 1893. We met
Supt. Simpson at the Depot and then all went to our Hotel,
the old Southern, where Supt. Simpson was Temporarily Staying. It was on the American plan and one of the best Hotels
that was then in Existence.

We went over the whole Case with Supt. Simpson that
night and I told him that St. Louis was to be the Battle
Ground for a while and that we would have to get our Start
from there. I told him that it was very suggestive to me, that
the fact of Hardin looking so bleached out when he Come to
Elrod's Gallery in St. Louis, that he had Come out of a Penetentiary somewhere. And Capt. Hume Said, "Dodge is
thougherly Convinced, and has offered Many good reasons,
that Hardin had just Come from a Penn." So Simpson said,
"If he has, we will soon get our Start." — but I could see lots
of work ahead. I said, "We do not Know his Penn name or
number. We have no Picture of him — and a man can be
thougherly lost to go to a Penn under an asumed name."
They all agreed on that.

I wired that night for Heck Thomas to Come into St. Louis
for there was still the Dalton Posse to settle up and I surely
wanted this off of my hands and I also had several Matters
that I wanted to Close out. And I closed it and Settled with
Heck Thomas and was through with the Case — and then we
got down to business.

Jim Hume had gone on to San Francisco, Cala. and Mr.
Simpson and I started on a long hard Case.

All that we had was the Name of Charlton Elrod to Start
with, and we did not have Hardin's name before he showed up
at Elrod's Gallery. We soon found out that Elrod and Hardin

were close friends, for they were always seen together. And we finally got hold of a Porter that used to work in the Gallery. He was a Negro but like all of his kind he could not remember Names, but he could identify the Girl if he could see her. He was sure that She worked in a Big Store somewhere in St. Louis. He Said that this Girl had a Sister who used to come to the Gallery to see the one that used to work there, and that he would know her if he saw her. He said that She worked in a big Store also.

So we had two Chances. All of the Big Stores used to close at 6 P.M. and all the help Come out a Small door at the back of the Store. (This was to prevent light fingered ones from getting away with many Articles.) We used to take this Porter, and after having a talk with the Proprietor, place our Selfs where we could see Every one that Come out. We could only take one Store a night and there were quite a number of Stores in St. Louis. We had worked about 3 when one night our Porter Saw the Sister but She become lost in the jam, for at this Store there was about 100 Girls and several Stores in a Neighborhood would put quite a bunch together. We had planned to Shadow the Young Lady home and get their number and Call later in the Evening — but we were up a tree. So we broke up and was to meet this Porter in the Morning, for we had the Store and could locate the Lady Easily the following day.

In the Morning, we took the Porter to the Store and very soon located the Young lady. We then went to the Private Office of the Man who had given us the permission to look the help over. This was one of the finest Stores in St. Louis and the firm was Vandervoot, Barney, and Co. The man we saw was Mr. Barney and he was one of the finest men that I ever met. Mr. Simpson and I got quite well acquainted with him and we both thought a lot of him.

We just told him the whole Storey about the $35,000 Case

and we wound up by telling him that the Girl's Sister was working for him there in the Store. Mr. Barney Sent for the Girl at once. When She Come into his Office he Explained the whole matter to her and She told him that her Sister was the one who used to work in the Photo Gallery of Elrod's, and that She was not working in the Store with her but She was working in another Store, the Golden Eagle. Mr. Barney Sent her at once to get her Sister and bring her back to his office and he also sent a Note by her to the Manager of the Store where the Sister was working and Mr. Barney told us the Sister would Come. We waited in his Office and was getting more aquainted with Mr. Barney all the time. Finally the Sister returned and had her Sister with her — and all that had been Said with refference to her looks was true and then some, for She was a very handsome Young Woman.

Mr. Barney told her what our business was, and that he (Mr. Barney) would guarantee that anything that Either one of us Said or promiced, that we would keep our word, and that he (Mr. Barney) would personally be responsible for us. We then Explained to her the fix that we were in and She told us at once that She did have a picture of Hardin and that we could come out to her house that Night and get it and She gave us the address and number of her house. This was on Tuesday, January 17th, 1893.

Mr. Simpson and I went there that night and we were Shown into the Parlor. There were several People there that Night but we did not see any of them. There was a Skating party on for that Night. We saw both of the Girls and met the Mother of both of these Girls. The Girls told us about the Skating party and this Girl who had the Picture Said that She had been unable to find it, but that her Mother would hunt for it and give it to us. Well, they went away and the Mother looked for It. Mr. Simpson helped her, but I did not do anything at all. I had a hunch that the Girl had put it away somewhere. The Mother was honest in her indeavor to find the picture but I was satisfyed that they Could not find it unless the Girl wanted to.

There had been Considerable talk in the room next to us and it dyed down some, like they were lowering their Voices, and I felt sure that some Man was taking a active part in that talk. I also Knew what they Could say about a Detective, that they never Kept their word and all that kind of stuff. We finally went away and had acomplished nothing.

Simpson Could see that there was something the matter with me and as soon as we got away from the House, he asked me what the matter was. He Said, "You did not act like yourself." And I told him that I would give him my reasons, as soon as we got to the Room. Mr. Simpson was Staying at the same Hotel, the Southern, as that Division had only just been opened and Wells Fargo & Co. had just acquired the [St. Louis & South Western] System and he had not had time to bring his Family to St. Louis from Omaha.

When we got to the Rooms I then told him that I had had a hunch that all was not right, that there was too much whispering going on in the next room at the Girl's house and that there was a man that had a lot to say. I told Simpson how the advice would go from a Young Man who undoubtedly was in Love with this Young Lady, that his advice to her would be for her to just keep out of the whole thing, to not give us any Picture and if she did, the probabilities were that she would see the Picture published in a News Paper and her name would be Connected with it. At any rate to postpone it for a few days anyhow — this would give him more time to make his argument good. I told Simpson, that he, this man, was partly right, for that was the way that a lot of these so-called Detectives would treat *any* Confidential information that they would receive. I went into the matter deep, and we talked it over from all its Standpoints.

Right at once when Mr. Simpson Come to St. Louis he had reason to become aquainted with the Chief of Police, Larry Harrigan, and through Mr. Simpson I had become aquainted with him and also the Chief of Detectives, William Desmond. We had all become quite good friends and they were both much interested in this "Brown Paper Case," the $35,-000 Loss. So Mr. Simpson and I agreed to take the whole thing to Larry Harrigan in the A.M. and see if he could help us out. Larry Harrigan was called the Zar of St. Louis and practically he was. He protected St. Louis and did not work for any other City. We called on him and we made arraingements for him to have an Interview with the Girl.

Mr. Simpson and I went to See the Young Lady that P.M. Simpson and the Girl's Mother Searched for the Picture, but they did not find it. The Girl and I did not Search much. We just Visited and I become thougherly sure that She had the Picture. Mr. Simpson was equally sure that She did not know where it was.

I had to leave for Cincinnatti that night and I was on the train all night. Col. Weir of the Adams Ex. Co. had wired me that they had some good information there and to come there. So I went. Col. Weir gave me all the Datta that he had and I started out to find the man that was Supposed to have known Hardin and I learned that he was in St. Louis and that all that he Knew was at St. Louis. I sent Several Telegrams to Mr. Simpson and left that night for St. Louis again.

I was there the Next Morning, met Mr. Simpson and we went to See the Chief of Police. This was on Saturday and a busy day for us. All business Houses Closed at one O'Clock P.M. This man that we were looking for was supposed to be working at Elrod's Gallery when Hardin Showed up there first. The Chief put the right men to looking for this Party and they found him and found where he lived. We went to see him. He also was a Negro but he could give us very little information for right about the time that Hardin Come there, this Porter got fired for getting drunk too often. He was no good to us — So we blew up again.

There was many Changes in the Express Service right about that time and as fast as they could be made, the Gen. Supt., Col. Evans, with headquarters at Omaha was going to New York as Vice-President. Mr. Amador Andrews, Supt. at Omaha, was made General Manager with Headquarters at Kansas City, And my Headquarters were changed from Houston, Texas to Kansas City with the General Manager and I was to have an Office there and a Stenographer who could be my Chief Clerk and also to Keep up my Files. So there was much moving to do for Kansas City had only the Headquarters of a Superintendent, Mr. C. W. Stockton, who was also a close friend of Mr. G. B. Simpson, Supt. at St. Louis — they had Started their Express work together at Portland, Oregon under Supt. Col. Dudley Evans. Col. Dudley Evans and Amador Andrews arrived in St. Louis the morning of January 25th, 1893, and we were advised of these changes that day.

The night before, Mr. Simpson had been to call on the Picture Girl but we did not do any good. We were becoming Stale there but we had made friends of the Family. This Picture Girl was our friend and I could see that there was something about her that She wanted to be otherwise. Mr. Simpson would use that against my opinion that She could find the Picture if She wanted to. (Col. Evans and Mr. Andrews took up most of our time while they were there, which was two days.)

Chief Harrigan had fixed up a plan to get the Picture Girl to his Office and have a talk with her and he made a success of getting her there and having the Talk but that was all. And when he went over this with us, He Said to me, "I will tell you this, Brother Dodge, She has got the Picture sure." This had a lot of weight with Mr. Simpson, for we both had a lot of Confidence in him, but we did not get much chance to talk it over for that night Col. Evans and Mr. Andrews left for Chicago and I left for Kansas City to meet Jim Hume. I was there in the A.M. and met Hume. We were in Kansas City all day and left that night for Chicago. We arrived in Chicago at 9:15.

The balance of the day we had a long talk with Capt. Murray and Billie Pinkerton. Murray had been to work on the Brown Paper Case and he told us that there was no question at all but Hardin was the Guilty Man and was sure of it, and that made Jim Hume feel pretty good. I did not have any doubt at all but what Hardin had made the Substitution. I told Murray and Pinkerton all about the Picture. They both knew Larry Harrigan, and Billie Pinkerton had known him for years, and when I told them what Harrigan had said after he had talked to the Girl, Pinkerton said then that I was right and that She had the Picture. Murray had been trying to get a Start on Hardin but had not got anywhere as yet.

Jim Hume's Nephew was Col. McCloughery and he was Warden of the Federal Penn at Leavenworth, Kas. and he had his Home in Chicago. Hume and I went out to see him but missed him and Come back down town. Jim Hume got a Message from his Wife that Sam, their Son, had been taken Suddenly and Seriously sick and Jim made arraingements to leave for California at once and he left at 10 P.M. for there. Jim gave me a letter to Col. McCloughery and I went out to see him. He had had much Experience with Criminals for he had been Warden of Several Penns. He was sure that I was on the right track for the Picture. I was in Chicago all the next day, Monday, January 30th, 1893, and left that Night at 9:20

for St. Louis and I was there in the Morning. That was Tuesday, January 31st, 1893.

Mr. Simpson had been out to see the Picture Girl the night before and we both went out that night again. Simpson was not so awfully sure about her and we Stayed up pretty late that night and I went over the whole thing again. But he was still unconvinced.

We went to bed and I made up my mind to just take the Bull by the Horns and get that Picture. I worked out a plan that night and was going to Start it in the morning. I had got well aquainted with the Golden Eagle People, and we had had the Girl at Simpson's Office Several times. But we had to be awfully Carefull, for if we got her name mixed up in any connection with this Case, we were blowed up on the Picture and Stood a chance for a Damage Suit and I was affraid that She was playing for that. It depended largely on what her Advisor was advising her. I told Mr. Simpson about it. He did not think much of it, but I was determined to bring it to a close. It was Picture or no Picture and I was sure She had it.

So I went to see her and made an appointment with her to meet me at Mr. Simpson's Office that afternoon and She agreed to it. I was there waiting, and She Come. I had Mr. Simpson there also, and I had told him that I was going to hang my Hat on that Picture or blow up right. Soon after She had come, I told her that I had a Story to tell her and that when I was finished, that it was just Simply up to her.

I then Started in at the Commencement and Step by Step I went through with it. I told her that there was two Express Companys that were interested in the Case. I told her that the Vice-President and the General Manager had both been there to see us, that they had Come Wednesday, Jan 25th, and that we had gone over the Whole Case, that the next night I had gone to Kansas City to meet another Official there who had come from San Francisco, Cala., that we had gone on to Chicago that night and next day we met the Vice-President and the General Manager and it was put up to me squarely, and that I had come back from Chicago. I also told her that the Pinkertons were in the Case and the Chief of Police of St. Louis also. I also called her attention to our meeting with her and what Mr. Barney had told her at that meeting, and that I wanted to, and would, Keep my Word with her in regard to her becoming Connected with the Case, and that I could and would keep the whole outfit from Connecting her with the matter untill Monday, but then I would be helpless. And if the Evening Papers Come out and She found her Picture and a long account of her being at Elrod's Gallery and all her Connections with the matter, that She must not blame me or Mr. Simpson for Neither one of us, would on any Circumstances whatever tell one thing, and would refuse to be interviewed by any one.

I then told her that Mr. Simpson had always been of the opinion that She did not have the Picture where She Could lay her hands on it, but that I had all the time held that they Could find the Picture if they had made a thougher Search of the House for it. I also told her that She would have got the Picture for us and have given it to us the first night if She could have found it, only for the Advice of some man who was in the Next Room to us. I described his Voice, and I just imagined what he would be saying — and then right there I thought that She was going to brake down tell the whole thing, but She did not, and then I had a Sure hunch that She had it and that we would get it.

This was Thursday, and I told her that She never had Stayed at Home and given her House a thougher Search for the Picture and I was sure that if She done so that She would find it. I then told her if she would do that I would see the

Golden Eagle People and make arraingements for her to Stay at home Saturday and make a thougher Search for it and She agreed to it, and from all the indications I was sure that we would get the Picture.

I had talked the whole afternoon and I had painted the whole line in words that was Convincing and picturest. I was talking for the Picture and I wanted it badly. When She left, Mr. Simpson said to me, "Well Fred, You have nearly Convinced me — you have painted a Picture that is hard to withstand. You have told the truth all the time, but while some of it has been Strained, still it was the truth. But if you are right about the talk in the room next to us the first night, I will say that you are a mind reader of the first class."

The next morning I went to see the Golden Eagle People and made the Arraingements for the Girl to Stay at Home on Saturday and I let her know about it. I also told her that I would be in Mr. Simpson's Office all the afternoon Saturday. I was there and about 2 P.M. the Girl Come in. I was sure about the Picture after looking at the Girl's Face. Although She said, "Well, I didn't find it."

It was a Cold day and She had on a heavy Coat, and I Could see just the Corner of something White sticking out of her Coat. I said to her, "I see that you did not find it," and I just reached over and took it from her Coat and it was Hardin all right and a fine Picture of him. She also had a very small one which She gave to me. We then made her quite a Substantial Present. She was not Expecting any thing like that, and that was where Mr. Simpson did Shine. Knew just what to say with all the Boquttes and he said it all.

We could do no more untill Monday when we were going to have Copys made So that we could get them going. We went down to Chief Harrigan's Office Sunday and showed him the Picture. He was very much Elated that we were finally successful in getting it. On Monday morning, we went to have copys of the Picture made by the best Photographer in the City.

The Girl told us that the first night that we were there that there was quite a number in the Room next to us, and this man that was going with her did Advise her not to let us have the Picture, to wait and see how it would come out, and he advised again against it. He also Said that we might pay quite a price for it, and this was Entirely against all the ideas that the Girl had for She was of the opinion that She did not want anything to do with the Picture or any one Connected with it. All she was afraid of was that She might be brought into the Case herself. They did not agree and Quarreled over it. Result — he lost a very Handsome Girl and She lost a stubborn, hard-headed man. She left Mr. Simpson's Office and He saw her Several times afterwards. But I never Saw her again.

[*That was the end of January 1893. If the Picture Girl had finished, Fred Dodge was just starting on a case which was to take him the better part of two years to bring to a close as far as the courts were concerned. It appears that the company pursued it still further. From the Dodge diaries in which entries are very brief — twenty-five or thirty words a day at the most — it is possible to piece together the outcome. Dodge worked with characteristic determination, in and out of Kansas City, Chicago, Washington, Louisville, and Nashville where the case finally was called on October 1, 1894. On October 10, Dodge noted in his diary entry for that day, "It now seems a certainty to me that the Defence have got the Jury." On October 12, he wrote, "Sure thing they have got the $35,-000 Jury." On October 17, 1894 at 9:30 A.M., the verdict was returned and Ketchum was pronounced not guilty. Feeling*

220

against the verdict was strong and Dodge who didn't swear in his diaries wrote, "Hell."

In the fall of 1895, J. J. Valentine, president of Wells Fargo and Company wrote Fred Dodge that the company was presenting him with a watch for his efforts on the $35,000 Brown Paper Case. The following day the watch arrived — a beauty, in a case decorated with engraved flowers and an elaborate monogram, F. J. D. On the back of the watch itself were engraved the words, "Fred J. Dodge for zeal, skill, and success in the Hardin Case 1892–'95 Wells, Fargo & Co."]

16

SOMETHING OF THE PERSONAL

[*Twenty-seven small diaries, most of them bound in maroon
leather, show the actual whereabouts, day and night, of Fred
Dodge from the year 1891 through 1918. It seems certain
that these books were what he used for reference as he developed his journals, calling on his own memory for details to re-
construct his years as a Special Agent for Wells Fargo. The
diaries contain little of a personal nature, but from time to
time there is a word or two about his family. In 1891, he mentioned writing home several times and receiving letters from
Patsy, his first wife. July 24, 1892, he noted "all day at Home
for one Sunday" — a rare entry. October 30 was another Sunday at home and he "took folks out riding — Taft and Family
with us" (Wells Fargo Route Agent G. A. Taft, frequently
mentioned in the journals). In November Dodge was in Kansas City and noted he went to the theater.*

*In 1893 he was at home two days over Christmas. The year
1894 was a busy one. Once in Chattanooga, he had a few
hours to spare and "went up on top of Lookout Mountain."
May 25 was a "tough day." He didn't elaborate, but he was on
the "$35,000 Brown Paper Case." July 2, they moved to a
house in Kansas City. The address was 345 Olive; the rent, $25
per month. In December, he visited his father for several days
in Sacramento, California.*

*In 1895, the family spent the summer in Colorado Springs
with trips to Cripple Creek by team and back via the Con-
tinental Divide. They returned to Kansas City in September*

and in October, Dodge received the letter and watch from Wells Fargo president J. J. Valentine for his part in the Hardin Case ("$35,000 Brown Paper Case," Dodge liked to call it.) In 1896, he noted two Sundays in a row at home and several days in July around Mexico City on business. His father died in October. November 3, Dodge voted for McKinley and Christmas found him at home in Kansas City.

Dodge made a trip to California in February of 1897 to settle his father's estate. He met Wyatt Earp in San Francisco February 15 and saw Capt. Hume of Wells Fargo "affraid for the last time." Hume had been ill. The Dodges bought a house in Kansas City in May of that year, and once more the man of the family was on the road for Christmas — that time in Tucson. In 1898, insights into his personal life were rare, but he was in Chicago in January and bought a piano.

In 1899, Patsy and Ada were with him for the month of August in Excelsior Springs and home was still Kansas City. In November, they all went to Texas. The hotel in Houston was twenty dollars a week for Patsy and Ada. Later, they went to San Antonio where they stayed until January 3, 1900. Vacation in 1900 was in Colorado Springs, June through September, when they moved to San Antonio and Ada started school October 1.

Patsy was quite ill early in 1901 and finally spent most of March and part of April in Santa Rosa Hospital in San Antonio. Later in April, they moved to 202 Fourth Street in San Antonio. Dodge bought another horse during the summer, also a new phaeton and harness. He noted President McKinley was shot September 6, and died of his wounds eight days later. Patsy accompanied her husband to New Orleans for four days in September. The December 21 entry noted the death of J. J. Valentine, president of Wells Fargo. Dodge spent Christmas in San Antonio and wrote December 31,

"Goodbye old year May I have a better New Year than the old one has been. I never want the worry again of the year 1901." (Workwise, he had been back and forth between the United States and Mexico on a seemingly discouraging case.)

In 1902, the family moved again to 503 Fifth Street, still in San Antonio. His vacation was during the month of September and he and Patsy camped first at Leon Springs, Texas, then Boerne, and for two weeks on the Guadalupe River, two miles from Waring. In November, he noted having a boat trip on the river in Kansas City. Christmas found Dodge in St. Louis.

In 1903, there is little of personal note except he was in quarantine in October for something and the quarantine was lifted by permit from the state health officer so Dodge could leave for Dallas. He was home for Christmas that year but spent the day working.

"Ada graduated" June 15, 1904, and she and her mother went with Dodge to Houston and New Orleans during July. Christmas, he was on the train en route to Denver. Vacation in 1905 was another camping trip in Striblings Pasture along the Guadalupe River and his Christmas was at home in San Antonio. August 16, 1906, the Boerne ranch was "now in our possession." He was home Christmas Day until the night train for Dallas, and not home again until February 25, 1907, though he noted seeing the family when he passed through San Antonio on the train February 11. "Christmas N.G.," he wrote, being on the train from New Orleans to Houston. The December 31 entry: "Good bye old year may the new year be somewhat less strenuous." That year of 1907 Dodge had traveled 37,252 miles.

In 1909, Dodge had pneumonia and spent twelve days in the hospital in Raton, New Mexico. June 18, he went to the Boerne Ranch "for a long rest" and stayed until August 14. December 9, Ada married and became Mrs. Zalmanzig. The following day, her father noted packing her wedding presents. She and her husband visited at the ranch in 1911 and New Year's Eve of that year, Dodge went deer hunting there.

September 18, 1912, Dodge was in a Dallas hospital. He wrote of that occasion, "Doctor wanting to operate on me. (NIX)." He got out in a week or so. During that year he was made "Supt of Stables and Equipment." On December 31, he wrote in part, "On the whole our blessings are usually more than our sorrows. Adios 1912." In November 1913, he drove a coach in the Houston Parade and "took all 1st prizes." He mentioned seeing Ada and her husband several times in 1914 and 1915. During the latter year, he saw the end of his duties as "Stable and Equipment Supt" and was glad of it. He was home for Christmas and wrote on New Year's Eve, "Good bye 1915, old year you have been a good one there is much I could say to your credit."

At the end of July 1916, Ada and her son, Fred Dodge Zalmanzig, sailed from Galveston for New York. September 23, Patsy was taken sick. Her death came October 31, and she was buried the following morning. November 5, Dodge noted that he talked to Ada and he spent the closing days of that year in New Orleans. In 1917, he married Jessie in New Orleans and during the remainder of the year, she frequently met him while he was on the road in Dallas, Houston, and New Orleans. They saw Ada a number of times. Christmas was spent in Dallas and on December 31, Dodge said, "Good bye old year, you have brought to me many blessings and much joy."

In April 1918, Jessie went with her husband to Houston and Dallas and in June they spent a few days on the ranch at Boerne. June 30, Dodge bade "Good bye Wells Fargo & Co — the passing of a good and old friend." July 1 in Houston he wrote, "Good morning American Railway Express Co."

Ada was in Houston with them briefly in July and Jessie joined her husband in Dallas before she went on to New Orleans for a visit. Westbound, she met Dodge on the train in Houston and they returned to San Antonio for the birth, December 22, of their son, Fred James Dodge, Jr., who with his wife, Elouise, is a resident of that city today.

The foregoing account is taken entirely from the diaries and while of utmost brevity still shows something of Fred Dodge apart from his career. He is, indeed, difficult to separate from his work but the reader's acquaintance with him should deepen through the Dodge correspondence with Wyatt Earp and Stuart N. Lake which follows.]

Part III
Letters in Retrospect

17

FRED DODGE RECOLLECTS

Dodge Ranch
Boerne, Texas
Sept. 18th, 1928

Mr. Stuart N. Lake
3916 Portola Place
San Diego, Cal'a

DEAR SIR

This to acknowledge receipt of yours of the 14th. To Commence with, it was good news to me, for I had heard sometime ago that Wyatt Earp was dead, and I am glad to Know that he is still with us. I am Constantly in receipt of letters for information for some one's Book and I am not giving any. I am quite liable to use it for my self. But it is different for Wyatt Earp for I want to help him in any way that I can, and I can furnish what you ask for regarding Curley Bill and in an understanding positive way, that Wyatt will know is right. Also other incidents wherein he figured and my opinion of him as a Man and an Officer. But first I must know that it is for Wyatt, and that it will benefit him from a pecuniary standpoint. Have him write me or give me his adress and I will write him.

Very truly yours,

[signature]

4004 West Seventeenth St.
Los Angeles, California
September 29, 1928

Mr. Stuart N. Lake
3916 Portola Place
San Diego, California

DEAR MR. LAKE:

. . . I want to thank you for the copy of the letter from Fred Dodge which you sent me; I much appreciate this. He is a fine companion and a wonderful friend, and I do not know of anything that has cheered me so much in a long time. I am writing him today and asking him to supply you with whatever information you desire, and I am sure he will.

Sincerely yours,

Wyatt S. Earp.

Dodge Ranch
Boerne, Texas
Oct. 8th, 1928

Mr. Stuart N. Lake
3916 Portola Place
San Diego, Cal'a

DEAR SIR:

I am today answering a letter received from Wyatt Earp, and I am enclosing to him a letter to you so he can check up on it and pass to you. He will likely show you my letter to him from which you can get my connection with Wells Fargo and Co. I did not come out from Under Cover until after I left that country which was in 1888, and this letter to him may

230

suggest other matters, and as stated in that letter I will do all I can. The loss of my Picture Collection was a serious loss to me. Billy Pinkerton said that I had the best private collection in existence.

Yours truly,

Dodge Ranch
Boerne, Texas
Sept. 8, 1928.

Mr. Wyatt S. Earp.
4004 West Seventeenth St.
Los Angeles, Cal.

MY DEAR WYATT:

Life certainly handed me a good thing when I learned that you were still on earth, and then to receive your letter was such an added pleasure that I can scarce yet believe it. To say that it also cheered me is drawing it mild. Yes, I think that you and I are probably all that are left of the old timers of Tombstone. At least I have no knowledge of any others. And we are both piling up the milestones. But you are of a long lived family as indicated by your brother's age of ninety-six and yours of eighty-one. I was seventy-four last August 29th, and still going strong. In 1896, looking forward to my time of retirement, I bought a ranch here in the most beautiful part of Texas or any other state. It is in the beautiful hill country, thirty-five miles north of San Antonio. We have an altitude of 1500 feet and the weather is seldom harsh either way. We came out here to live seven years ago when I was retired from the service. At that time I was down and out from overwork, but I now enjoy excellent health. You will recollect that I am a native Californian, born at Spring Valley, Butte Co., August 29, 1854. I have a girl forty years old born at Tombstone. She is married and has a family and lives at San Antonio. Her Mother died some years ago. Later I again married and have a son ten years old. They say he is a chip off of the old block. He rides and ropes and is a thoroughly active outdoor boy. Above all stories, he loves tales of the old west, and is very familiar with your name and Morgan's.

I am glad that the story of your life is being written. It is a good thing to have a record of those days as they were. They are worth remembering but the true facts are becoming clouded by hearsay evidence and blood-and-thunder criminal histories so called. I am only too glad to corrobarate and assist in any way that I can.

I too have not been strong for this sort of thing in the past, and was known among reporters from New York to San Francisco as the man who could not be interviewed. But of late years, reading some of the distorted accounts that have appeared, I have changed my point of view.

Before I tell you about Curley Bill I want to explain to you something that you likely have not known. When I went to Tombstone I was employed by John J. Valentine as under cover man for Wells Fargo, and reported direct to him. No one other than Mr. Valentine had any knowledge of my connection with the Company. For this reason I had accurate information about the death of Curley Bill, and I will give that information under another heading which you may use with Mr. Lake. But I want to give you, personally, my sources of information.

You will recollect that J. B. Ayers kept the saloon in Charleston that was the headquarters for all the outlaw and rustler element. This man Ayers, for personal reasons that would take too long to tell, supplied me with reliable information. Through him I got in touch with several others. Johnny Barnes, who you will recollect was in the fight at Iron Springs, gave me much information, not only of that but of many other things, before he was killed. Afterwards all that they said with reference to Curley Bill was corroborated by Ike Clanton himself.

It was my report to Mr. Valentine with reference to Curley Bill that brought John Thacker out there. I will give a full account of this matter in a letter which you can use with Mr. Lake. I have only one picture that would be of use to you. A few years ago I lost most of my pictures in a fire and have this because it was given to me by old Jim Matthews who used to be at Dodge and Las Animas. This one will take you back and may interest you if you have not a similar one. I am sending this picture under separate cover. I attended Luke Short's funeral at Fort Worth.

Now Wyatt, I note that you are going to spend your winter at the mine, and I certainly hope to hear from you and your good wife while you are there. There is hardly any chance of my visiting there unless I made the trip on the hurricane deck of a sore backed pony. And it is a long ride. It is pleasing to know if there is any way in which I can be of help to you. We both send you and Mrs. Earp our kindest and best regards. Through me Mrs. Dodge has come to know you well. Let me know if there is any way in which I can be of help to you. We will hope that some turn of life's wheel will bring us together again.

Sincerely your old friend,

Fred J. Dodge

PS I am sending Mr. Lake's letter to you that you may check up and then pass to him. I am also sending him a letter advising him of this arraingement.

Yours,
FRED

Dodge Ranch
Boerne, Texas
Oct. 8, 1928

Mr. Stuart N. Lake
3916 Portola Place
San Diego, Cal.

DEAR SIR:

Referring to your letter of Sept 14. You ask for information about the death of Curley Bill. By reason of my connection with Wells Fargo and Co., and also because of my association with Wyatt Earp and others of his party, I had full information concerning the fight at Iron Springs in which Wyatt Earp and party were ambushed by Curley Bill and party.

Immediately after this fight I interested myself in ascertaining the true facts about the death of Curley Bill. J. B. Ayers, a saloon keeper of Charleston, where the outlaws and rustlers headquartered, told me that the men who were in the fight told him that Wyatt Earp killed Curley Bill and that they took the body away that night and that they buried him on Patterson's Ranch, on the Babocomari. Johnny Barnes, who was in the fight and was badly wounded, and was one of the Curley Bill party, told me that they opened up on the Earp party just as Wyatt Earp swung off his horse to the ground and they thought they had hit Wyatt but it was the horn of his saddle that was struck. That Wyatt Earp throwed down

234

on Curley Bill right across his horse and killed him. That the Earp party made it so fast and hot that all of the Curley Bill party that could, got away. I made this report direct to John J. Valentine, President of Wells Fargo & Co., and in substance it was the same as the above. Mr. Valentine sent Thacker out there, and he, as you know made a full investigation. Some time after this Ike Clanton himself told me that Wyatt Earp killed Curley Bill.

You ask for my impressions about Wyatt Earp in Tombstone as a Peace Officer and as a man. As a man he was Ace high, and as a Peace Officer he WAS the Peace. I have been a witness to many incidents connected with the life of Wyatt Earp in Tombstone. At the time of the big fight with the Clantons and McLowerys on Fremont street, almost in front of the Sheriff's office, Morgan and Virgil Earp were both wounded. After they had been taken to their homes I came up Fremont street with Wyatt Earp. When about opposite the Sheriff's office Johnny Behan, the Sheriff, intercepted us and said "Wyatt, I have got to arrest you." Wyatt told him that he had two brothers wounded and that things were looking bad and that he (Behan) knew that he was not going to leave town, but that if he was God Almighty himself he could not arrest him then. And Behan didn't made any attempt to arrest him.

I saw Wyatt at the time that Virgil brought Johnny-behind-the-deuce from the Last Chance to Vogan's saloon in Tombstone and a mob was following from Charleston and a mob of miners came off the hill all coming to hang Johnny. Wyatt's resourcefulness and Quiet courage never showed to better advantage. They saved the situation and Johnny was taken to Tucson to jail without a fight.

Another time when the cool quiet nerve showed was the night that Fred White, the City Marshal, was killed by Curley Bill. White was killed at the back end of a cabin occupied by Morgan Earp and myself. When Morgan and I and several others reached Wyatt who was by the chimney of the cabin, the shooting was lively and the balls were hitting the chimney and the cabin. All of the men were squatted down on their heels. Wyatt said "Someone put the fire out in Fred's clothes." Fred White had been shot at such close range that his clothing was afire. In all that fusillade of shots Wyatt's voice sounded as even and quiet as it always did.

Through all the trying times I never knew Wyatt Earp to be other than quiet, cool, and courageous. His head was always clear, which showed that he was absolutely devoid of fear.

Those Tombstone days were of a kind to cut deep memories into the mind and if you find that I can be of assistence in filling in any details of events there I shall be glad to do so.

Very truly yours,

F. J. Dodge

Dodge Ranch
Boerne, Texas
March 9th, 1929

My Dear Mr. Lake,

Your letter of Feb 7th was received and to say that it was a Shock to me was drawing it quite mildly. It was the first news that I had had of the passing of Wyatt. . . . The Photo that I sent to Wyatt was a group picture. It was in his younger days at Dodge City. Himself, Luke Short, Bat Masterson and 2 or 3 that I do not at the Moment recall, but the Names are all on the Picture. You should have it. Luke Short and Bat Masterson I Knew intimately but the others I only Knew by what Wyatt told me of them years ago. Yes, "And what a man he was." The Kind, unasuming, Gentleman, with Nerve of Steel, The heart of a Lion, The swiftness of the Tiger and the Certainty of the Cool fearless Man. Of Couse I am not aware of all that you have for the Book but if there is anything that you want, corroboration, Information, etc that you think I could supply, Call on me. There may have been Men as brave and fearless as Wyatt. But none ever surpassed him, and in my long experience in the West and Elsewhere, I have never Known his Equal.

Mr. Lake, I have, in a way, formed a long distance acquaintance with you, and I would be glad to hear from you whenever time and inclination permits.

Sincerely yours,

[signature]

[William Barclay "Bat" Masterson's fascination for the frontier led him West when he was scarcely sixteen. He met Wyatt Earp for the first time in 1872 on the Salt Fork of the Arkansas where both were buffalo hunting and, from Wyatt's kindness to the younger boy in the buffalo camp developed the mutual respect and loyalty of friendship which lasted as long as either man lived.

In 1876, after service as a civilian scout with the army, Bat happened into Dodge City as Wyatt, who had been appointed marshal there by then, was looking for another deputy. The job was Bat's. Later, in 1877, he was elected sheriff of Dodge. By 1881, Bat had come to Tombstone and there, Wyatt considered him a good man on a posse.

Still later, after serving as U.S. Marshal of the state of New

York, Bat, with his background of adventure on the frontier, was a newspaperman on the New York Morning Telegraph where, in 1921, he died, not with his boots on perhaps, but at any rate, at his desk.]

> Dodge Ranch
> Boerne, Texas
> Sept. 15th, 1929

Stuart N. Lake
3916 Portola Place
San Diego, Cala.

DEAR MR. LAKE

I was writing a letter to Mrs. Earp and in it I said that I had not heard from you in a long time. Just then some folks Come out from town, and brought our mail, and in it was your letter of Sept 11th. I have been away most of the Summer. My Wife, our Boy and myself left here June 1st and returned August 31st. We visited my Wife's relatives in Ohio and traveled over Considerable of that State, then we visited her brother and his Wife who live in Niagara Falls, and while there we took in some of Canada. We traveled 5994 miles, 6000 round figures. We made the entire trip in our car and I drove every mile of the trip. On our return trip we Come into Texas Aug. 29th my Birthday and it was my 75th. When we arrived here I was feeling fine and *None* the worse for wear. So you see I am still going strong, feel like I was about 40 or 45. So much for my summer, and now I will get down to hard pan and try and give you the information that you ask for.

When John Thacker got to Tombstone, I got in his way so that he would Come to me, and I personally gave him the Names of the men to go to. They all talked to him, but Ike Clanton would have nothing to do with him, but he got all the information that he required and was thougherly and completely satisfyed beyond a doubt that Wyatt had killed Curley Bill and that Bill was buried on the Patterson Ranch. I am sure that Thacker *did not* have the body dug up, and I am Equally sure that if he had done so I would have Certainly Known it. I am quite sure also that at the time of John Thacker's visit there, that there Could not have been an identifycation made, by reason of decomposure. You will Know that at that time and in that Country there were no means of preserving a Corpse. . . .

It would take a long time to explain just how I Could get all this information from these Kind of men, but my Key to the whole situation was J. B. Ayers. It was not an easy job and Keep the hair on my head at the same time. . . .

No, Wyatt did not Kill John Ringo. You are right Wyatt had left Arizona some little time.

John Ringo was found dead sitting up with his back to a tree, where he had been placed. Johnny-behind-the-deuce Murdered him. There was bad blood between the two and Johnny-behind-the-deuce was affraid of Ringo. Johnny was not in the same class as Ringo. So Johnny made a sure thing of it and Murdered Ringo. this all worked out through friends of both parties. Johnny-behind-the-deuce went the same way. I did Know H. C. Hooker, but do not Know anything about his daughter in law, but I am willing to bet *all* the Cheap Pools that she never got the Ringo End from Wyatt. There has been many Stories about that Country and men in it, but very few have Ever had even a little actual Knowledge to help on their imagination. With my kindest personal regards I am

Sincerely yours,

F. J. Dodge

Dodge Ranch
Boerne, Texas
September 30, 1929

Mr. Stuart N. Lake
3916 Portola Place
San Diego, Cal.

DEAR MR. LAKE:

Your letter of Sept 21 reached me at a rather inopportune time as I was in bed with an attack of dengue fever. But what is a little dengue fever when John Ringo and his friends are on hand. However as I am still very weak I will have to reply briefly, and will take up the Ringo matter at once.

I was riding in that part of the country quite a little bit right at that particular time. Frank Leslie did not kill John Ringo. Those two and myself were together a couple of days before Ringo was found dead. Ringo was found by Pony Deal and some one else that I do not, at this time, remember. They were coming in from the opposite side to where we were. In the intervening time I saw Frank Leslie several times — one night we stayed over on White River together — and he had no possible chance to get where Ringo was found and back before the news of the killing came in. Pony Deal was a bosom friend of John Ringo's.

Johnny-behind-the-Deuce had his camp in the vicinity of the killing and had had it there for some time. This was known to Frank Leslie as well as to myself and when we went over to where Ringo was, which we did at once, we went on to where this hideout of Johnny's was and found that he was gone and had taken all his camp equipment with him, and his pack horse and saddle horse. It was easy for one who knew about those things to see that camp had been stripped quite recently. We acquainted Pony Deal and his companion with these facts and it was a surprise to them to know that Johnny was on this side of the line at all. There can be no mistake about these facts as I had been seeing Johnny frequently because I had been trying to arrange to use him in getting hold of some things I wanted to know in my under cover work for Wells Fargo, and he knew me and trusted me as far as it was possible for him to trust any one. We believed that Johnny had seen Ringo riding in that vicinity and probably thought he was looking for him — Johnny — and got scared up. Only a few days later Johnny-behind-the-Deuce was found dead. While Pony Deal never would admit it to me there was enough circumstancial evidence to warrant thinking that he had done the killing . . .

First I will give you a description and location of the cabin occupied by Morgan and myself [*in Tombstone*]. The lot faced on Allen St. with one lot intervening, I believe, between that and Sixth St, on the south side of Allen. The cabin was about eighteen feet long by twelve wide. At the south end was built in a very large and heavy adobe fireplace and chimney. There was an open space on each side of this cabin that gave back from Allen St. This is the cabin that held the lot upon which the celebrated and notorious Birdcage Theater was afterward built.

On the night that Curley Bill killed Fred White we were all fully aware that the town was full of rustlers and we were rather expecting trouble. There was an occasional shot scattered around over town. After a short time several shots were fired up towards our cabin. Fred White was evidently in his cabin, which was quite a little distance to the rear of ours. Morg and I were in front of Vogan's saloon. We started toward our cabin. Wyatt and one or two more went running by and Wyatt got one of my pistols from me and continued on ahead only slightly in advance of Morg and me. When Wyatt left us he said, "Look out for yourselves now." When we got to the opening of our lot, that is to the open part in front of the cabin, which sat well back on the lot, the shooting had become quite general. Coming from the rear of our place in a sort of depression there was down there. You have the description of what occurred there in my letter of Oct. 8 Page 2, Par. 2.

As soon as things quieted down a little bit and Fred White's body had been cared for, we took Curley Bill right back across to where the little calaboose stood. This was a small but very sturdy affair. We put Curley Bill in there and Morgan and I were made guards over him, while Wyatt, with Holliday, Turkey Creek Jack, and some others started out to round up the town. Before leaving Wyatt agreed with us on a signal, as it was dark and we would want to know whether any one coming was he and his party or some one else. This to avoid a surprise attack. This was done and we halted every body fifty feet away from the little jail, regardless of who they were. Before Wyatt and his party finished they had rounded up every thing there was in town, which included all those you name and some others, but I do not remember who they were. We never learned of any attempt to lynch Curley Bill.

Pony Deal worked mostly in his class with Johnny Barnes, and they were stage robbers and were implicated in most of the stage holdups in that vicinity in those times, but we could never get sufficient evidence to convict them. Pony Deal was killed in a little Mexican town near Fronterras in Sonora, Mexico.

Now with reference to Johnny Barnes, I had much to do, one time and another, with him. He never recovered from the wounds that he received at Iron Springs, and in one other skirmish. My main connection with him was after Iron Springs, and started through J. B. Ayers, his strongest personal friend.

All of these stage robbery episodes had to do, of course, with Wells Fargo and Co. and the men that he was most associated with were men of the same caliber as himself. These robberies had occurred at intervals for some time before the Iron Springs fight. I presume that Wyatt has made you acquainted with several men that we knew were implicated in these robberies. The night that Virgil was shot in Tombstone, Johnny Barnes and Pony Deal were there; and Johnny Barnes was the man who fired the shot that tore up Virg's arm. I don't know who Wyatt attributed that shot to, but Johnny Barnes was the man. As I said, Johnny never recovered from his wounds and finally died of them in Charleston, where he was being cared for by Ayers.

I have known of a good many rumors and much mis-information that comes from men like Billy Claiborne, including the suicide theory of John Ringo, and think I have cleaned up this matter.

Will you please sent me John P. Clum's address. [*Clum at that time was a resident of Los Angeles.*]

With kindest personal regards, sincerely,

H. J. Dodge

Dodge Ranch
Boerne, Tex.
Dec 5th, 1929

Stuart N. Lake
3916 Portola Place
San Diego, Cal'a.

DEAR MR. STUART,

We have been having some bad weather and very cold, but we have a big fireplace and plenty of wood and I put in most of my time near it. The hunting season is now open. Nov. 16th to Dec. 31st inc. Deer and Turkey and we have a lot of them in our big Pasture. I leased the hunting priveledge to the man who has the lease on our place and he looks after it Carefully. We have lots of Company, for the latch string is always on the outside at the Dodge Ranch, and Mrs. Dodge has a wide reputation for Coffee and they *all* want Coffee and there is always something to go with the Coffee when they are hungry. Of course there is always venison hanging on the back porch. Wish you were here. How is the Book coming along? I am going to write to John P. Clum, I hope that he made the trip to Tombstone. I see by the papers that old Tombstone has lost the County Seat. Am sorry for it was all she had left. Bisbee has it now and it will be quite unhandy for a lot of people. Tombstone was near the center but Bisbee is right close to the Edge of the County. Let me hear from you whenever time and inclination permits. Mrs. Dodge joins me in our Kindest personal regards to you and Mrs. Lake.

Sincerely yours,

Dodge Ranch
Boerne, Texas
Sept. 11, 1930

DEAR MR. LAKE:

This is to acknowledge the receipt of your letter of Aug. 16th — nearly a month ago — Geting the Boy ready for School — Ex of Eyes — Teeth — New clothes, New Uniform etc made many trips to San Antonio, and with other matters also, I have been a pretty busy man — we take Fred Jr. to the School next Sunday, ready to blow Reveille Monday Morning 6:30 A.M. — Then next week I am Calculating to answer Correspondence and you come first. And I will answer fully. Am awfully glad to have met you and do Certainly wish that the visit could have been longer. With kindest regards from all of us to you and yours — I remain

Sincerely yours,

F. J. Dodge

Dodge Ranch
Boerne, Texas
Sept. 18, 1930

Mr. Stuart N. Lake
3916 Portola Place
San Diego, Cal.

DEAR MR. LAKE:

Referring to your letter of Aug. 16th, and also to your short visit with us, which we both enjoyed very much, I will answer the questions that you have asked.

Referring to the arrest of Frank Stilwell at Bisbie. Neither Breakenridge nor Neagle had any thing to do with it whatever. Both of them had quit the posse and gone on ahead into town some little time before we got into Bisbee. Wyatt and I were both off from our horses when we found the bootheel while we were trailing the robbers in the Mule mountains. When we got to Bisbee we were satisfied as to the man who had done

245

the job and Wyatt went to question the shoemaker and I
slipped down where Frank Stilwell and Pete Spence hung
out. There I found that Frank Stilwell had one new boot
heel. Wyatt found out from the shoemaker that he had put a
new heel on Frank Stilwell's boot. We arrested Frank Stilwell and Pete Spence. On our way in to Tombstone Stilwell
and Spence both swore they would get Wyatt, Morg, and myself for this arrest.

Mrs. Dodge knows all about me and everything that I have
been connected with, but Fred Jr. is naturally not so well in-
formed. He is now back in school and we are just getting settled down.

Yes, "Doc [*Holliday*] was a tough citizen and a bad egg,"
and I was fully aware of the situation between Doc and
Wyatt. Doc never played square with any one in that country.
Bill Leonard was as hard as nails and was a stage robber and
everything else in the line of crime. Marshall Williams did do
some tipping off, but Doc was a full fledged member of the
gang that Leonard was in with. I know who was present at the
holdup at the time Bud Philpot was killed and I know who
killed him. It was Bob Paul, though, that they were after. If
Wyatt has not told you, out of respect to his memory I will say
nothing more about Doc Holliday, except to tell you the place
where he died. He died at Glenwood Springs, Colorado. I do
not remember the date, but a letter of inquiry to that place
should get the record.

I would like very much to see a copy of Breakenridge's book.
[*Helldorado*] Knowing the man I can imagine much that
the book probably contains, but I do certainly want a photograph of Morg, Virg, and Wyatt, and would much appreciate
your sending them to me.

Both Mrs. Dodge and myself are looking forward to that
promised visit. We trust that it will not be long until you

again can come to Texas, and then with no strings to your time and movements. The latchstring at the Ranch is out to you and we hope you will pull it whenever you can. And don't forget that you have promised to bring Mrs. Lake when you come again.

Very truly yours,

F. J. Dodge

Dodge Ranch
Boerne, Texas
Dec. 16, 1930

Mr. Stuart N. Lake
3916 Portola Place
San Diego, Cal.

DEAR MR. LAKE:

No doubt you are wondering what has become of me, that you have had no acknowledgement of the two books you so kindly sent. For some weeks we have been more or less cut off from the world, for Fred Jr. contracted scarlet fever. But now we are fumigated and free from danger of sending germs abroad, and can communicate with our friends once more.

Breackenridge was what might be termed a civil deputy. If his book shows his view point, it is interesting as a viewpoint. But if it is intended to show the truth it falls far short of the whole truth in Cochise County. He often speaks of there having been no warrants for the rustlers, or he would have known of it. But makes no mention of the fact that the rustlers were in power, and closely allied with the sheriff, and naturally did not issue warrants for themselves. This is only one of many discrepancies. Such description as he gives of the situation is wholly onesided.

I have already written you with reference to the Frank Stilwell and Pete Spence arrest. In his account of this, I note only one truth — what he says about me.

With reference to "Saint Johnson," for absolute distortion. of facts and complete disregard for truth it beats anything I have ever had the misfortune to read. It is a shame that such a near-libel could be printed. I am glad that the true facts that you have gathered into your book will clear away the fictional mists that have accumulated about Wyatt. He was too much of a man to be made the lay figure for such trash as this "Saint Johnson."

I read with interest your very well written series of articles in the *Saturday Evening Post*, and have heard many complimentary comments on them. As an old timer I feel myself a competent judge of them, and I congratulate you on the way you rung the bell.

Mrs. Dodge joins me in kindest regards to you and Mrs. Lake. We trust that you may have a Merry Christmas and a Happy and Prosperous New Year.

Very Truly Yours,

F. J. Dodge

Dodge Ranch
Boerne, Texas
May 14, 1931

Mr. Stuart N. Lake
3916 Portola Place
San Diego, Cal.

DEAR MR. LAKE:

Do you people in California hibernate during the winter? We have not heard from you for so long that we wonder if you are still among those present. How is the Book getting along? I read your articles in the *Post* with much interest, and know by them that you are keeping fairly busy. You must have gotten in with some good old timber to get the stuff you did for the Ranger article. It was great.

We have had a long, wet, gloomy winter and a cold spring. But now the weather man is doing better and everything looks fine. If you could see this country now you would not ask why I preferred it to California.

Trusting this finds you well, and hoping to hear from you again some time soon,

Very truly yours,

F. J. Dodge [signature]

3916 Portola Place
San Diego, California
Sept. 11, 1931

DEAR CAPTAIN DODGE:

There is some hesitancy on my part about the content of this letter, which I am sure you will appreciate as you read it;

but, I do feel that you and I are well enough acquainted to have you let me know of your attitude frankly and with perfect assurance that I will understand it. Let me tell you the story in proper order:

The Pacific States Building and Loan Co., one of the oldest and biggest banking houses on the coast with banking houses in every important city, has long been much interested in Western history, to the extent that for years they have devoted their bank windows to historical displays made up of items obtained from the best museums and the best authenticated private collections in the country. Each exhibit is built around some central theme of pioneering days — the last window in their San Diego bank having been an accurate portrayal of the ships which have carried traffic between the East Coast and the West, models of old clippers, galleons, early steamboats, etc. etc. — which attract throngs. Now, they wish to build such a display around the oldtime peace officer, the frontier marshal, using Wyatt as the finest of them all and building the exhibit around my book. Houghton Mifflin are providing them with all the copies of the book they need, and a lot of special material, enlargements of some of the old photographs, etc. etc. Some of my friends in Dodge City are sending out a collection of items connected with Wyatt's days there, and I have one or two little things that Wyatt left me — including that Indian-made buffalo-bone walking stick which Senator Hearst gave him after the two had finished their *pasear* in the Huachucas, also an enamel inlay ivory chip out of Luke Short's faro-bank, etc. etc. The bank plans to open its display in their big window on Broadway, Los Angeles on October 6, the day before the book goes on sale in the stores, and from then on for four months, running through the Christmas holidays and the best buying season of the book year, it will be shown in every community of importance, Los

Angeles, Long Beach, San Diego, Pasadena, Santa Barbara, Bakersfield and so on up the line. It should sell a tremendous lot of books, at least it will make Wyatt known to a multitude of people. And here is the question I wish to ask you:

Would you be willing to send over to me that sawed-off Wells Fargo gun and the six-gun which you let Wyatt take the night Curly Bill killed White? And, any other items you may have which you think might be of interest?

If you do not wish to do this you should have no hesitancy in telling me so. But if you will lend them, I can tell you that the bank has had for its window displays over a period of years loans from many museums public and private and from individuals, and has never lost or harmed an item. Each will be fully covered and protected by a special insurance policy in addition to the fact that I, too, will hold myself liable for their safe return. Charles Lockwood, who used to be around Tucson, is letting us take an old Wells Fargo treasure box — he has loaned to the bank on many occasions, and around the book we will build a display of great interest. Tom Drummond is letting me take his father's old Sharp's-50 buffalo gun which he used with Wyatt in the Kansas camps of 1871–73, and the addition of the two pieces which you have, and any others you'd care to send would help alot. I should have these in hand here by September 22 if you will entrust them to me, and if you will you may send them insured express, collect. At any rate will you let me know your decision promptly, and feel perfectly free to express your true mind.

So much for that. Marvin Hunter [*Publisher of* Frontier Times] writes you spent a day with him lately and tells me how much he enjoyed it. Also, the book will be out October 7, but don't you go buying yourself your own copy. I want to send that to you, for you to read and Fred, Junior, to keep. I should get it to you in advance of sale date — I am having it sent here to me first instead of direct to you from Boston, so that I can write a brief word on the forepage—but if the shipment is a day or so late, I'd like to have you know that this copy will be coming. Then, when you read it, I wish you'd write me with all frankness *exactly* what you think of it — no hedging because you might tread on a toe or two, but speaking right out in meeting as one friend to another, because if I can't take friendly and authoritative criticism I ought to go back and start over living.

Did you ever know a Tom Rynning, of Texas and Arizona? He's written a book "Gun Notches" which reads fishy to me. If so, what do you know about him?

Meanwhile I'm hoping to get through Texas soon again, this time with Mrs. Lake whom you should know, as she's got it over me like blue sky as family representative. Suppose Fred, Jr. has returned to school, but my remembrances to him, with my best to Mrs. Dodge and yourself.

Sincerely,

Stuart N. Lake

Dodge Ranch
Boerne, Texas
Sept. 17th, 1931

Mr. Stuart N. Lake
3916 Portola Place
San Diego, Cal.

DEAR MR. LAKE:

Your letter of Sept. 11th received and contents carefully noted. It will be a pleasure to me to lend you these guns as a

252

personal favor to you, and in respect to Wyatt's memory, though, as you know, I have hitherto refused to let them out of my possession even for a short time. As I understand your letter you will want them for about four months from Oct. 6th; that is until the second week of Feb. or thereabout. Only your assurance that you will be personally responsible for them induces me to part with them, even for this short time, as I count them among my most treasured possessions. I am having a box made for the purpose and will ship them to you within the next few days, by Express. I can't think of anything else that I have that would be of use to you in this proposed exhibit.

We are all much interested in the advertising plans as you outlined them and it looks as if the Book would have a rattling good sendoff. My copy will be doubly valuable to me, coming as a gift from you, and both Fred, Jr. and I are awaiting its coming with high expectations. We read the page on the poster and want more of the same. I will read it carefully and write you "with all frankness EXACTLY" what I think of it.

I never heard of Tom Rynning, or his book. He may be one of the later editions now posing as authority — on second hand knowledge.

Whenever you and Mrs. Lake come to Texas you will find the latch string out and the watch dog chained at the Dodge Ranch. You are always welcome, and if Mrs. Lake is as superior to yourself as you say we can't afford to miss knowing her.

Mrs. Dodge and Fred Jr. join me in kindest regards to both of you.

Very sincerely and cordially yours,

F. J. Dodge

Dodge Ranch
Boerne, Texas
Oct. 12th, 1931

Mr. Stuart N. Lake
3916 Portola Place
San Diego, Cal'a.

DEAR MR. LAKE:

On Sept 18th I shipped to you by Express the shotgun and the sixshooter that you asked for, the shotgun is the one that Wyatt used when he killed Curley Bill [*and the sixshooter by*] Dep. U.S. Marshal Heck Thomas when he killed Bill Doolin a member of the Dalton gang. If ever you have seen Doolin's picture you can see the efficiency of this gun.

Soon after this killing, while riding at night my horse fell and broke the stock all to pieces and otherwise scarred it up I sent it to the factory and had a new stock put in and repolished.

Fred Jr. is at the Peacock Military Academy in San Antonio. At present Mrs. Dodge and I are both well and we unite in our kindest regards to you and Mrs. Lake.

Sincerely Yours,

[signature: F. J. Dodge]

3916 Portola Place
San Diego, California
October 17, 1931

Captain F. J. Dodge
Boerne, Texas

DEAR CAPTAIN DODGE:

The shot gun and sixshooter arrived in fine condition, and

254

now are being shown in the Los Angeles bank window in connection with the interest-arousing work we are trying to do for the book . . .

Meanwhile rest assured that the guns are safe and well-cared for, and that I am awaiting with much interest your comment on the biography.

Our best remembrances to Mrs. Dodge and yourself, and my greetings to Fred Jr. when you write. Tell him, will you, that when he has had a chance to read Wyatt Earp's story I should appreciate very much his frank opinion. As a matter of fact, the criticisms of youngsters are apt to be worth twice as much as those of their elders who are more apt to conceal true feelings from consideration for another's — a consideration which is seldom really as kind as the intentions to which it is due. You've told Fred, Jr. enough about the old days to give him a pretty sound idea of what it's all about. That's another reason why I'll be interested in his fresher approach to the subject.

Most sincerely,

Stuart N. Lake

Dodge Ranch
Boerne, Texas
Oct. 26, 1931

Mr. Stuart N. Lake
3916 Portola Place
San Diego, Cal.

DEAR MR. LAKE:

. . . Now for the Book. You may be sure that I have read it with greatest care and interest, but before I comment on it I want to thank you for it, and for the presentation you wrote in

255

it. It will be doubly precious to me always because of it, and to Son Fred after me.

As you know, until I met the Earp boys in Tombstone I knew none of them personally. And all that I know of Wyatt previous to that time is what he and his brothers have told me, and the various stories of them that were current. Of course I am thoroughly familiar with the Tombstone part of their lives. So that part of your material I know is accurate, and handled in a most masterly manner. I must congratulate you in the way you have made Wyatt to stand out from his background without in any way changing values or atmosphere. You have drawn an accurate picture of one of the coolest and bravest men I have ever known, and made it alive. It is a pity he could not have lived to see this book, which should go so far to refute the many blood and thunder stories that have been told about him.

Naturally the part that was familiar to me was of deepest interest to me — and right here I want to thank you for the way you have handled my double life in Tombstone — but the whole book is so interesting and so true that I feel that you have done a real service to my generation on the frontier. Fred Jr. knows that the Book is here, and he and I are planning to read it aloud together during his first vacation. We have only had time for little bits, so far, and are looking forward to making the whole a family affair.

Mrs. Dodge joins me in kindest regards to you and Mrs. Lake. You couldn't be human without being a bit puffed up, for you have done a good job of work, and I hope sales are satisfactory and that you are having a good time after your hard work.

Sincerely your friend,

J. F. Dodge

Dodge Ranch
Boerne, Texas
March 24, 1932

Mr. Stuart N. Lake
Wells Fargo Bank & Union Trust Co.
Market and Montgomery,
San Francisco, Cal.

DEAR MR. LAKE:

. . . I am glad to learn that the history of Wells Fargo has at last fallen into your competent hands. I was not greatly surprised to learn that you had undertaken to write it, as I had felt, from something you said in our conversation, that you were interested in it, and wish you all success in the undertaking. Mr. Lipman [*then President of Wells Fargo*] (who I do not know) will be very helpful to you. I am sorry that the death of Mr. Andrew Christeson has deprived you of that great source of information. Am glad you have been in touch with Mr. LaForrest. He is all gold and thoroughly reliable.

Jim Hume was methodical and dependable in all ways. Perhaps Thacker will need a little extra checking.

You have four dependable assistants in your sorting, and ought to get along rapidly with so much good help.

The Boston man was Mr. Cheney [*Benjamin P. Cheney, in 1867 a director of Wells Fargo*] a very close personal friend of Mr. Valentine's. He was for many years on the Board of Directors of the Atcheson, Topeka, and Santa Fe Ry. Confidentially, I think it was through this friendship that Mr. Valentine succeeded in getting the contract for Wells Fargo on that railroad.

I am glad that the old guns are able to do their bit for Wyatt and for you, and note all that you say concerning their care and return. I trust that the book is getting the recognition it so richly deserves.

I also note what you say about Mr. Valentine's daughter and the material that she has turned over to you. I feared that much had been lost in the fire, as I knew he had most of it in San Francisco.

You speak of coming to San Antonio soon and we look forward to that with pleasure. If Mrs. Lake accompanies you, Fred's horse and saddle and plenty of hill scenery and wide open country are here for her use. Mrs. Dodge is anxious to meet her and hopes she will come along with you.

With kindest regards to you both,

Sincerely yours,

F. J. Dodge

Dodge Ranch
Boerne, Texas
July 27th, 1932

Mr. Stuart N. Lake
3916 Portola Place
San Diego, Cal.

DEAR MR. LAKE:

The guns reached me day before yesterday, perfectly packed and in excellent condition. I did not wire you because we now have no telegraph office at Boerne, and so am sending this to you by Air Mail.

Referring to yours of the 9th. You know just right when you say that Mrs. Dodge and myself will be pleased to hear of the expected addition to the Lake family. There is nothing like a child to give zest to life, and while many new burdens come with one, the blessings far outweigh the other things. I

258

know you are as proud and pleased as can be, and we rejoice with you.

Fred Jr. has been home some little time. He is coming along nicely, and we talk of you often and wish you might drop in on us again, but suppose there is no hope of it this season. I am fair though Mrs. Dodge keeps a wary eye on me at all times. Women can be awful bossy at times.

How is the work on the Wells Fargo book progressing? Mr. LaForrest wrote me that he had seen you several times, but not lately, and he wondered what had become of you. All the old timers are naturally interested. A good many people have tackled the history of the old Company, but nothing of value seems to have come of it. We, having seen what you did with Wyatt's life, are hoping much for this.

With very kindest regards, and sincere best wishes to Mrs. Lake and yourself, in which Mrs. Dodge and Fred join me.

Most truly yours,

Dodge Ranch
Boerne, Texas
Oct. 14, 1932

Mr. Stuart N. Lake
3916 Portola Place
San Diego, Cal.

DEAR MR. LAKE:

The letter with the good news reached us just as we were leaving to go to Fred's school, and as we did not get back until yesterday I have had no opportunity to answer. Congratulations and all good wishes to you and Mrs. Lake, and many long and interesting years to young Carolyn. [*Little did he think that one of the most interesting I would spend working with his own journals. C.L.*]

Mrs. Dodge joins me in all good wishes, and we trust that this will find the whole Lake family in the best of health and spirits. Remember, I am always glad to hear from you.

Very truly your friend,

[signature: Fred Dodge]

Dodge Ranch
Boerne, Texas
Sept. 14, 1934

Mr. Stuart N. Lake
3916 Portola Place
San Diego, Cal.

DEAR MR. LAKE:

It has been a long time since I heard from you direct, and it occurs to me that I may owe you a letter. A few weeks ago I had a letter from my old friend, Mr. Ben Cheney of Boston, [*son of the Mr. Cheney referred to in the Dodge letter dated March 24, 1932*] in which he mentions having called on you in San Diego and having a most interesting time with you, and says he fell in love with your Den. I wish I might have a like privilege.

My health has not been at all good this past year, and I do not get about much. A while ago I had an accident in getting out of the car, and dislocated my shoulder, which adds to my general disability. But I am still interested in you and your work and hope I may soon see your book on the grand old Company in print. How is it coming along?

This country is suffering from drouth, but owing to the steady irrigation of Relief Money supplied by a free handed Government the drouth is about the only thing we suffer, as yet. Of course we still have to face what is to come in the way of settlement.

Mrs. Dodge and Fred Jr. join me in best regards to you and Mrs. Lake and Miss Lake, and trust that all is well with you. Fred is doing well. We have finally found a medicine that seems to control his illness, and he is apparently free from that. He is six feet tall, and strong as they come.

With all good wishes to you and yours,

Very truly your friend,

[signature]

[Fred Dodge died on December 16, 1938. He was eighty-four and one of the last surviving peace officers of the frontier where he had been cool, quick, and a dead shot, and where his native ability as a detective was widely known and respected.

In an obituary on December 22, 1938, the Boerne, Texas, Star wrote in part, ". . . his keen sense of justice made him so square with all men, even lawbreakers that many times those who had served out their time turned to him for help in getting a new start in life. And none appealed in vain.

"He had no patience with the rising tendency to glorify early day outlaws as picturesque heroes. He knew them for what they were . . .

"We cannot mourn his passing," the Star continued. "He was very tired and he had earned his rest."

With his inheritance of pioneer resourcefulness, innate wisdom, and quiet courage, Fred Dodge, his own modesty notwithstanding, made a place for himself in the history of law enforcement and in the history of his country.]

Boerne, Texas
April 1, 1941

Mr. Stuart N. Lake
3916 Portola Place
San Diego, Cala.

DEAR MR. LAKE:

Hearing from you after so long was a pleasant surprise to us. Fred Jr. and I have often wondered about you, and Fred Sr. had you much in mind during his last months. The history of Wells Fargo which you had proposed doing was to him a most cherished project. So I at once searched out the diaries you asked for and shipped them to you yesterday, by express. I sent those from 1891 to 1918 inclusive. His earlier ones were lost some years ago when the building where they were stored burned. I do not know that these will be of much use to you except in fixing dates, but am glad to entrust them to you because I know Fred would have wanted it so. I also sent some of the notes he wrote about his own life, as they had a lot of details about his cases. There were six of those. And as a last minute idea sent his account of "the brown paper case," as he always called it.

This last because, when searching out a box for shipping I ran across that one. It had been stored in an out building at the Ranch and had not been opened in twenty years. We could find no key to fit it, so pried off one of the back boards. In it were the original packages of the brown paper, seals and all, packed in that paper I used in packing the diaries and note books. [*Yellow tissue paper copies from an express company receipt book.*]

Fred Jr. and I decided that one of those packages would be an interesting souvenir of old Wells Fargo for you. So, if you would care for it, we will send it to you. And if there is anything further that I can do or send to help you please let me know. For I feel that in doing it I will be doing what Fred would have been happy to do.

If Mr. Cheney is still there please give him our best regards. His never failing kindness helped much to make Fred's last years happier — indeed really helped to prolong his life.

Fred Jr. seems to be outgrowing his illness. He is six feet two and mostly bones, but developing in a most hopeful way. His general health is excellent, and I am always well. I trust your family are in good health. The young lady will be quite a young lady by now.

With every good wish for your success, and best regards to yourself,

Sincerely,

Jessie Dodge.

Index

INDEX

Adams, killer of Ike Roberts, 62, 63

Adams Express Company, 199, 203, 204, 205, 206, 207, 208, 214

Alexander, Minton "Kid": in Teague case, 180, 181, 185–191

Alhambra Saloon, 26

American Railway Express Company, 225

Ames, Andy, 57, 58, 59, 61

Andrews, Amador, 153, 154, 159, 162, 163, 177, 215, 216

Aransas Pass, 155

Archer: in Houston depot robbery, 148, 149, 150, 152

Ardmore, Oklahoma, 119

Arizona Historical Review, 25

Arkansas City, Kan., 131, 156, 163

Arkansas River, 130, 164, 171, 176

Armington, G. W., 190

Armstrong, Noah: in Coleman train robbery, 179–181, 186–191; wife testifies, 189–190

Arnold, Jim, Dallas Police Chief, 116

Atchison, Topeka and Santa Fe Railroad, 123, 133, 155, 157, 163, 164, 172, 180, 257

Atlanta, Ga., 130

Augusta, Kan., 163

Ayers, Coffeyville, Kan. banker, 174

Ayers, J. B., undercover saloon-keeper, 17, 18, 19, 26, 40–44. 52, 232, 233, 234, 239, 242, 243

Bakersfield, Calif., 250

Ball Hutchings & Company, 198, 199

Ballinger, Tex., 178

Bangor, Calif., 5

Barnes, Johnny, 20, 24, 28, 38, 52, 233, 234, 242

Barry, messenger in Coleman Y train robbery, 178

Bartell, Sam, 124, 127, 134, 138, 157, 158

Behan, John H., Tombstone Sheriff, 13, 15, 20, 24, 27, 35, 36, 37, 39, 91, 235

Belton, Bell County, Tex., 179, 181

Benson, Ariz., 11, 12, 17, 41, 69, 84, 87, 94, 95, 102

Berwin Indian Territory, 123

Bird Cage Theater, 10, 24, 241

Bisbee, Ariz.: holdup, 45; 13, 14, 15, 41, 42, 43, 44, 47, 51, 55, 80, 244, 245, 246

Bitter Creek. *See* Slaughter Kid

Black Hawk War, 1832, 125

Cincinnati, Ohio, 199, 202, 203, 206, 207, 208, 209, 214
Cisco, Calif., 5
Claiborne, Billy, 26, 35, 36, 243
Clanton, Joseph Isaac (Ike), 26, 35, 36, 37, 38, 233, 235, 238
Clanton, William (Billy), 26
Clanton brothers, 35, 235
Clifton, Ariz., 53
Clum, John P., *Epitaph* editor, Tombstone's first Mayor, 20, 24, 25, 36, 37, 243, 244
Cochise County, Ariz: created, 20; 43, 44, 247
Coffeyville, Kan., 172, 173, 174, 176, 177, 184, 193, 196
Cohn, Dave, 30
Cohn, Ike, 30
Coleman, Tex., 181, 185, 187, 190
Coleman Y train robbery, 178–181, 185–190
Collins, "Shotgun," 12
Colorado Springs, Colo., 222, 223
Colwell, Charley, 57, 58
Columbus, Kan., 131
Connor, J. T. M., Dallas agent, 119, 121
Cook, Sheriff, Oswego Co., Mo., 192, 193, 195
Cooley, Lou, stage driver, 8
Cox, Burrell, posseman, 137, 138, 139, 162, 164, 165, 166, 167, 169, 170, 171, 177
Crane, Jim, outlaw, 24
Crawford, Wells Fargo employee, 155
Creek Nation, 137, 138, 140
Cripple Creek, Colo., 83, 222
Crossin, Tom, D.A., Teague case, 180, 186, 188
Crowe, Dallas Route Agent, 116
Crowley, La., 147

Cruz, Florentino (Indian Charlie), 38
Crystal Palace Saloon, 28, 103
Cuba, Mo., 191
Cuero, Tex., 154, 155
Cunningham, Charley: shoots Charley Smith, 81–82
Curley, Bud, Dallas Chief of Detectives, 116

Dallas, Tex., 116, 119, 153, 154, 159, 185, 224, 225, 226
Dalton, Ben, 126
Dalton, Bill, 175, 176, 183, 184, 185
Dalton, Bob, 124, 126, 133, 135, 138, 156, 157, 158, 166, 168, 172, 173
Dalton, Emmett, 124, 126, 138, 157, 158, 166, 169, 172, 173, 175, 176; reforms, 177
Dalton, Grat, 126, 158, 166, 169, 172, 173, 174
Daltons, 127, 132, 133, 135, 139, 141, 157, 158, 159, 162, 163, 168, 174, 254
Dana, Dallas Route Agent, 116
Daniels, Bill, Bisbee Deputy Sheriff, 47, 48, 49, 51, 52, 53
Deadwood, Colo., 32
Deal, Pony, 20, 240, 241, 242, 243
Deep Fork Bottom, Okla., 131, 158
Deitrect, Cincinnati Chief of Police, 209
Delaney, Wells Fargo Agent, Guthrie, 167, 171, 172
Delaney, William, 51
Deming, N. M., 53
Denver, Colo., 224

LaForest, Emil, Superintendent of Wells Fargo's San Francisco stable of 300 horses during earthquake and fire, 257, 259
La Junta, Colo., 135
Lake, Carolyn (daughter of Stuart L.), 260, 261
Lake, Marion K. (wife of Stuart L.), 244, 247, 248, 252, 253, 254, 256, 258, 259, 260, 261
Lake, Stuart N., 20, 27, 38, 226, 229–262 passim
La Morita, Sonora, Mexico, 51
Langsford, James, 144
Lansing, Kan., 177
Las Animas, Colo., 133, 233
Las Vegas, N.M., 102, 156
Lathrop, Calif., 44
Lazzard, Tombstone troublemaker, 81–82
Leavenworth, Kan., 216
Ledbetter, Bud, 161
Leon Springs, Tex., 224
Leonard, Bill, 24, 246
Leslie, Frank, 79, 240
Levy, Ike, 29–31, 32
Lilly, Deputy U.S. Marshal, 131
Lima, Ohio, 209
Lipman, Frederick L., Wells Fargo President, 257
Little Ax, Seminole Indian, 132
Little Rock, Ark., 196
Lockwood, Charles, 251
Long Beach, Calif., 250
Long Tom, Seminole Indian, 132
Lordsburg, N.M., 97
Los Angeles, Calif., 108, 111, 177, 230, 231, 243, 250, 255
Lot jumpers, Tombstone, 34–35
Louisville, Ky., 203, 204, 206, 208, 209, 220
Lynch, Tim, 30

McAlester, Okla., 137
McBryan, attorney for Bill Chadborn, 195, 196
McCann, Dan, 25, 27, 28
McCloughery, Col. (nephew of James B. Hume), 216
McGinness, Nick, Agent at Fort Worth, 119
McKinley, William, President of the U.S., 233
McLowery, Frank, 26
McLowery, Tom, 26
McLowery brothers, 35, 36, 235
McMasters, Sherman, 12, 33, 39
McMullen, S. R., Route Agent, 119
Madsen, Cris, 132
Manuel, Yaqui Indian trailer for Fred Dodge: posseman on Bisbee holdup, 47, 48, 49, 50, 51, 52; trails on first Pantano train robbery, 83, 84, 85, 86, 87; on second Pantano train robbery, 89, 90; helps in ice business, 104
Mason, Jeff, 190
Masterson, William Barclay "Bat," 236; career sketched, 237
Matthews, Jim: on Wharton train robbery case, 133, 134, 135, 233
Maxey, U.S. Judge, 153
Meade, W. K., U.S. Marshal: on second Pantano train robbery, 89, 90, 91, 92, 93; on second Steins Pass train robbery, 100
Mexico City, Mexico, 223
Miller, of Adams Express Company, 203
Miller, Henry, 138, 140
Minas Prietas Mine, 49, 51, 52
Missouri, Kansas and Texas Railroad (Katy), 164

274